Urban Crime and Social Disorganization in China

Haiyan Xiong

Urban Crime and Social Disorganization in China

A Case Study of Three Communities in Guangzhou

Springer

Haiyan Xiong
International Institution of Criminal Justice
Southwest University of Politic Science
and Law
Chongqing
China

and

Department of Sociology
University of Oxford
Oxford
UK

ISBN 978-981-10-1315-7 ISBN 978-981-287-859-5 (eBook)
DOI 10.1007/978-981-287-859-5

Springer Singapore Heidelberg New York Dordrecht London

Softcover re-print of the Hardcover 1st edition 2016

Printed on acid-free paper

Springer Science+Business Media Singapore Pte Ltd. is part of Springer Science+Business Media
(www.springer.com)

Foreword

This book is Dr. Haiyn Xiong's first English publication. Doctor Haiyan Xiong is the first doctor supervised by me in the University of Macau and can be said to have learned a lot from me. I do criminological research in USA. Status and disciplinary systems of criminology are different in China and America. In the United States, Criminology is a key discipline. It is an interdisciplinary subject relating law, sociology, statistics, and even some natural scientific fields. However, what Dr. Haiyan Xiong has received is pure, orthodox legal education. This is clearly not enough for criminological research. So she studied professional knowledge of sociology and statistics to make her qualified to do criminological research. At the same time, her professional background of Law enabled her to make deeper analysis of social problems.

This book focuses on urban crime and social disorganization in temporary China. The author noticed that modern China was in extremely rapid social transition. Social changes in China are reflected in many social phenomena such as rapid economic growth, the speed of urbanization, and significant changes in urban spatial patterns. It is well known that high crime rates always co-occur with rapid social transition. China is also encountering high crime rates in its profound social transformation without exception. This book summarizes the index of rapid Chinese societical transition as rapid economic growth, high urbanization speed, significant changes in urban spatial patterns, population mobility, prominent urban poverty, gradually disorganized social norms, and spiraling crime growth.

It could be realistically significant to explore the relationships between urban crime and social disorganization against a macro background of rapid social transition. In the early 1930s of the last century, Yan Jingyao, the famous sociologist, criminologist and jurist in China, who was the first Chinese doctor of criminology from the US, as well as the first Ph.D. in criminology in Chinese history, was concerned about this issue and wrote his doctoral book "Relationship Between Crime and Social Change in China." China was experiencing early modernization in the 1930s. Chinese society was undergoing multilevel, multidirectional changes, and "social changes arouse conflicts between the old and the new points of law and ethics, so many people have lost direction due to rapid social change. They could not tell right from wrong. They could not understand suddenly emerged new laws and would break them naturally."

Perhaps coincidentally, perhaps inevitably, a century later China is also facing a series of social problems caused by rapid social changes during rapid economic development—urban spatial structural spread, social disorganization, increased differentiation between rich and poor, centralized poverty, structural unemployment, frequent population flow, ethnic heterogeneity, and so on. On the issue of crime, Chinese society has greeted the fifth crime peak in 1998 and it continues today after experience of four crime climaxes. What relationships exist between China's crime and social change under the new historical circumstances? Whether it is as Louis Shelley (1981) argued, "Modernization process has significant and lasting impact on crimes of all countries...Modernization is a process combining both creation and destruction. It provides new opportunities and new prospects on price of human dislocation and pain." Is crime rate bound to rise in a period of rapid social change? Are all indexes of social change related to crime? What distribution patterns do crime rates have in various areas and communities even if the national crime rate is rising. How do changes in urban spatial structure impact crime? Are urban ecological changes in China radiating outwards as concentric circles like Chicago? How law and crime themselves vary in a social transiting period? What kind of influence do tradition, morality, culture and institution have on crime? These questions torture us in the social change whirlpool. It is no doubt that the study of crime, especially the relationship between crime and social disorganization against the great background of social change, has an immeasurable significance for crime control and prevention.

The theoretical contribution of this book lies in critical development on the basis of the inheritance of previous achievements in research on the social disorganization theory. The concept of "social disorganization" itself is actually a very obscure concept, known as the most "complex" concept in Western Criminology. There is no existing unified and clear definition of "social disorganization." Durkheim believed that uncertainty and unexpectation of the future caused social disorganization; Shaw and Mckay believed a large amount of poor population, big ethnic difference, and frequent migration are often the three structural reasons for community disorganization; Sampson defined social disorganization as a community that does not have the ability to realize its common value. And lack of a unified conclusion is definitely the vitality of criminology which can stimulate innovation and generate tests. While affirming the historical significance of the "concentric circles" theory of the Chicago School, this book also points out the limitations of the theory. Initial distribution is gained through the location of 1483 crime cases collected by techniques of GIS in Guangzhou. The author finds that the distributions of spatial density and demographic density of crime in Guangzhou show themselves in an irregular circle, waning from the city center to the suburbs. On the basis of empirical research, the author then proposes her own "punctate distribution" theory.

Compared with other books on criminology, the methodology in this book may deserve special attention. Due to various kinds of limitations, the author did not use sampling, but used news gathering instead to collect data. She used GIS technology to locate data on the map, resulting in the density distribution of all crime cases. Practical problems are actually solved by using scientific methods, although there are still some defects in research methods. To make up for the deficiency of the case collecting method, the author selected three communities in Guangzhou to make detailed in-depth interviews, and also found a number of interesting results. Relationships between crime and some factors relative to social disorganization are distinctly different from the West, including economy, unemployment, marriage and family, residential stability, ethnic heterogeneity, social justice, social capital, social order and social control, social isolation and social exclusion, community cohesion, trust, fear, tradition, morality, religion, language, etc. It is also a new trend to try to combine these two methods to study relative issues on crime and society in recent years.

I am pleased to preface on the forthcoming book. I hope this book should be a bridge to make Western society better understand contemporary China, and to make this new concept and new scientific research method be also accepted and spread in Asia.

Macau, February 2015

Jianhong Liu
President of the Scientific Commission
of International Society for Criminology

Preface and Acknowledgments

Nowadays, modern China is experiencing extremely rapid social transition. Social changes in China are reflected in many social phenomena such as rapid economic growth, the speed of urbanization, and significant changes in urban spatial patterns. It is well known that high crime rates always co-occur with rapid social transition. China is also encountering high crime rates in its profound social transformation without exception.

This book focuses on the relationship between social transition and crime in the context of rapid Chinese social changes. Chinese society has experienced rapid social change. Accompanying this profound change, crime and social disorganization has increased significantly in urban China. Few empirical studies have been conducted to examine community social disorganization in China. For the purpose of my book I have selected Guangzhou as a research site to study the patterns of crime and social disorganization. My book combines methods of content analyses with ethnographic fieldwork to overcome the difficulty of scarce data. Official data has many well-known limitations and there are no community-level data available. This research first selects 1483 crime cases reported by the influential Southern Metropolis Daily in 2013 to characterize the general pattern of crime distribution. The findings suggest that both spatial and demographic density distributions of criminal cases in Guangzhou show a gradient circle pattern from city center to suburb. Focusing on three selected typical communities, this book finds important patterns of crime and social disorganization that are very different from Western research. These findings are organized along major correlates of social disorganization, such as unemployment, marriage and family, residential stability, ethnic heterogeneity, social equality, social capital, social control, social isolation and exclusion, community cohesion, trust and fear, traditions, morals and beliefs, and language. These findings extend and elaborate the Social Disorganization Theory in urban China.

In completing the manuscript and adapting it to the current book, nearly four years have been spent on this project. In these four years, I received assistance from many generous sources and now I write the following text with a grateful heart.

Thanks to my colleagues and friends in the internationalized city of Macau. Thanks to my friends in Guangzhou. Thanks to my sponsor Prof. Federico Varesse, who invited me to visit Oxford University as an academic for one year. Thanks to many scholars off-campus in the field of criminal law and criminology giving me a lot of encouragement and guidance in my study process.

Finally, thanks to my parents, husband, and child. Completing such a book would have been impossible without their undying support and encouragement, and for this I can never thank them enough.

Oxford, February 2015 Haiyan Xiong

Contents

List of Figures

List of Tables

Abstract

Chinese society has experienced rapid social change. Accompanying profound change, crime and social disorganization has increased significantly in urban China. Few empirical studies have been conducted to examine community social disorganization in China. The present book selects Guangzhou as a research site to study patterns of crime and social disorganization. The book combines methods of content analyses with ethnographic fieldwork to overcome the difficulty of scarce data. Official data have many well-known limitations and there are no community-level data available. The research first selects 1483 crime cases reported by the influential Southern Metropolis Daily in 2013 to characterize the general pattern of crime distribution. The findings suggest that both spatial and demographic density distributions of criminal cases in Guangzhou show a gradient circle pattern from city center to suburb. Focusing on three selected typical communities, the book finds important patterns of crime and social disorganization that are very different from Western research. These findings are organized along major correlates of social disorganization, such as unemployment, marriage and family, residential stability, ethnic heterogeneity, social equality, social capital, social control, social isolation and social exclusion, community cohesion, trust and fear, traditions, morals and beliefs, language, and others. These findings extend and elaborate Social Disorganization Theory in urban China.

Chapter 1
Introduction

1.1 Experienced Social Disorganization in Contemporary China

Social disorganization and crime in China seems a new focus of peculiar research interest. Social disorganization often occurs in periods of rapid social change and is always accompanied by a sharp rise in crime rate. This phenomenon has circled many times in human history, and normally attracted the attention of a large number of social scientists (Breetzke 2010; Kim and Pridemore 2005; Konings and Walsh 1999; Makinen 2000; Radulescu and Barlow 2002; Zeitler 2005).

Nineteenth was an age of grand turmoil created by the arise of the 1789 French Revolution and by the speedy industrialization of French society. It was the part of a more common effort to reconstruct a rational society out of the ruins of the traditional one. The famous sociologist of the day, Emile Durkheim, who has been called "one of the best known and one of the least understood major social thinkers" (LaCapra 1972), coined the phrase "anomie" to describe the orderless social process, which refers to state a society that has lost the ability to control and regulate its members. Human society maintains in the process of social change involving in industrialization from the more primitive mechanical form into the more advanced organic form. Durkheim believes that crime is a "normal" functional part of all society; it is an inevitable product when a mechanical society changes into an organic one. Crime is definitely a societal necessity as it permits members of a society, through punishing those who offend the law, to remold their social values, and thus develop the collective conscience and reinforce social solidarity. (Durkheim 1951, 1964).

In the 1930s when the United States was similarly undergoing dramatic industrialization, a group of scholars in the University of Chicago concentrated on the expansion process of industrialization and how it affected human society. In adjusting Durkheim's theory to American society, Shaw and McKay held

H. Xiong, *Urban Crime and Social Disorganization in China*,
DOI 10.1007/978-981-287-859-5_1

Durkheim's opinion about rapid social transition but shifted the attention from societies to neighborhoods. With Chicago city as their situational basis of study, they focused on the relationship between social disorganization and crime at the community level (Shaw 1942). They noticed the similar process of invasion, dominance, and succession of human community to biotic state in nature and identified a parallel between the distribution of plant life in nature and the organism of human life in societies (Hawley 1981). As Shaw and Mckay's colleague, Burgess continued to propose concentric circles as zones, and pointed out that cities rather have a tendency to spread radially from their center in patterns of concentric circles each moving gradually outward than merely growing at their edges. In this period, the first time the concept "social disorganization" was presented and examined (Blanchard and Kremer 1997).

Following prior studies, the sociologist Merton (2000) also noted that there was an increase in the crime rate during periods of rapid social change. Despite his research focusing more on the relationship between strain and crime on an individual level, his conclusions can be acknowledged and utilized in a greater understanding of social disorganization. Durkheim has described anomie as a breakdown in the ability of society to control the natural desires of individuals, while Merton holds that severe strain would be placed on people who cannot achieve culturally identified success through institutionalized means. Delinquency is just one of the various ways in which an individual can respond to the problem of anomie.

These scholars experiencing sharp social change or even unrest were acutely aware of unusual fluctuations in crime rates in the specific period. Their works stand with landmark significance in respective fields. Shaw and McKay's social disorganization method has been accepted and advanced by numerous criminologists to explain deviant behavior and crime. To explain these newly emerging changes in today's urban areas, a new concept, "collective efficacy," has been created by Sampson et al. (1997). Collective efficacy emphasizes the combination of neighbors' mutual trust and shared willingness to take action to strengthen community informal control effects. They hold that "the willingness of local residents to intervene for the common good depends in large part on conditions of mutual trust and solidarity among neighbors" (Sampson et al. 1997). This is an important extension of social disorganization theory because collective efficacy theory distinguishes between community's resource potential and expectations for action (Mazerolle et al. 2010).

Broadly speaking, a rapidly changed society has several signs, while social disorganization is fundamental one of them. Social disorganization is a term to describe community features from the perspective of community's ecological characteristics. Although the concept of social disorganization has not been clearly expressed so far, we can still describe a society in the state of social disorganization from the community's ecological geographical features and the anthropological characteristics it encompasses. Profound social disorganization might be represented by collapse of value system, upset norms, increased volume of deviance, highly transient or kinetic neighborhoods, mixed used buildings in a community, infrastructure, elevated street crimes, and drug use patterns. It might be understood through social conditions and physical aspects. According to Traub and Craig (1985),

> social organization (social order) exists when there is a high degree of internal cohesion binding the individuals and institutions in a society closely together. This cohesion consists largely of consensus about goals worth striving for (values) and how or how not to behave (norms). When consensus concerning values and norms is upset and traditional rules do not appear to apply any longer, conflict, social disorganization, and the volume of deviance are all apt to increase.

Disorganized social conditions include misconduct in public spaces such as drinking, drunkenness, rowdy and unsupervised teen groups, tramping, neighbors fighting or quarreling, solicitations for prostitutes, and drug sales. Physical disorganization includes graffiti, litter, trash-filled vacant lots, broken windows, abandoned cars, fired housing, and shuttered stores. These types of social and physical disorganizations allegedly produce fear of crime and urge residents to remove from the community, which weakens both formal and informal social control, and finally induces concentration of crime and delinquency. Such areas become hotbeds for criminal behaviors given the lack of supervision. The elevated crime rates in these disorganized communities are in stark contrast to the organized communities and this has been proven by empirical research (Choi and Choi 2012; Esbensen and Huizinga 1990; Lyons 2007; Patchin et al. 2006; Rose 2000; Ye et al. 2015; Zhang et al. 2010).

However, social disorganization itself is such a complex concept that we cannot directly measure the concept itself without any other indexes (Alanezi 2010; Moravcova 2014; Queen 1941). Because of this, we are only able to measure the concept via some of its indicators. While social disorganization can reflect in many of its indicators such as poverty, economic recession, unemployment, and fear, we cannot say that these indicators can be measured with precision. On the contrary, in fact these indicators prove to be complex in nature and must be divided into secondary and even tertiary levels to develop a greater understanding of the characteristics of social disorganization. The relationship between social disorganization and crime is an interesting topic in the western world; however, it remains highly controversial. Even more controversial is this analysis in China. Because of this, most of the historical researches have been based out of western countries and the issue of social disorganization in China has often been overlooked. Moreover, researcher's focus on social disorganization is in western society; the issue of Chinese social disorganization is seldom mentioned. As far as China is concerned, it maintained an economic growth rate of 8 % in the modernization process, so studying the relationship between social disorganization and crime is not only necessary but also integral to fully understand global patterns of social disorganization.

The relationship between social change and crime involves some concepts that are fundamental to Western Criminology and constitutes the main body of Western criminological research. For instance, concepts such as social disintegration, social cohesion, community cohesion, population mobility, urbanization, social inequality, and unequal distribution combine to build the basis for this field of study (Arthur 1992; Bernburg 2002; Braga and Clarke 2014; Miethe et al. 1991; Torry 2001). Generally speaking, social disorganization theory has originated and been developed primarily in the US. Subsequently, a fraction of cross-national studies has examined its application in other countries (e.g., Mazerolle et al. 2010; Sampson and Wikstrom 2008; Zhang et al. 2007). However, rare study is from a non-Western culture, let alone China. Therefore, studying the relationship between social change and crime has theoretical significance for the longitudinal expansion of criminology as a whole.

Research on the relationship between social change and crime is also important in understanding the criminal phenomenon of transitional China. The West often ignores criminal justice policies and practices of the East. This is mostly due to the lack of cross-cultural research (Lambert and Jiang 2006). While intra-cultural research is vital to generate and develop a theory, cross-cultural studies permit scholars a more thorough understanding of the generalizability of a theory. Cross-cultural investigations "help to reveal not only intriguing differences between countries and cultures, but also aspects of one's own country and culture that would be difficult or impossible to detect from domestic data alone" (Jowell 1998). This situation also suits to research on social disorganization approach and other criminological theories. China is a perfect non-Western culture to examine the generalizability of crime patterns found in the U.S. in general and correlates of social disorganization in particular. Although both nations are market economies, significant different cultures, economic developed manners, political systems, and criminal justices distinguish them from each other (Lambert and Jiang 2006). In addition to this, it is important to analyze and asses the effects of these various factors of crime, and how they affect society. This can provide various countries and their governments with evolutionary ideas in the formulation of crime prevention and control measurement, as well as rethinking of criminal legislation, and hence ameliorating the whole judicial system. This topic is related to regional economics, population geography, urban space, law, public administration, sociology, agriculture, economic management, and other disciplines, so it has theoretical significance for the lateral extension of criminology.

This book focuses on the relationship between social transition and crime in context of rapid Chinese social changes. Social changes in China are mainly reflected in rapid economic growth, the speed of urbanization, and significant changes in urban spatial patterns. The characteristics of Chinese society in the period of transition will be briefly summarized in the following manner as the characteristics are all closely related to social disorganization or represent social disorganization itself.

Rapid economic growth: According to the Encyclopedia Britannica, economic growth refers to the national wealth growing process (Edens 1975). Therefore, economic growth also means expansion and improvement of the factors that determine productivity. People supporting economic growth think that it can increase the wealth of a nation and provide more employment opportunities, which are generally considered to be the embodiment of overall economic prosperity (Peters et al. 2010; Sugden 2014; Victor 2010). Since its reform, the Chinese economy

Table 1.1 Rapid economic growth in China, 1978–2013

Year	GDP (Unit: 100,000,000 ¥)
1978	3645.2
1979	4062.6
1980[a]	4545.6
1981	4891.6
1982	5323.4
1983	5962.7
1984	7208.1
1985	9016.0
1986	10,275.2
1987	12,058.6
1988	15,042.8
1989	16,992.3
1990	18,667.8
1991	21,781.5
1992	26,923.5
1993	35,333.9
1994	48,197.9
1995	60,793.7
1996	71,176.6
1997	78,973.0
1998	84,402.3
1999	89,677.1
2000	99,214.6
2001	109,655.2
2002	120,332.7
2003	135,822.8
2004	159,878.3
2005	183,217.4
2006	211,923.5
2007	257,305.6
2008	300,670.0
2009	340,902.8
2010	401,512.8
2011	473,104.1
2012	519,470.1
2013[b]	568,845.2

Source Statistics Database of National Bureau of Statistics
[a]Since 1980, the difference between the Gross Domestic Product and the Gross National Income (formerly, the Gross National Product) is the net factor income from the rest of the world
[b]Data of 2013 were preliminary estimation. The same applies to the relevant tables following

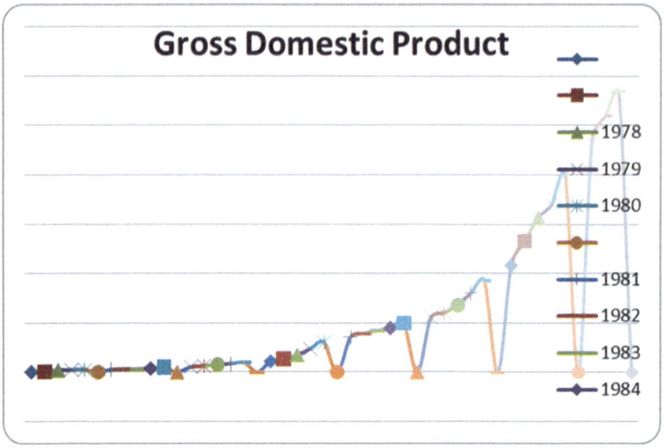

Fig. 1.1 GDP growth in China, 1978–2013. *Source* Statistics Database of National Bureau of Statistics

has experienced 30 consecutive years of rapid growth (Ke 2015) (see Table 1.1; Fig. 1.1). GDP increased to 56.885 trillion Yuan in 2013 from 364.5 billion Yuan in 1978, which increased almost 150 times in 35 years. This is a miraculous increase in economic history (Baum 1996). The economic reform has brought about significant social and cultural changes to the nation, although the political structure of the state remains basically intact. It can be said that all the changes in Chinese society, including social disorganization, are formed on the basis of rapid economic growth. Table 1.1 and Fig. 1.1 describe GDP growth in China from 1978 to 2013.

High-speed urbanization: Urbanization is an inevitable loop in the process of economic development all over the world (Chen et al. 2014), and with this comes the increase in population in urban centers during this time period. After British industrialization in the nineteenth century, the population in the ten big cities increased from 16 to 23 % in 1801–1851 (Button 1976). The Japanese economic recovery after World War II pushed the industrial development and urbanization process. For instance, 70 % of the urban population is concentrated in the three city circles—Tokyo circle, Osaka circle, and Nagoya circle. The three city circles account for only 10.4 % of the land area, whereas the concentrated population accounts for 43.5 % of the total population in 1970 (Otsu et al. 2004).

As a developing country, China began its urbanization process much later than the West (Bai et al. 2012). Urbanization rates increased to 17.92 % in 1978 from 10.6 % in 1949, which increased only 7.3 % in nearly 30 years (Chen et al. 2011). The pace of urbanization was very slow. With the rapid economic development, a wave of urbanization has swept over China in the past two decades (Yang 2013). The urban population ratio skyrocketed from 17.92 % in 1978 to 53.73 % in 2013 in a country with more than one billion people (Chen and Song 2014) (see Tables 1.2 and 1.3; Fig. 1.2 describes national and regional proportion of urban

Table 1.2 Proportion of urban population in China, 1978–2013

Year	Total population (100,000 persons)	Urban	
		Population (10,000 persons)	Percent (%)
1978	96,259	17,245	17.92
1980	98,705	19,140	19.39
1985	105,851	25,094	23.71
1990	114,333	30,195	26.41
1991	115,823	31,203	26.94
1992	117,171	32,175	27.46
1993	118,517	33,173	27.99
1994	119,850	34,169	28.51
1995	121,121	35,174	29.04
1996	122,389	37,304	30.48
1997	123,626	39,449	31.91
1998	124,761	41,608	33.35
1999	125,786	43,748	34.78
2000	126,743	45,906	36.22
2001	127,627	48,064	37.66
2002	128,453	50,212	39.09
2003	129,227	52,376	40.53
2004	129,988	54,283	41.76
2005	130,756	56,212	42.99
2006	131,448	57,706	43.90
2007	132,129	59,379	44.94
2008	132,802	60,667	45.68
2009	133,450	64,512	48.34
2010	134,091	66,978	49.94
2011	134,735	69,079	51.27
2012	135,404	71,182	52.57
2013	136,072	73,111	53.73

Source Statistics Database of National Bureau

population in year 2013). It is widely admitted that urbanization is not only an outcome of rapid accelerating economy, but also plays a key role in China's spectacular economic growth. Moreover, it is beyond doubt that will maintain its impetus and continue to be a momentous motive force for China's economic growth at least in the next one decade (Li et al. 2012; Meng 2012).

Unfortunately, China's urbanization has developed relatively far ahead of its economic growth (He et al. 2014). As a result, China's urban economic bonuses are being counteracted by the ceaseless urban curses of overcrowding, urban land expansion and deteriorated urban ecology (Li and Ma 2014), air and water pollution, rural–urban migration, environmental degradation, contagious disease, and crime at the same time (Faria and Mollick 1996), yet we are absolutely ignorant of

Table 1.3 National and regional proportion of urban population in 2013

Areas	Total Population (10,000 persons)	Urban population	
		Population (10,000 persons)	Percent (%)
National	136,072	73,111	53.73
Beijing	17,454	594.2942	86.30
Tianjin	12,150	273.6350	82.01
Hebei	60,517	451.7419	48.12
Shanxi	29,957	307.2808	52.56
Neimenggu	20,613	285.9667	58.71
Liaoning	36,231	824.0193	66.45
Jilin	22,707	373.3951	54.20
Heilongjiang	31,651	520.2461	57.40
Shanhai	19,932	674.1399	89.60
Jiangsu	65,526	999.3187	64.11
Zejiang	45,376	759.6981	64.00
Anhui	49,765	419.6828	47.86
Fujian	31,148	440.1215	60.77
Jiangxi	37,321	222.3878	48.87
Shandong	80,331	930.8403	53.75
Henan	77,688	563.6599	43.80
Hubei	47,860	584.0288	54.51
Hunan	55,219	401.0819	47.96
Guangdong	87,847	1849.4043	67.76
Guangxi	38,947	267.2388	44.81
Hainan	7389	69.1822	52.74
Chongqing	24,512	304.7787	58.34
Sichuan	66,904	555.9873	44.90
Guizhou	28,905	187.0355	37.83
Yunan	38,680	227.7135	40.48
Xizang	2575	10.0073	23.71
Shanxi	31,063	300.2620	51.31
Gansu	21,311	180.1481	40.13
Qinghai	4769	47.3375	48.51
Ningxia	5399	73.0768	52.01
Xinjiang	18,688	226.7041	44.47

Source Chinese Statistical Yearbook 2014

the following reason. The obvious significance of the issue has triggered a growing literature devoted to picturing the elementary patterns involved in urbanization in China.

Urban expansion is one of the geographic patterns of China's urbanization. Landless peasant issues and problems related to land transfer are often derived from urban expansion (Hao 2012; Hao et al. 2012, 2013). For instance,

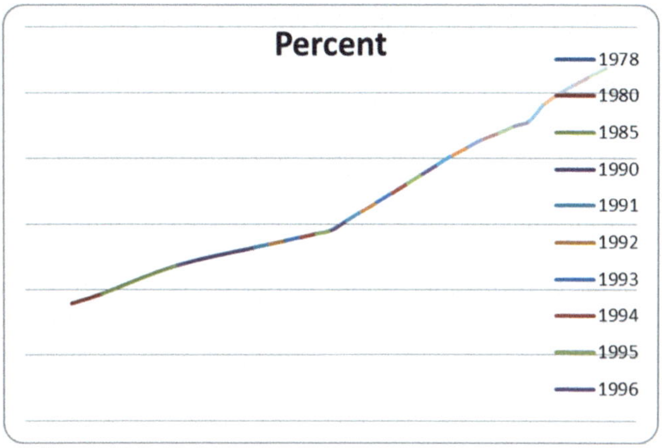

Fig. 1.2 Urbanization rate in China, 1978–2013. *Source* Statistics Database of National Bureau of Statistics

innumerable landless peasants crowded into cities during periods of social change, which resulted in cramped urban living spaces and placed constraints on urban public resources. Data show that from 1990, the annual loss of farmland amounts to 10,000,000 mus (a Chinese unit of area, =0.0667 ha), which causes at least 400,000,000 unemployed farmers to rural China, reaching 8 % of the total rural labor force (Yang and Cao 2004).

Rural–urban migration is another basic component involving in rich dynamic process of urbanization. To speak historically, the dominant form of current Chinese urbanization has been donned "townization turning into incomplete urbanization" (Li 2004a, b). In this stage, a large number of the rural population migrate to the city to engage in "long-distance, cross-border" (Li 2004a, b) employment mobility. They encountered a state of anomie which meant that traditional morality and values have collapsed, while new values and social order have not yet been established in social interaction with urban residents. This proves that the intrinsic culture, ethics, and values of either original inhabitants or the migration will be influenced and infiltrated by each other. Moreover, China's rapid developed urbanization has also generated a severe labor shortage in its rural areas. By 2013, 262 million people had migrated to the urban. The bulk of the rural-to-urban migrants are adult men, who seek higher wages in cities but have to leave their children, spouses, and aging parents in rural hometown. The number of unattended children increased from 22 million in 2004 to 58 million in 2010, and the women and aging parents staying home reached more than 47 million and 40 million, respectively. These three groups now take up more than 22 % of China's total rural population. The rural left-behind children were often related to critical economic and social problems. The latter are evidently considered as a potent resource of juvenile delinquency.

Significant changes in urban spatial pattern: Urban expansion and ecological structural changes are the basic results of urbanization and modernization on geographical and spatial levels. From the nineteenth century onwards when capitalism expanded, urbanization all over the world developed rapidly in the drive for industrialization (Ma and Lian 2011). Since the 1950s, the speed of urbanization in each country has accelerated, causing population trends to migrate to the big city. Because of this, metropolitan economic functions are becoming more prominent (Aunan and Wang 2014). As the population and wealth gathered into the metropolitan area, overall development of the city ensued (Fay 2014). This occurred specifically in the area of infrastructure, as urban lands gradually expanded outwards toward and the boundary between urban and suburban areas became blurred. Urban areas also reveal contiguous developmental trends in what described as the "city spread" (Goldstein 1990). In the late 2005, there were 661 cities and 35,894 urban people in all of China. Urban areas reach 412,700 km^2, including 32,500 km^2 of developed land, with an urban population density of 870 person/km^2.

Urban ecological patterns change as well (Liu 2006) and this is especially prevalent in the Pearl River Delta. Guangzhou serves as the regional center and therefore expands rapidly. At the present time, there is also no geographic border between cities of Guangzhou and Foshan, which is important to note that the farmland that separated the two districts has now been utilized for developmental purposes. It can be said that with decades of the development of cities, ecological patterns are also important to analyze to fully comprehend the changes that are taking place in China's city centers (Liu et al. 2014).

The most significant social effect in urban spatial pattern change in criminological sense is how it generates "social isolation" and crime hot spots. In general terms, with the change of urban spatial structure, a considerable number of higher-price residential communities will appear outside the city, especially in suburban areas. Closed-end managements are popular in these residential communities as fences, security guards, and video-monitoring systems are implemented. These communities are the so-called "gated communities." Unlike Western countries, Chinese "gated communities" in China locate not only outside the city, but also in urban central areas and transitional regions. Essentially, there is large number of lower-class population in urban village, living next to luxury upper-class communities in most major Chinese cities (Fig. 1.5). This phenomenon is determined by the unique Chinese cultural tradition, law, and land systems.[1]

Given all this, the community distribution for various social classes and the reasons for shaping such features will be discussed in detail in this book (in a typical case study). Community isolation is one of the factors aiding in the reshaping of community distribution. Blakely and Snyger (1997) indicate that community isolation tends to aggravate the socioeconomic stratification and division, privatize

[1]Land systems in China are different from other countries. There are two types of land in current China. One is urban land, and the other is rural land. Urban land is belonging to the state, while rural land belongs to the villager collective. Rural land cannot be in trade freely.

Fig. 1.3 'Hand-in-hand' buildings and thin strip of sky (By Xiong 2014)

public space while unbalance the residential social process, reduce social participation, and inhibit its workings. Concentrated poverty is another significant consequence of social isolation at the community level. Geographic concentration of poverty makes communities in which poor people live much more degenerated. Because of this, a deteriorated community environment will create many adverse effects (Liu et al. 2009), such as juvenile delinquency, drug abuse, prostitution, premarital pregnancy, abortion, and so on. Urban village is definitely such a typical degraded, social isolated community experiencing concentrated poverty, severe disorganization, and high crime rates (Li et al. 2007) (Figs. 1.3, 1.4, 1.5 and 1.6).

Population mobility: Thirty years of Reform has not only brought a boom in China's economy, but also an increase in all areas of development and urbanization. As a result, floating population has emerged and played a dominant role in economic development and social transition (Buckley 2014). As we know, before China's economic reform, a strict household registry system was put in practice in China which prevented rural dwellers and urban residents from relocation. Since its economic reform, China's household registration policy has been gradually adjusted to less control and less restriction on population movements, and allowed people to move from one place to another for jobs (Huang and Zhan 2005).

Fig. 1.4 Iron gates in 'hand-in-hand' building in urban village (By Xiong 2014)

Consequently, there has been a trend of large-scale population mobility in China (Murphy 2002). For example, the number of nationwide floating population doubled in just 10 years as it went from 70 million to 140 million in 2003. The "floating population" is always treated as special social group as they are facing many difficulties, unrest, and instability within the social strata (Research Group of State Labor and Social Security Ministry 2005). A period with large population flow is inevitably a period with a relatively large scale of instability. Population mobility in China is somewhat different from many western countries due to its special historical, cultural, and traditional driving factors. These features also make China encounter more instable status during periods of large-scale population mobility. As migrant workers provide the main base of China's economy, the floating population proves to be vastly different from what of western countries (Curran 1998). For example, worldwide statistics show that the migration rate for children under five is quite high, whereas China's migratory patterns do not reflect these characteristics. Table 1.4 shows provinces and territories with proportion of migrants more than 10 %; Table 1.5 indicates thee number of floating population in 2000, 2005, and 2010–2013.

Fig. 1.5 Breakfast stall in urban village (By Xiong 2014)

One of the main reasons for China's floating population administration dilemma is that migrant workers make up the majority of the floating population (Knight 2013; Buckley 2014). By the National Bureau of Statistics of China, the total number of migrant workers once reached 225.42 million persons in 2008, including 140 million migrant workers who work outside their hometowns (NBSC 2009). Large scales of migrant workers who came into cities for jobs were not permitted to settle down (actually they have no ability to settle down in city) in the place where they worked because of the household registration system; they have to return hometown mainly by train or interurban coach in major festivals. Consequently, there is a unique seasonal movement of migrant workers in China.

Due to the lack of economic ability to set up family in the city (Wang 2014; Xu 2000; Becker 2014), coupled with institutional discrimination and a series of other social problems (Wang 2013; Qin 2015; Li et al. 2014), these migrant workers often leave their children in their city of origin to be cared for by their parents (Zhan 2014). This induces a unique population phenomenon in China as "left-behind children" reflect the complex nuances of China's population (Qiu et al. 2011; Hong 2011). The increasing number of migrant workers and left-behind children also produces a series of social concerns (Li 2013). The crime rates

Fig. 1.6 Shrine in house corner in urban village (By Xiong 2014)

Table 1.4 Provinces and territories with proportion of migrants more than 10 %

	Beijing	Tianjin	Shanxi	Neimenggu	Liaoning	Jining	Hei Nongjiang	Shanghai
Proportion of migrants	33	22	11	16	15	11	10	32
	Jiangsu	Zejiang	Fujian	Guangdong	Hainan	Qinghai	Ningxia	Xinjiang
Proportion of migrants	12	18	17	29	12	10	12	15

Source Chinese Statistical Yearbook 2014

Table 1.5 Number of floating population Unit: a hundred million persons

Year	Population of residence–registration inconsistency	Floating population
2000	1.44	1.21
2005		1.47
2010	2.61	2.21
2011	2.71	2.30
2012	2.79	2.36
2013	2.89	2.45

Source Chinese Statistical Yearbook 2014

become affected by the issues as social equity and equal education opportunities (Gui et al. 2012; Lo and Jiang 2006).

Deteriorated urban poverty: Before 1978, China was in overall poverty with an extremely small income per capita and low living standard. The World Bank declared in 1978 that the population in poverty in China reached 2.6 billion, while 100 million of which was concentrated in rural areas (Fan et al. 2003). Subsequently, by some researchers' reckoning, China's urban poverty population proportion in 1996 accounted for at least 5 % of urban population which was estimated to be 1200 myrias. (Appleton et al. 2010). These statistics, however, refer to the absolute poverty population only. If measured by relative poverty, the urban poverty population would even reach more than 2400 myrias (Appleton et al. 2010).

Generally speaking, macroeconomy maintained long-term rapid and steady development since the Reform in China. It gave the Chinese farmers in rural areas the opportunity to get out of poverty in some extent. In China's urban areas, however, along with urban residential average incomes and the living standard improving during the period of rapid economic growth, it must be added, went a strong relative, or even absolute poverty (Cho 2013; Cook 2000; Hammond 2013; Park and Wang 2010). This is partly due to the increase in the number of laid-off workers affected by the rapid institutional reformation (Shouhai 2015). Obviously, the efficacy of China's current strategy of emphasizing economic growth over redistribution results partly insharpening of polarization between the rich and the poor. Poverty and relative poverty are often associated with concepts such as social deprivation, social injustice, and social exclusion, which are all factors causing social disorder and social instability (Fan et al. 2003; Solinger and Hu 2012; Wang 2004). A substandard income not only affects the ability of families, but also their living standard Wu (2010). Table 1.6 shows income per capita of China's urban and rural households and Engle coefficient in 2013. Table 1.7 and Fig. 1.7 describe annual purchases of major commodities and annual purchases of yogurt per capita of urban households by the level of income in turn. Registered urban unemployment, number of the poverty, as well as national and regional urban poverty rates in China from 1990 to 2013 are shown in Tables 1.8, 1.9, and 1.10 and Fig. 1.8, respectively.

Although there have still no powerful evidence that poverty leads to crime directly, it is clear that long-term poverty, concentrated poverty, and polarization of wealth are all relative to crime (Appleton et al. 2010). To a certain extent, floating population's clustering in urban village is partly responsible for urban concentrated poverty. Floating population simply cannot do anything but to rent in urban village due to their low personal income, limited social networks, and relatively cheaper rent of villagers' houses. As the case study site, the number of registered migrants of Guangzhou from other cities reaches 6,869,700 (2014 Guangzhou Census). Given the hidden nature of population migration, multiple unregistered floating population were estimated by the official and the estimated total number of floating population in Guangzhou reached 8,370,000, even a bit more than local residents. Most of the floating population lived in renting housing in urban

Table 1.6 Per capita income of Chinese urban and rural households and Engle coefficient in 2013

Year	Per capita disposable income of urban households		Per capita net income of rural households		Urban households	Rural households
	Absolute number (Yuan)	Index (1978 = 100)	Absolute number (Yuan)	Index (1978 = 100)	Engel coefficient (%)	Engel coefficient (%)
1978	343.4	100	133.6	100	57.5	67.7
1980	477.6	127	191.3	139	56.9	61.8
1985	739.1	160.4	397.6	268.9	53.31	57.8
1990	1510.2	198.1	686.3	311.2	54.24	58.8
1991	1700.6	212.4	708.6	317.4	53.8	57.6
1992	2026.6	232.9	784	336.2	53.04445	57.6
1993	2577.4	255.1	921.6	346.9	50.3167	58.1
1994	3496.2	276.8	1221	364.3	50.03928	58.9
1995	4283	290.3	1577.7	383.6	50.0906	58.6
1996	4838.9	301.6	1926.1	418.1	48.76093	56.3
1997	5160.3	311.9	2090.1	437.3	46.59502	55.1
1998	5425.1	329.9	2162	456.1	44.66099	53.4
1999	5854.02	360.6	2210.3	473.5	42.06798	52.6
2000	6280	383.7	2253.4	483.4	39.44218	49.1
2001	6859.6	416.3	2366.4	503.7	38.19902	47.7
2002	7702.8	472.131	2475.6	527.9	37.67637	46.2
2003	8472.2	514.6	2622.2	550.6	37.1	45.6
2004	9421.6	554.2	2936.4	588	37.7	47.2
2005	10,493	607.4	3254.9	624.5	36.7	45.5
2006	11,759.5	670.7	3587	670.7	35.8	43
2007	13,785.8	752.5	4140.4	734.4	36.28948	43.1
2008	15,780.76	815.7	4760.62	793.152	37.88906	43.67
2009	17,174.7	895.4	5153.2	860.6	36.5	41.0
2010	19,109.4	965.2	5919.0	954.4	35.7	41.1
2011	21,809.8	1046.3	6977.3	1063.2	36.3	40.4
2012	24,564.7	1146.7	7916.6	1176.9	36.2	39.3
2013	26,955.1	1227.0	8895.9	1286.4	35.0	37.7

Source Chinese Statistical Yearbook (1978–2014)

village or self-built dilapidated shelters. For instance, Shipai Village, as one of the most famous urban villages in Guangzhou where 20,000 closed-circuit television cameras have been installed to guard against deviance and crime, has over 42,000 floating population, which is more than 4 times of local residents. Undeniably, the inburst of floating population leads naturally to environmental deterioration and public disorder. Moreover, high mobility makes them neglect the social affairs, lack of social responsibility, and needless to say tackle their marriage and children's education.

Table 1.7 Annual purchases of major commodities per capita of urban households by level of income in China in 2013

	Poor families	Middle-income families	High-income families
Edible vegetable oil (kg)	8.26	10.72	10.37
Pork (kg)	11.17	20.06	23.15
Beef (kg)	1.23	2.38	2.7
Mutton(kg)	0.89	1.39	1.29
Egg (kg)	7.65	11.37	11.71
White spirits (kg)	1.74	2.33	1.9
Wine (kg)	0.06	0.2	0.49
Beer (kg)	2.95	5.59	6.39
Tea (kg)	0.17	0.3	0.39
Cake (kg)	2.29	5.05	6.72
Milk (kg)	6.66	15.84	22.37
Milk powder (kg)	0.32	0.61	0.71
Yogurt (kg)	1.36	3.74	5.49
Dress (piece)	3.06	7.73	14.3
Shoes (pair)	1.5	2.85	3.92

Source Chinese Statistical Yearbook 2014

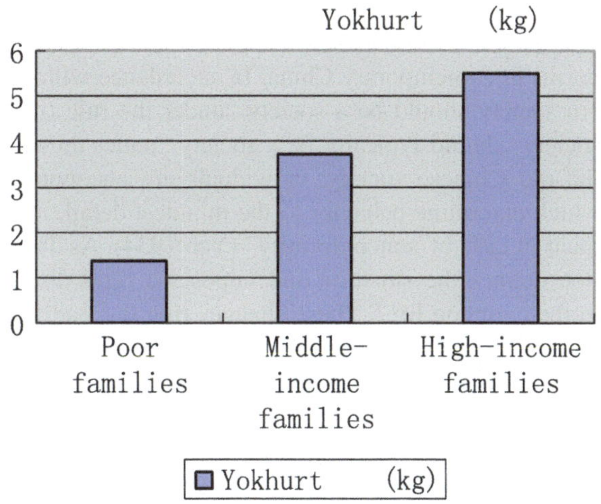

Fig. 1.7 Annual purchases of yogurt per capita of urban households by level of income in China in 2013. *Source* Chinese Statistical Yearbook 2014

Gradually disorganized social norms: In the early nineteenth century, the famous sociologist Emile Durkheim made a wonderful description on chaos and the collapse of French social norms (Durkheim 1951): If anomie is a crime, it is because it makes the society in tribulation. Society would never survive without social cohesion and regulating force. Crime is irreplaceable for society to evolve

Table 1.8 Registered urban unemployment in China, 1990–2013

Year	Registered urban unemployed population (%)	Registered urban unemployment rate (%)
1990	383	2.5
1995	520	2.9
2000	595	3.1
2001	681	3.6
2002	770	4.0
2003	800	4.3
2004	627	4.2
2005	839	4.2
2006	847	4.1
2007	830	4.0
2008	886	4.2
2009	921	4.3
2010	908	4.1
2011	922	4.1
2012	917	4.1
2013	926	4.1

Source Statistics Database of National Bureau of Statistics

and retain itself and that there is no society without crime for a society that does not have crime would be in a state of anomie (Durkheim 1964).

Heavy transitional and mixed color is now becoming a regular feature of social norms in contemporary China. In accordance with the view of Fei (1998), a modern society should be a society "under the rule of law," and the traditional rural society should typically be a society "under the rule of *Li*". In other words, "in the old Chinese society, individuals are encountered with inveterate traditions, which determine behavior to the minutest detail, and are assured of swift punishment in case of nonconformity" (Yen 1934). As Thomas says, "Custom and tradition defines the situation and imposes a rigid discipline on all who participated in the common life." These changes ruin the traditional manner of living, and the crowning *li*, which has molded the Chinese behavior for thousands of years, has begun to decompose, and then produces maladjustment and social disorganization. However, social and legal rules have not completely formed in Chinese society. Society now shows a "multiplex mixed rule" interwoven by legal rule, moral rule, and rule of the Patrilineal Clan (Cao 2007).

Economic and political restructuring and social changes have a tremendous impact on Chinese morals and cultural practices in the modernization process (Tang 1997). "Moral norm vacuum and moral criteria confusion are caused by severe social changes" (Zhao 2008). "The original ethical rules greatly lost social integration function, while the new moral standards and ethical rules have not established … … it is the so-called 'loose morality'" (Cao 2007).

Spiral crime growth: Contemporary China, however, has observed a dramatic growth of economy and crime (Cheong and Wu 2015). Many investigations

Table 1.9 Number of the poverty in China in 2013

Areas	Number of urban residents in minimum living guarantee	Number of urban households in minimum living guarantee	Number of rural residents in minimum living guarantee	Number of rural households in minimum living guarantee
Unit	Person	Household	Person	Household
National total	23,330,910	11,415,731	48,404,296	23,280,262
Beijing	147,190	74,747	80,032	42,924
Tianjin	182,354	88,600	75,132	31,808
Hebei	900,670	441,419	1,787,219	1,167,546
Shanxi	942,236	438,394	1,194,210	828,346
Neimenggu	872,054	449,298	1,195,907	847,823
Liaoning	1,299,803	623,511	919,763	496,571
Jilin	1,209,666	617,658	984,291	491,766
Heilongjiang	1,536,288	738,997	1,086,377	507,694
Shanghai	365,499	204,768	101,622	62,159
Jiangsu	460,838	220,554	1,384,352	746,997
Zhejiang	92,563	55,942	571,311	344,734
Anhui	925,284	500,124	2,124,165	1,068,847
Fujian	186,619	84,331	707,982	301,277
Jiangxi	984,711	447,087	1,495,830	612,567
Shandong	617,145	273,135	2,015,243	1,225,059
Henan	1,487,037	700,857	3,623,193	2,092,239
Hubei	1,452,677	675,340	1,781,709	869,726
Hunan	1,492,523	774,485	2,663,940	1,091,422
Guangdong	404,284	168,868	1,726,052	685,562
Guangxi	638,124	315,014	3,101,752	1,210,015
Hainan	181,531	75,636	223,682	92,695
Chongqing	697,143	358,859	1,165,941	591,644
Sichuan	1,886,237	1,002,916	3,925,619	1,933,623
Guizhou	521,669	260,392	3,617,364	1,565,804
Yunnan	907,117	527,035	3,384,724	1,745,726
Xizang	39,415	17,901	230,000	58,385
Shanxi	858,723	380,630	2,310,379	935,690
Gansu	834,011	348,410	2,933,689	835,320
Qinghai	221,345	98,850	379,999	133,613
Ningxia	208,431	95,017	305,135	186,556
Xinjiang	777,723	356,956	1,307,682	476,124

Source Chinese Statistical Yearbook 2014

Table 1.10 National and regional urban poverty rate in China in 2013

Areas	Number of urban residents in minimum living guarantee (10,000 persons)	Total number of urban residents (10,000 persons)	Urban poverty rate (%)
National total	2333.09	60,667.00	3.85
Beijing	14.72	1439.06	1.02
Tianjin	18.24	908.22	2.01
Hebei	90.07	2928.32	3.08
Shanxi	94.22	1538.53	6.12
Neimenggu	87.21	1248.14	6.99
Liaoning	129.98	2590.98	5.02
Jilin	120.97	1454.76	8.32
Heilongjiang	153.63	2119.27	7.25
Shanghai	36.55	1673.18	2.18
Jiangsu	46.08	4168.77	1.11
Zhejiang	9.26	2949.12	0.31
Anhui	92.53	2484.68	3.72
Fujian	18.66	1798.40	1.04
Jiangxi	98.47	1819.84	5.41
Shandong	61.71	4482.60	1.38
Henan	148.70	3397.27	4.38
Hubei	145.27	2581.37	5.63
Hunan	149.25	2689.17	5.55
Guangdong	40.43	6048.03	0.67
Guangxi	63.81	1837.79	3.47
Hainan	18.15	409.92	4.43
Chongqing	69.71	1419.22	4.91
Sichuan	188.62	3043.61	6.20
Guizhou	52.17	1104.06	4.72
Yunnan	90.71	1499.19	6.05
Xizang	3.94	64.89	6.07
Shanxi	85.87	1583.80	5.42
Gansu	83.40	844.94	9.87
Qinghai	22.13	227.00	9.75
Ningxia	20.84	278.00	7.50
Xinjiang	77.77	844.65	9.21

Source Chinese Statistical Yearbook 2014

have indicated that China's crime rate has increased virtually accompanied with the sweeping economic growth (Bakken 1993; Dai 1995; Rojek 1996; Dutton 1997; Liu and Messner 2001; Liu 2005a, b). The transition from the highly centralized planning system to a market economic system leads to the breakdown

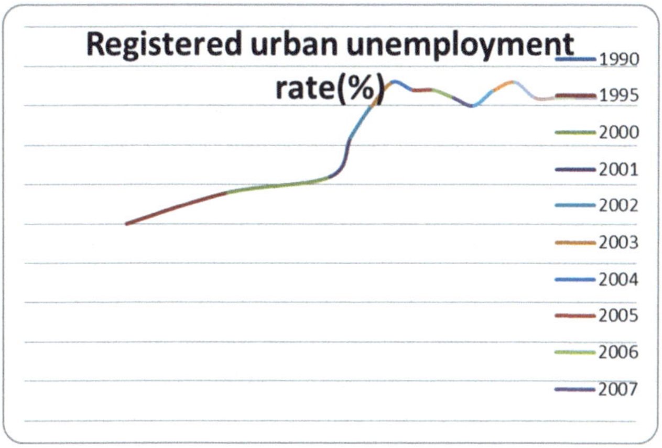

Fig. 1.8 Registered urban unemployment rate in China, 1990–2013. *Source* Statistics Database of National Bureau of Statistics

of traditional forms of social bonds and long-accepted social organizations. Consequently, crime rates have uprisen due to the lack of social control and social integration. Furthermore, the market-oriented economic systems are not perfect yet and still in the process of improvement, leaving many individuals and groups marginalized during the period of economic reform, which results in an exasperation of economic inequality which further raises the crime rate.

We can clearly see that there have been five crime waves since the national founding in 1949 in China. Table 1.11 and Fig. 1.9 based on criminal statistical data clearly reflect the spiraling process of crime rate and the six crime peak periods.

The first wave of crime appeared in the early days after the foundation of People's Republic of China (PRC). There were bandits, spies, and ruffians left by Kuomintang regime that seriously disrupted social order in China during that day. During that period, the national crime rate reached 93 per 100,000 people in 1950, 59 per 100,000 people in 1951, and 42 per 100,000 people in 1952, which reduced to 29 per 100,000 people in 1956.

After 1957, there was a second wave of crime that took place in 1961 due to severe economic recession. In that year, national crime rates reached 64 per 100,000 people. Social order improved following a decreased crime tendency with the improvement of the national economy. National crime rates kept in 30–40 per 100,000 people from 1962 to 1965.

After 1978s reform and opening up, society became more liberal in its initial stage of economic reform, resulting in social structural change, which increased crime rates through social members' moral anomie and ideational alienation. There occurred the third crime wave in 1981 with a crime rate of 89 per 100,000 people. After that, crime rates declined year after year and stabilized in 50 per 100,000 people in 1987.

Table 1.11 National statistics of criminal cases investigated by police, 1978–2013

Year	Criminal cases investigated by police (10,000)	Criminal cases investigated by police per 100,000 persons
1978	53.6	56.0
1979	63.6	66.0
1980	75.7	77.0
1981	89.0	89.0
1982	74.8	74.0
1983	61.1	60.0
1984	51.4	50.0
1985	54.2	52.0
1986	54.7	51.9
1987	57.0	54.0
1988	82.8	77.0
1989	197.2	181.5
1990	221.7	200.0
1991	236.6	215.0
1992	158.3	138.5
1993	161.7	140.0
1994	166.1	140.0
1995	169.0	142.3
1996	160.1	130.9
1997	152.8	123.6
1998	198.6	159.1
1999	229.0	182.0
2000	363.0	286.5
2001	446.0	349.5
2002	433.7	337.6
2003	439.4	340.0
2004	471.8	363.0
2005	465.3	355.9
2006	466.6	355.0
2007	474.6	359.2
2008	488.5	367.8
2009	558.0	418.1
2010	597.0	445.2
2011	600.5	445.7
2012	655.1	483.8
2013	659.8	484.9

Source Statistics Database of National Bureau of Statistics

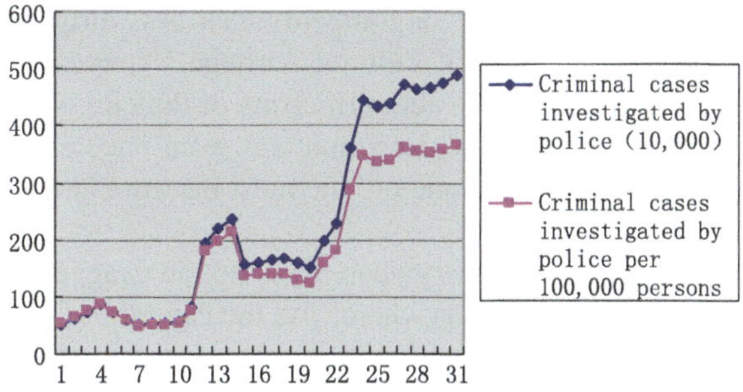

Fig. 1.9 National statistics of criminal cases investigated by police, 1978–2013. *Source* Statistics Database of National Bureau of Statistics

Since 1988, crime rates began rising dramatically, and reached the peak in 1991, with national crime rate 215 per 100,000 when the fourth crime wave surfaced. There kept a downward trend of crime rate since 1997 which reduced to 123 per 100,000 people. Crime rate climbed again year after 1998. There has been a national crime rate of 159 per 100,000 people in 1998, and 182 per 100,000 people in 1999. Crime rates reached the peak in 2000 and surged to 286 per 100,000 people.

Since 2001, national crime rates reached another high and have continued since then. National crime rate crested in 2008 at 367.8 per 100,000 people, and then continued at 484.7 per 100,000 people in 2013.

1.2 Taking to the Field—About Guangzhou

To speak frankly, Guangzhou is a strange city full of contradictions: it is the richest "City" in the whole country but houses many impoverished people. It is also one of the most modern cities but also the oldest city in China with a history of more than two thousand years which flourished from the Qin Dynasty,[2] 33 years Qin Shi Huang,[3] 214 BC) (Liu 2005a, b) (Ancestral shrines in some communities even have existed nearly a thousand years.) There are more other contradictions as it is one of the most urbanized cities in China, while it also has a large number of well-known "urban villages" at the same time. Its residential population is the same as outsider populations, while the latter is somewhat successfully absorbed by the former.

With a Google search, you will find many positive comments about the city on the Internet; conversely, at the same time you can also find a lot of negative

---

[2]Qin Dynasty (Chinese: 秦朝; pinyin: qíncháo). The first imperial dynasty of China, lasting from 221 to 206 BC.

[3]Qin Shi Huang, (Chinese: 秦始皇; pinyin: qínshǐhuáng), the King of the state of Qin (r. 246–221 BC) who conquered all other Warring States and united China in 221 BC.

evaluations about it: ongoing overcast sky, dirty streets, "strange planned city," "noisy city," "lack of cultural heritage," "mercantilism," and so on. Above all, one of the most persistent criticisms of the city is its social order. Condemned for its high crime rate, Guangzhou was even once elected as "city with worst social order in China" and one of "the most insecure cities" in China (Information Times 2006).

City with gold everywhere: It is not an exaggeration to describe Guangzhou as a "city with gold everywhere." As the capital of Guangdong Province, Guangzhou is also political, economic, and cultural center of this province. The city is one of the five national key cities established by the State Council in 2008. Industry and tertiary industry have been developed rapidly after the Reform. In addition to this, the GDP and per capita GDP of Guangzhou continue to increase. For example, in 2009 its GDP was ranked third, while the per capita GDP was ranked first in all of China.

Floating city: Immigrants play an increasingly important part in Guangzhou's regional economic growth. Between 1978 and 2013, Guangzhou's permanent population rose from 4,820,000 to 12,926,800 persons, an increase of 8,106,800 or 1.68 times. This increase was more than quadruple the national rate of 40.67 % in the same period. Owing to this sustained and rapid increase, Guangzhou's permanent population climbed to third place nationwide in 2013. In the three decades after reform and opening up, Guangzhou became one of the four largest first-tier cities in China not only in point of overall economic output but also in point of permanent population.

Known as the capital of Guangdong Province, Guangzhou is also famous as an ancient center of culture and migration. Renxiao[4] in the Qin Dynasty was the first city's architect. As an old poetry said, "warlords fight for Central Plains[5] while the multitude go to southern border," Guangzhou was one of the major shelters harboring thousands of refugees trapped by war, drought, and famine during the five migrating waves and continued to be the land of dreams of innumerable peasant workers after the Reform (Shen 2010). There is another well-known bard song saying that "East, South, West, North, and Centre, anywhere you come from, all making money in Guangdong" (Cantonese) (Ming Pao Daily 2011). Furthermore, different from Beijing, Shanghai, and Shenzhen, where consensus has clearly shifted in favor of raising the immigration threshold, Guangzhou continues to hold tolerant attitudes toward extraneous people. It entitles more outsiders to make money, get job, and dwell in this city. Furthermore, different from Beijing, Shanghai, and Shenzhen, which have begun to set threshold to outsiders, Guangzhou continues to hold tolerant attitudes toward outsider earning one's crust and seeking livelihood in it, which attracts more outsiders immigrating into Guangzhou (Xiaoliu 2010). However, it must be pointed out that migrant workers

[4]Ren Xiao (Chinese: 任嚣; pinyin: rénxiāo). The first Governor of Guangzhou historically.

[5]The Central Plain, or Zhongyuan or Chungyuan (Chinese: 中原; pinyin: zhōngyuán), refers to the area on the lower reaches of the Yellow River which formed the cradle of Chinese civilization.

proceed to make up the largest parts of outsiders (Jian 1996). In recent years, the birth rate of the inflowing population in Guangzhou showed a rise as well. At the same time, social problems cropped up with the influx of extraneous population swarming into Guangzhou. The surge of outsider populations generated enormous wealth as well as diverse hard issues (Paik 2014). Due to limited city capacity, public facilities, and employment opportunities, the city cannot handle the overflow, while the city management system has been met by a challenge, especially its public-security administration experienced considerable pressure caused by the surge of transient populations. Robbery and theft happen highly, especially in urban villages. Moreover, relative survey shows that 80 % of prisoners were foreign population, of whom nearly 90 % lived in rental house before arrest (Zhu et al. 2006).

Chocolate City: Guangzhou is one of leading open cities in China. As a window of foreign trade, it attracts many foreign people. Trade between China and Africa has spread dramatically since Chinese accession to the World Trade Organization in 2001 (Zheng 2009), and African communities in South-East China have grown significantly in recent years (Bodomo 2009).

Guangzhou's population increased greatly during 1978–2013, with additional high levels of unregistered migration (Wu 2001). At the same time, the number of foreign visitors in Guangzhou is growing rapidly. Of these, some 20 % are African. The municipal figure for Africans has reached into 200,000 persons in 2013, an annual increase far steeper than other nationalities (Huanqiu Net 2014).

Guangzhou's Africans are clustered for both housing and work. Different with foreign elites clustering in the city's new Central Business District (CBD), Africans gather in poorer areas mentioned above, handy for transport to the port, wholesale market and manufacturing centers, and offering cheap accommodation in flat blocks, hostels and inns (Li et al. 2007). This mirrors gradually increasing social stratification and social isolation of today's Chinese cities. Chinese society shows signs of xenophobia, particularly toward Africans, notably in the housing market (Hu and Kaplan 2001; Li et al. 2007; Nyamwama 2004). Racism still exists to varying degrees. Generally, Guangzhou's Africans tend to concentrate in small streets of Yuexiu District and Baiyun District such as Dengfeng Road, Kuangquan Road, and Sanyuanli Street (Guangzhou Bureau of Tourism 2014).

In Guangzhou, increasing transnational activities gradually form the existence of an African diaspora (Lyons et al. 2008). Furthermore, the almost complete vacuum of opportunity for insertion into local employment markets means that entrepreneurship is a basement of this diaspora and maintains a strong characteristic for the long term. The difficulties of getting residency visas purport that most members of the African diaspora in Guangzhou city are short-term migrants or even unlawful presencers (Lyons et al. 2012). The Africa's swarming into Guangzhou makes the city the 'forefront of a migration wave' (Bertoncelo and Bredeloup 2007), and challenges the city's public administration ability.

In addition to this, illegal immigration appears a new social issue. Statistics show that the number of Africans moving in Guangzhou increase at an annual rate of 30–40 %; it was also referred that the total number of blacks is more than

200,000 (Lan 2015). This influx of foreigners to Guangzhou has brought so many social problems that criminal cases related to Africans have risen drastically in recent years. Furthermore, on July 15, 2009, there were minor clashes between Africans and the authorities in a police station in Kuangquan Street Yuexiu District (Guangzhou Municipal Bureau of Tourism 2011). This influx of foreigners brings new security issues in Guangzhou as some negative social emotions such as impugnation and resentment are raised because of racial appearances, ethnic habits, religious differences, and economic and living frictions. There are also more and more social problems caused by Chinese sympolyandria with foreigners, especially blacks, which force the entire Chinese society to pay attention to problems of heterogeneity.

Urban village—wound behind prosperity:

The 'urban village' is direct production of typical urban expansion's Pearl River Delta Model. Because of its unique position as the capital of province Guangdong and its designation as one of the 14 first-open coastal cities back at the beginning of Reform and Open, Guangzhou is an expanding market attracting foreign investment from around the globe and has stimulated buck migration to its newly established manufacturing industry. The urban area has expanded remarkably in the last 30 years and, accordingly, Rapid urbanization has swallowed up a great quantity of villages at the fringes of the city. The city authority usually only requisitions farmland, while ignoring the existing residential village areas, as the latter demand much more compensation and involved in several thorny legal relative problems. Consequently, many villages do not evolved into mature urban areas, but are nevertheless succeeded by urban sprawl. In this way, they become recognizable as 'urban villages,' characterized by their rural essence under urban appearance. "Deprived of their traditional agricultural resources, the villagers, out of necessity, become 'builders'. The 'illegal' constructions they erect then serve as housing for mass migrants, who are institutionally and economically excluded by the urban system. Consequently, urban villages become migrant enclaves, characterised by high-density and overcrowding" (Lin et al. 2011).

As far as Guangzhou is concerned, urban spread has been dramatically accelerated during the 2000s, with its built-up area getting to 990 km^2 in 2013, while only 58 km^2 in 1978 (Nanfang Daily 2013). The average annual increase is 26.6 km^2 and spread rate is 2.94 %. A large number of natural villages in the suburb originally were swallowed by urban land expanding and became urban villages. By 2013, there were 139 villages in urban built-up area in Guangzhou, with a total area reaching 80.6 km^2, holding 8.14 % of urban built-up area. Affected by city and countryside, the urban fringe is habitat of urban development and change. Urban villages are basically located at such areas and distributed along the traffic arteries. Accompanied with rapid urbanization, urban village expands and accumulates massive collective wealth due to its perfect location and large expropriation compensation from local government (Zhou 2014). Simultaneously, a large number of peasant workers swarm into city to fish for jobs and local residents in

Table 1.12 Number of criminal case-filing and rate of case-filing per 100,000 persons in Guangzhou in 1995 and 1998–2013

Year	Total population (100,000 persons)	Number of criminal case-filing	Number of criminal case-filing per 100,000 persons
1995	64.67115	59,775	924
1998	67.414	45,415	674
1999	68.50024	43,411	634
2000	70.06896	141,930	2026
2001	71.25979	123,554	1734
2002	72.06229	113,901	1581
2003	72.51888	116,146	1602
2004	73.7672	111,745	1515
2005	75.05322	105,364	1404
2006	76.0722	94,775	1246
2007	77.34787	79,770	1031
2008	78.41695	68,699	876
2009	79.46154	59,900	754
2010	127.008	53,700	423
2011	127.514	56,500	443
2012	127.951	115,100	900
2013	129.268	240,600	1861

Source Guangzhou Statistical Yearbook (2000–2014)

urban village strive to build so many low-quality and high-density renting houses, which produce a series of social and physical problems.

Unlike several of their parallels in other backgrounds, Guangzhou's urban villages are representatively low-ending communities, housing many of the most discriminated against and disadvantaged members of the population (Wei and Yan 2005a, b). "Their development characteristics share a number of similarities with some informal settlement types in other developing countries. For instance, the growth of these settlements is often driven by rural-to-urban migration and the growth of the poor urban population" (O'Hare and Barke 2002; Mobrand 2008), while urban spread often produces the proliferation of new settlements at the fringe of urban areas (Harris and Wahra 2002; O'Hare and Barke 2002).

"Urban-village" is not only a structural abnormality, but also a social disease (Xie and Chen 2003). Guangzhou's urban villages have extremely high housing density of 70 % and a surprising floor area ratio of more than 5. Although the total area of the 138 urban villages in Guangzhou amounts roughly to only 20 % of the whole urban area, they house about 70 % of migrants, which is approximately 40 % of the total urban population. The officially documented densest urban village is 500 persons per hectare in 2000 (Li 2004a, b). As too large coverage and

Table 1.13 Comparison of rate of case-filing per 100,000 people between Guangzhou and the whole Country

Year	Rate of case-filing per 100,000 persons in Guangzhou	National rate of case-filing per 100,000 persons
1998	674	159.1
1999	634	182
2000	2026	286.5
2001	1734	349.5
2002	1581	337.6
2003	1602	340
2004	1515	363
2005	1404	355.9
2006	1246	355
2007	1031	359.2
2008	876	367.8
2009	754	418.1
2010	423	445.2
2011	443	445.7
2012	900	483.8
2013	1861	484.9

Source Guangzhou Statistical Yearbook (2000–2014), website statistics database of National Bureau of Statistics

abnormally high plot ratio as well as disorderly building arrangement, it would make a sociologist cast professional eyes on dysfunctional aspects of an urban village or its components. Gathered floating population proves difficult to manage and concentrated poverty deteriorates citizens' living conditions (Ding and Xing 2007). As far as urban crime is considered, urban village can be said the blind area of public order in a city. With this common set of factors in place, the social traditional institutions at the neighborhood level are powerless to perform their socialization and social control functions, and goes criminal activity. Family, relatives, friends, and neighbors cannot handle the dysfunctional impacts of the urban village which bring about social disorganization and criminal behaviors.

The most danger city in China: In 2006, magazine "*Xiaokang*[6]" held a readership survey about social security in 37 large Chinese cities to decide the five best and five worst cities in regards to public order. According to the feedback, Guangzhou was ranked as the most insecure city in China (Information Times 2006). Some of this could be attributed to the fact that the absolute number of criminal case-filing and rate of case-filing per 100,000 people are quite high in Guangzhou. Table 1.12 shows the number of criminal case-filing and rate of case-filing per 100,000 people in Guangzhou in 1995 and 1998–2013 (Guangzhou

[6]Xiaokang (Chinese: 小康社会; pinyin: xiǎokāngshehui) refers a moderately prosperous society composed of a functional middle-class.

Bureau of Statistic 2014). Table 1.13 makes a comparison of rate of case-filing per 100,000 people between Guangzhou and the whole country. The result shows that rate of case-filing per 100,000 people in Guangzhou is much higher than the national average.

1.3 Street and Community

Street and community are common study units of crime research. Determining a research unit is a necessary prerequisite for any study. Research units can be chosen by researchers according to the specific circumstances of his or her project, such as a continent, a country, a state, a province or a city. If a city is elected as study goal, you can also choose districts, streets, or communities as research units. Those listed above are all macro-level research units. In addition, many studies are from the individual level, which is called micro-level research. For the empirical criminology, the initial research was based on individual units.

The theory of "*born criminals*" founded by Lombroso, the founder of West empirical criminology, was based on anthropometric and the physiognomic analysis of "101 Italian criminal skulls" and "1279 Italian criminals" (Lombroso 1891). The Chicago School began to study crime on macro-level in 1830s, and then made the famous "concentric circles theory" (Vold et al. 1998). Consider that macro-level researches are more objective and reliable in terms of methods and can withstand the test of science. Then macro-level research units are chosen basically in West studies on criminology, such as anomie theory, strain theory, and so on.

1.3.1 Street

China is a centralized country with hierarchically distributed structure. Junior governmental officials are appointed by senior office and report to these higher authorities. Common hierarchy in China's large cities (e.g., Guangzhou) is as follows: at the top is the city council, then district council, and then street offices. Street office is officially recognized as the smallest official unit in China. Each lower office is responsible to its higher authorities.

In Guangzhou, a street office generally covers nearly 60,000 residents. Since the population at the street is quite large, street is then divided into several communities. A community is an unofficial unit normally with 1000–3000 families or 3000–9000 dwellers although a small part of communities are beyond this range (Jiang et al. 2010, 2013).

Choices of criminological research units are in detailed description above to make a simple introduction for research units for the purposes of this paper, and the geographical research scope is limited to Guangzhou City. The research units are as follows: City—District—Street—Community. Considering that the statistics about crime, demography, economy, and other information are mostly on level of district, larger than street level, for the purposes of this paper, I have chosen a city, district, and street as research units when using statistic data. Here, I will explain in detail the districts and streets in Guangzhou (Materials from Guangzhou Statistical Yearbook 2009).

Current administrative divisions of Guangzhou are as follows:

10 districts: Yuexiu District, Haizhu District, Liwan District, Tianhe District, Baiyun District, Huangpu District, Panyu District, Huadu District, Nansha District, Luogang District.

Two County-level cities: Zengcheng city and Conghua city

There are 84 streets and 78 towns in total in Guangzhou City.

Twenty-two streets are administered by Yuexiu District: Hongqiao, Guangwei, Beijing, Liurong, Liuhua, Dongfeng, Guangta, Shishu, Daxin, Renmin, Donghu, Nonglin, Dadong, Datang, Zhuguang, Baiyun, Jianshe, Huale, Meihuacun, Huanghuagang, Kuangquan, and Dengfeng.

Nine streets are administered by Yuexiu District: Yuzhu, Huangpu, Nangang, Dasha, Wenchong, Hongshan, Suidong, Changzhou, and Lilian.

Twenty-two streets are administered by Liwan District: ShaMian, HuaLin, DuoBao, ChangHua, FengYuan, LongJin, JinHua, CaiHong, NanYuan, XiCun, ZhanQian, LingNan, QiaoZhong, ChongKou, HuaDi, ChaJiao, BaiHeDong, ShiWeiTang, DongJiao, DongSha, HaiLong, and ZhongNan.

Eighteen streets are administered by Haizhu District: ChiGang, XinGang, BinJiang, SuShe, HaiZhuang, FengYang, LongFeng, ShaYuan, RuiBao, JiangHai, NanHuaXi, NanShiTou, JiangNanZhong, ChangGang, NanZhou, PaZhou, GuanZhou, and HuaZhou.

Twenty-two streets are administered by Tianhe District: ShaHe, WuShan, CheBei, YuanCun, ShiPai, TianHeNan, LinHe, ShaDong, XingHua, TangXia, LieDe, XianCun, TianYuan, HuangCun, YuanGang, ZhuJi, XinTang, LongDong, FengHuang, QianJin, and ChangAn.

Fourteen streets and four towns are administered by Baiyun District: SanYuanLi, SongZhou, JingTai, TongDe, HuangShi, TangJing, XinShi, TongHe, JingXi, YongPing, JinShaJie, ShiJing, JiaHe, JunHe, JiangGao, RenHen, ZhongLuoTan, and TaiHe.

Seven streets and 10 towns are administered by Panyu District: ShiQiao, QiaoNan, DongHuan, ShaTou, LuoPu, DaShi, XiaoGuWei, ShiBi, NanCunZhen, ZhongCun, ShaWan, ShiQi, ShiLou, XinZao, HuaLong, LanHe, DongYong, and DaGang.

One street and seven towns are administered by Huadu District: TiMian, HuaShan, TanBu, ChiNi, ShiLing, HuaDong, and YaYao.

Four streets and are administered by Luogang District: XiaGang, LianHe, DongQu, and LuoGang.

One street and three towns are administered by Nansha District: NanSha, WanQingSha, HengLi, and HuangGe.

1.3.2 Community

According to relative acts, a community is an autonomous mass organization and normally has a residents' committee. The committee exercises multiple neighborhood functions and powers to distribute and promote policies and regulations from all higher authorities, settling disputes in neighbors, assisting local police to maintain public order, rehabilitating drug abusers, helping former offenders reintegrate into the society, household registration, holding community events, and a variety of other public services to the local residents.

The residents' committee usually comprises five to nine members with one director and one or two vice directors. Although they may receive some assistance from the city or street offices, the committee members are not public servants. Therefore, the residents' committee is considered as a "mass organization" in China. As Troyer (1989) declared, however, the residents' committees "are not voluntary associations in the US sense; they are government organized and controlled entities." They function as government offices.

We can clearly see the number of communities governed by a street in an administrative division map of Guangzhou City. These communities are usually same as neighborhood committees. The number of neighborhood committees in Guangzhou reaches a total of 1572 according to summary of each street. Communities in the whole city might be divided into four types in the light of respective characteristics of each neighborhood, such as nature-type community, biotope-type community, organ-type community, and mixed-type community.

Nature-type community:

This type of communities mainly shapes on historical, geographical, and other natural factors, such as Xian Village in Tianhe District. Xian village is located near the new CBD of the city, and is a geographical community developed from a natural village. As a result, a large number of houses are let to extraneous population, and then the village has one of the city's greatest concentrations of migrants. All in all, urban villages in Guangzhou at large belong to nature-type community.

Biotope-type community:

This type of community is basically often new living areas with new buildings, which are generally equipped with perfect property service, recreational facilities, and mature commercial outlets. These communities are closed or semi-closed with fences or gates on safety grounds. The security purpose makes this type of communities geographically independent.

Organ-type community:

University employees and governmental staff usually dwell in the communities near to universities and government agencies they work in, and thus shape organ-type communities. This third type of community is often formal dormitory areas of state-owned companies, government agencies, and other colleges or universities, or mixture with the above. This typical community is generally located in relatively open areas out of city center. A complete set of self-contained social service systems has formed in these relative concentrated spaces. Social space is administrated, and because of this, excludability occurs. In addition, the lifestyles in organ-type communities are strongly homogeneous in spite of their different divisions of labor, which are different from heterogeneous characteristics of urban societies. Community culture is formed with characteristics of the units or companies where residents working in. Residents in organ-type community were relatively stable and well equipped with educational or even medical facility before the open and reform. Since the open and reform, especially after the 1990s, most university and government staff maintain to dwell in the same communities, and their relative economic status is better than the working class but worse than the rich class.

Mixed-Type Community:

This type of community is strongly heterogeneous. Typically, government organizations and units, commercial plaza and hotel restaurants, as well as scattered inhabitants co-exist within a mixed community. You can see not only old residential buildings but also new high-rise offices, state-owned enterprise dormitories and private houses, wide streets, and also narrow alleys in these mixed communities. Mixed-type community is universal in contemporary Guangzhou and has a very heterogeneous inhabitant in it.

It should be pointed out that the "community" studied in this book and the official definition of "community" belongs to two different categories, respectively. The "community" here is spatially smaller than a neighborhood committee, and generally refers to a housing estate, a residential area, a state-owned factory, or a natural village. Considering that rare statistical data based on neighborhood levels are reported in China, specifically on the community level, the author had to select 'street' as a research unit to study spatial distribution of crimes. Since 'community' is a research unit, it will be analyzed in a more in depth manner. Residents from organized and disorganized communities have been selected as interviewees to qualitatively analyze the relationship between social disorganization and crime in following study.

Crime is a special social phenomenon existing for thousands of years. Due to different political systems, economic systems, national traditions, and cultural backgrounds, crime presents different patterns in different countries. Rapid social transition accompanying economic growth and system transformation make crime a serious social problem. Social transition affects social life in all directions and induces social disorganization in every respect. Its influence to crime proves that it is easy to cause a power vacuum due to social institutional change, and negatively affect crime prevention and social control; it is easy to produce negative psychological phenomena such as anomie, stress, resentment, and confusion due to disorganization and reconstruction of social order and social norms, which results in frequent anomie and deviant behavior (Zhou 1999). Considering the complicated realities around the concept of crime, sociologists hunt to understand how crime itself may be affected by changing social, political, psychological, and economic conditions and the form of the legal, law enforcement, and penal responses made by society. Altogether, crime is the natural product of rapid social transition (Zhou and Cao 2007). A study on the relationship between social disorganization and crime in China has irreplaceable significance to clearly understand criminal phenomenon in periods of China's social transformation. Correct crime prevention and control measures could be made through a deep study on the influences of various factors of social disorganization on crime. Thus criminal legislation could be improved.

References

Alanezi, F. (2010). Juvenile delinquency in Kuwait: Applying social disorganization theory. *Digest of Middle East Studies, 19*(1), 68–81.

Appleton, S., Song, L., & Xia, Q. (2010). Growing out of poverty: Trends and patterns of urban poverty in China 1988–2002. *World Development, 38*(5), 665–678.

Arthur, J. (1992). Social-change and crime rates in Puerto Rico. *International Journal of Offender Therapy and Comparative Criminology, 36*(2), 103–119.

Aunan, K., & Wang, S. (2014). Internal migration and urbanization in China: Impacts on population exposure to household air pollution (2000–2010). *Science of the Total Environment, 481*, 186–195.

Bai, X., Chen, J., & Shi, P. (2012). Landscape urbanization and economic growth in China: Positive feedbacks and sustainability dilemmas. *Environmental Science and Technology, 46*(1), 132–139.

Bakken, B. (1993). Crime, juvenile delinquency and deterrence policy in China. *The Australian Journal of Chinese Affairs, 30*, 29–58.

Baum, R. (1996). China after deng: Ten scenarios in search of reality*. *The China Quarterly, 145*, 153–175.

Becker, J. (2014). *Social ties, resources, and migrant labor contention in contemporary China: From peasants to protesters Lanham*. Maryland: Lexington Books.

Bernburg, J. G. (2002). Anomie, social change and crime. A theoretical examination of InstitutionalAnomie theory. *The British Journal of Criminology, 42*(4), 729–742.

Bertoncelo, B., & Bredeloup, S. (2007). The emergence of new African "trading posts" in HongKong and Guangzhou. *China Perspectives, 1*, 94–105.

Blakely, E. J., & Snyder, M. G. (1997). *Fortress America: Gated Communities in the United States, Washington, DC and Cambridge*. MA: Bookings Institution and Lincoln Institute of Land Policy.

Blanchard, O., & Kremer, M. (1997). Disorganization. *Quarterly Journal of Economics, 112*(4), 1091–1126.

Bodomo, A. (2009). The African trading community in Guangzhou: An emerging bridge for Africa-China relations'. *China Quarterly, 203*, 693–707.

Braga, A. A., & Clarke, R. V. (2014). Explaining high-risk concentrations of crime in the city. *Journal of Research in Crime and Delinquency, 51*(4), 480–498.

Breetzke, G. (2010). Modeling violent crime rates: A test of social disorganization in the city of Tshwane, South Africa. *Journal of Criminal Justice, 38*(4), 446–452.

Buckley, M. (2014). On the work of urbanization: Migration, construction labor, and the commodity moment. *Annals of the Association of American Geographers, 104*(2), 338–347.

Button, K. J. (1976). *Urban economics. Theory and policy*. London: The MacMillan Press Ltd.

Cao, L. (2007). Returning to normality: Anomie and crime in China. *International Journal of Offender Therapy and Comparative Criminology, 51*(1), 40.

Chen, Q., & Song, Z. (2014). Accounting for China's urbanization. *China Economic Review, 30*, 485–494.

Chen, J., Guo, F., & Wu, Y. (2011). Chinese urbanization and urban housing growth since the mid-1990s. *Journal of Housing and the Built Environment, 26*(2), 219–232.

Chen, P., Yuan, H., & Li, D. (2013). Space-time analysis of burglary in Beijing. *Security Journal, 26*(1), 1–15.

Chen, M. X., Zhang, H., Liu, W., & Zhang, W. (2014). The global pattern of urbanization and economic growth: Evidence from the last three decades. *Plos One; PLoS One, 9*(8).

Cheong, T. S., & Wu, Y. (2015). Crime rates and inequality: A study of crime in contemporary China. *Journal of the Asia Pacific Economy, 20*(2), 202–223.

Cho, M. Y. (2013). *The specter of "the people": Urban poverty in northeast China*. Ithaca, N.Y.: Ithaca, N.Y.: Cornell University Press.

Choi, C. G., & Choi, S. O. (2012). Collaborative partnerships and crime in disorganized communities. *Public Administration Review, 72*(2), 228–238.

Cook, S. (2000). In Jolly S., Institute of Development Studies (Brighton, England) and China Women's College (Eds.), *Unemployment, poverty and gender in urban China: Perceptions and experiences of laid off workers in three Chinese cities*. Brighton: Institute of Development Studies.

Curran, D. J. (1998). Economic reform, the floating population, and crime: The transformation of social control in China. *Journal of Contemporary Criminal Justice, 14*(3), 262–280.

Dai, Y. (1995). Expanding economy and growing crime. *CJ International, 11*, 9–16.

Ding, H., & Xing, H. (2007). Problem, cause and management measures of urban village. *Chinese Real Estate, 12*, 55–57. 丁洪建, 刑海峰. (2007). 城中村的问题、成因及规划管理对策.《中国房地产》, *12*, 55–57.

Durkheim, É. (1951). In J. A. Spaulding & G. Simpson (Eds.), *Suicide: A study in sociology*. Glencoe, Illinois: Free Press.

Durkheim, É. (1964). In G. Simpson (Ed.), *The division of labor in society*. New York: London: New York: Free Press; London: Collier-Macmillan.

Dutton, M. (1997). The basic character of crime in contemporary China. *The China Quarterly, 149*, 160–177.

Edens, T. C. (1975). Economic growth. *Science (New York, N.Y.), 189*(4201), 410.

Esbensen, F., & Huizinga, D. (1990). Community structure and drug use: From a social disorganization perspective. *Justice Quarterly, 7*(4), 691–709.

Fan, S., Fang, C., & Zhang, X. (2003). Agricultural research and urban poverty: The case of China. *World Development, 31*(4), 733–741.

Faria, J. R., & Mollick, A. (1996). Urbanization, economic growth, and welfare. *Economics Letters, 52*(1), 109–115.

Fay, M. (2014). Role of green governance in achieving sustainable urbanization in China. *China & World Economy, 22*(5), 19.

Fei, X. (1998). *Native Chinese fertility system*. Beijing: Peking University Press. 费孝通, (1998).《乡土中国生育制度》, 北京:北京大学出版社.

Goldstein, S. (1990). Urbanization in China, 1982–1987—effects of migration and reclassification. *Population and Development Review, 16*(4), 673–701.

Goldstein, A., & Goldstein, S. (1987). Varieties of population mobility in relation to development in China. *Studies in Comparative International Development, 22*(4), 101–124.

Guangzhou Bureau of Statistics. (2014). Guangzhou statistics yearbook 2014. Beijing: China Statistics Press. 广州市统计局, (2014).《广州统计年鉴2014》. 北京: 中国统计出版社.

Guangzhou Bureau of Tourism. (2014). Foreigners in Guangzhou, Guangzhou travel guide net, http://gzlyzn.com/a/gzlvyou/guangzhou/. 广州市旅游局. (2014). 广州市外籍人士情况, 广州旅游指南网, http://gzlyzn.com/a/gzlvyou/guangzhou/

Gui, Y., Berry, J. W., & Zheng, Y. (2012). Migrant worker acculturation in China. *International Journal of Intercultural Relations, 36*(4), 598–610.

Hammond, D. R. (2013). Policy entrepreneurship in China's response to urban poverty. *Policy Studies Journal, 41*(1), 119–146.

Hao, L. X. (2012). Cumulative causation of rural migration and initial peri- urbanization in China. *Chinese Sociological Review, 44*(3), 6–33.

Hao, P., Geertman, S., Hooimeijer, P., & Sliuzas, R. (2012). Spatial analyses of the urban village development process in Shenzhen, China. *International Journal of Urban and Regional Research.*

Hao, P., Hooimeijer, P., Sliuzas, R., & Geertman, S. (2013). What drives the spatial development of urban villages in China? *Urban Studies, 50*(16), 3394–3411.

Harris, R. & Wahra M. (2002). The urban geography of low-income housing: Cairo (1947−96) exemplifies a model. *International Journal of Urban and Regional Research. 26*(1), 58−79.

Hawley, A. H. (1981). Human ecology: Persistence and change. *American Behavioral Scientist, 24*(3), 423–444.

He, C., Huang, Z., & Wang, R. (2014). Land use change and economic growth in urban China: A structural equation analysis. *Urban Studies, 51*(13), 2880–2898.

Hong, Y. (2011). *Labor, class formation, and China's informationized policy of economic development*. Lanham, Md.: Lanham, Md.: Lexington Books.

Hu, X. H., & Kaplan, D. (2001). The emergence of affluence in Beijing: Residential social stratification in China's capital city. *Urban Geography, 22*(1), 54–77.

Huang, P., & Zhan, S. (2005). *Internal migration in China: Linking it to development.* Presented at the Regional Conference on Migration and Development in Asia, Lanzhou, China, Mar 14–16, 2005.

Huanqiu Net. (2014). Guangzhou has been the largest rallying point in Asia for Africans, *Sina News*, http://news.sina.com.cn/c/2014-08-29/054630762026.shtml 环球网. (2014). 广州成亚洲最大非洲人聚集地, http://news.sina.com.cn/c/2014-08-29/054630762026.shtml

Information Times. (2006). Chinese internet users focus on city's security: The best in Hangzhou while the worst in Guangzhou, Xinhuanet, Sept 21, 2006. http://bbs.hefei.cc/. 信息时报. (2006). 网民热议中国各地治安:最好是杭州最差为广州, 新华网2006年9月21日http://bbs.hefei.cc/.

Jian, X. (1996). Increasing pressure: Impacts of migration on cities. *China Population Today, 13*(5–6), 21.

Jiang, S., Wang, J., & Lambert, E. (2010). Correlates of informal social control in Guangzhou, China neighborhoods. *Journal of Criminal Justice, 38*(4), 460–469.

Jiang, S., Land, K., & Wang, J. (2013). Social ties, collective efficacy and perceived neighborhood property crime in Guangzhou, China. *Asian Journal of Criminology, 8*(3), 207–223.

Jowell, R. (1998). How comparative is comparative research? *American Behavioral Scientist, 42*, 168–177.

Ke, S. (2015). Domestic market integration and regional economic growth—China's recent experience from 1995–2011. *World Development, 66*, 588–597.

Kim, S., & Pridemore, W. (2005). Poverty, socioeconomic change, institutional anomie, and homicide. *Social Science Quarterly, 86*(5), 1377–1398.

Knight, J. B. (2013). In Q. Deng & S. Li (Eds.), *The evolution of the migrant labor market in China, 2002–2007.*

Konings, J., & Walsh, P. P. (1999). Disorganization in the process of transition—firm-level evidence from Ukraine. *Economics of Transition, 7*(1), 29–46.

LaCapra, D. (1972). *Emile Durkheim: Sociologist and Philosopher*, Cornell University Press, Ithaca, NY; reissued in 1985 by University of Chicago Press.

Lambert, E., & Jiang, S. (2006). A comparison of Chinese and US college students' crime and crime control views. *Asian Criminology, 1*, 37–49.

Lan, S. (2015). State regulation of undocumented African migrants in China: A multi-scalar analysis. *Journal of Asian and African Studies, 50*(3), 289–304.

Li, S. (2004a). Population migration and urbanization in China: A comparative analysis of the 1990 population census and the 1995 national one percent sample population survey. *International Migration Review, 38*(2), 655-685.

Li, J. (2004b). *Transformation of urban villages* (pp. 26–30). Beijing: Science Press. 李俊夫. (2004). 《城中村的改造》. 北京:科学出版社, 26–30.

Li, Q. (2013). China's labor transition and the future of China's rural wages and employment. *China and World Economy, 21*(3), 4.

Li, S. S., & Ma, Y. (2014). Urbanization, economic development and environmental change. *Sustainability, 6*(8), 5143–5161.

Li, Y., Chen, Y., & Li, H. (2007). Closed or open: Spatial analysis of urban village—a case study of village Chebei in Guangzhou, City Issues, *7*(144), 63–70. 黎云,陈洋, 李郇, 封闭与开放: 城中村空间解析——以广州市车陂村为例, 《城市问题》, 2007, *7*(144), 63–70.

Li, Z., Xue, D., Lyons, M., & Brown, A. (2007b). Ethnic enclaves of transnational migrants in Guangzhou: a case study of Xiaobei. *Acta Geographika Sinica, 63*(2), 208–218.

Li, H., Li, L., Wu, B., & Xiong, Y. (2012). The end of cheap Chinese labor. *Journal of Economic Perspectives, 26*(4), 57–74.

Li, J., Chang, S. S., Yip, P., Jordan, L., Tang, Y., Hao, Y., & Zeng, Q. (2014). *Mental wellbeing amongst younger and older migrant workers in comparison to their urban counterparts in Guangzhou city, China: A cross-sectional study* (p. 14). Bmc Public Health: BMC Public Health.

Lin, Y., de Meulder, B., & Wang, S. (2011). Understanding the 'village in the city' in Guangzhou. *Urban Studies, 48*(16), 3583–3598.

Liu, W. (2005a). Guangzhou city: On mighty mountains, facing the south China sea, south China begins flourish, southern metropolis daily, Sept 8, 2005.刘炜茗. (2005). 广州建城 负山险,阻南海,岭南始风流,《南方都市报》2005年9月8日.

Liu, J. (2005b). Crime patterns during the market transition in China. *British Journal of Criminology*, *45*, 613–633.

Liu, J. (2006). Modernization and crime patterns in China. *Journal of Criminal Justice, 34*(2), 119–130.

Liu, J., & Messner, S. F. (2001). Modernization and crime trends in China's reform era. In J. H. Liu, L. N. Zhang, & S. F. Messner (Eds.), *Crime and social control in a changing China* (pp. 119–130). Westport, CT: Greenwood Press.

Liu, J., Messner, S., Zhang, L., & Zhuo, Y. (2009). Socio-demographic correlates of fear of crime and the social context of contemporary urban China. *American Journal of Community Psychology, 44*(1), 93–108.

Liu, D., Song, W., & Xiu, C. (2014). Spatial patterns of violent crimes and neighborhood characteristics in Changchun, China. *Australian & New Zealand Journal of Criminology*, 0004865814547133.

Lo, T., & Jiang, G. (2006). Inequality, crime and the floating population in China. *Asian Journal of Criminology, 1*(2), 103–118.

Lombroso, C. (1891). *The man of genius*. London: Walter Scott.

Lyons, C. (2007). Community (dis)organization and racially motivated crime. *American Journal of Sociology, 113*(3), 815–863.

Lyons, M., Brown, A., & Li, Z. (2008). The "third tier" of globalization reconsidered: African traders in Guangzhou. *City, 12*(2), 196–206.

Lyons, M., Brown, A., & Li, Z. (2012). In the dragon's den: African traders in Guangzhou. *Journal of Ethnic and Migration Studies, 38*(5), 869–888.

Ma, H., & Lian, L. (2011). Rural-urban migration and urbanization in Gansu province, China: Evidence from time-series analysis. *Asian Social Science*, *7*(12).

Makinen, I. (2000). Eastern European transition and suicide mortality. *Social Science and Medicine, 51*(9), 1405–1420.

Mazerolle, L., Wickes, R., & McBroom, J. (2010). *Community variations in violence: The role of social ties and collective efficacy in comparative context*

Meng, X. (2012). Labor market outcomes and reforms in China. *Journal of Economic Perspectives, 26*(4), 75–101.

Merton, R. K. (2000). Insiders and outsiders. *American journal of sociology*, *78*, 9–27.

Miethe, T., Hughes, M., & Mcdowall, D. (1991). Social-change and crime rates—an evaluation of alternative theoretical approaches. *Social Forces, 70*(1), 165–185.

Ming Pao Daily. (2011). Lack of work every year, the most this year in PRD, Chinanews Net, Feb 10, 2011. http://www.Chinanews.com/hb/2011/02-10/2832161.shtml 香港明报. (2011). 珠三角年年缺工 今年最心慌，中新网2011年2月10日．http://www.Chinanews.com/hb/2011/02-10/2832161.shtml

Moravcova, E. (2014). Social disorganization theory and its relevance for the socio-spatial analysis of crime. *Sociologia, 46*(5), 534–553.

Murphy, R. (2002). *How migrant labor is changing rural China*. Cambridge: Cambridge University Press.

Nanfang Daily. (2013). Average annual new constructive land has reached 38.6 km^2, July 30, 2014. http://epaper.southcn.com/nfdaily/html/2013-07/30/content_7211849.htm. 南方日报 (2014). 近十年年均新增建设用地38.6平方公里, 南方日报2014年7月30日. http://epaper.southcn.com/nfdaily/html/2013-07/30/content_7211849.htm

National Bureau of Statistics of China. (2014). Chinese Statistical Yearbook 2014. Beijing: China Statistics Press. 国家统计局 (2014).《中国统计年鉴2014》. 北京:中国统计出版社.

Otsu, A., Araki, S., Sakai, R., Yokoyama, K., & Scott Voorhees, A. (2004). Effects of urbanization, economic development, and migration of workers on suicide mortality in Japan. *Social Science and Medicine, 58*(6), 1137–1146.

Paik, W. (2014). Local village workers, foreign factories and village politics in coastal China: A clientelist approach*. *The China Quarterly, 220*, 955.

Park, A., & Wang, D. (2010). *Migration and urban poverty and inequality in China*. London: Routledge.

Patchin, J. W., Huebner, B. M., McCluskey, J. D., Varano, S. P., & Bynum, T. S. (2006). Exposure to community violence and childhood delinquency. *Crime and Delinquency, 52*(2), 307–332.

Peters, G. P., Guan, D., Hubacek, K., Minx, J., & Weber, C. (2010). Effects of China's economic growth. *Science, 328*(5980), 824–825.

Qin, L. (2015). Health status and earnings of migrant workers from rural China. *China and World Economy, 23*(2), 84.

Qiu, P., Caine, E., Yang, Y., Chen, Q., Li, J., & Ma, X. (2011). Depression and associated factors in internal migrant workers in China. *Journal of Affective Disorders, 134*(1–3), 198–207.

Queen, S. A. (1941). The concepts social disorganization and social participation. *American Sociological Review, 6*(3), 307–319.

Radulescu, R., & Barlow, D. (2002). The relationship between policies and growth in transition countries. *Economics of Transition, 10*(3), 719–745.

Research Group of State Labor and Social Security Ministry. (2005). Quantity, structure and characteristics of current migrant workers' flowing employment, *China Labor and Social Security News*, Aug 3, 2005. 劳动与社会保障部课题组. (2005). 当前农民工流动就业数量、结构与特点,《中国劳动保障报》, 2005年8月3日.

Rojek, D. G. (1996). Changing Directions of Chinese Social Control. In C. B. Fields & J. R. H. Moore (Eds.), *Comparative criminal justice: Traditional and nontraditional systems of law and control* (pp. 234–249). Prospect Heights, IL: Waveland.

Rose, D. (2000). Social disorganization and parochial control: Religious institutions and their communities. *Sociological Forum, 15*(2), 339–358.

Sampson, R. J., Raudenbush, S. W., & Earls, F. (1997). Neighborhoods and violent crime: A multilevel study of collective efficacy. *Science, 277*, 918–924.

Sampson, R. J., & Wikström, P. H. (2008). *The social order of violence in chicago and stockholm neighborhoods: A comparative inquiry*

Shaw, C. R. (1942). In H. D. McKay (Ed.), *Juvenile delinquency and urban areas: A study of rates of delinquents in relation to differential characteristics of local communities in American cities*. Chicago, Ill.: The University of Chicago Press.

Shen, H. (2010). More beautiful Guangzhou, China's National Religion Net, Nov 11, 2010, http://www.mzb.com.cn/html/report/153454-1.htm 沈海滨. (2010). 越秀越美的五羊城,中国民族宗教网2010年11月11日, http://www.mzb.com.cn/html/report/153454-1.htm

Shouhai, D. (2015). Employment in township urbanization in China. *Social Sciences in China, 36*(2), 152–167.

Solinger, D. J., & Hu, Y. (2012). Welfare, wealth and poverty in urban China: The Dibao and its differential disbursement. *The China Quartely, 211*, 741–764.

Sugden, A. M. (2014). The cost of economic growth. *Science, 345*(6198), 783.

Tang, S. (1997). From social control to disorganization: Official corruption in China. *Social and Economic Studies, 46*(1), 135–147.

Torry, W. (2001). Social change, crime, and culture: The defense of provocation. *Crime, Law and Social Change, 36*(3), 309–325.

Traub, S. H., & Craig, B. L. (Eds.). (1985). *Theories of deviance* (3rd ed.). Berkeley and Los Angeles: University of California Press.

Troyer, R. J. (1989). Chinese social organizations. In R. J. Troyer, J. P. Clark, & D. G. Rojek (Eds.), *Social control in the People's Republic of China* (pp. 26–33). New York: Praeger.

Victor, P. (2010). Questioning economic growth. *Nature, 468*(7322), 370–371.

Vold, G. B., Bernard, Thomas J., & Snipes, Jeffrey B. (1998). *Theoretical criminology*. New York: Oxford University Press. 123.

Wang, Y. P. (2004). *Urban poverty, housing and social change in China*. London: Routledge.

Wang, H. (2013). Discrimination in migrant workers' welfare entitlements and benefits in urban labour market: Findings from a Four-City study in China. *Population, Space and Place, 21*(2), 124.

Wang, Z. (2014). China's "labour shortage" and migrant workers' lack of social security. *International Labour Review, 153*(4), 649.

Wei, L. H., & Yan, X. (2005a). Sustainable urban-rural relation in rapid urbanization areas-case of transformation of "urban village" in Guangzhou. *Chinese Geographical Science, 15*(3), 212–218.

Wei, L., & Yan, X. (2005b). Village: transition under the premise of existence—on the feasibility model of urban village's reconstruction. *City Plan, 9*. 9–13.魏立华、闫小培. (2005). 城中村:存续前提下的转型——兼论城中村改造的可行性模式.《城市规划》*9*, 9–13.

Wu, W. P. (2001). Temporary migrants in Shanghai: Housing and settlement patterns. In J. Logan (Ed.), *The New Chinese city: Globalization and market reform* (p. 21226). Oxford: Blackwell.

Wu, F. (2010). *Urban poverty in China*. Cheltenham: Cheltenham: Edward Elgar.

Xiaoliu, Y. (2010). Research on the adjustments of population migration policies in Guangzhou province since the reform and opening period. *Chinese Sociology and Anthropology, 43*(2), 6–24.

Xie, Z., & Chen H. (2003). Urban village: urbanization disease in Chinese context, http://www.drcnet.com.cn, Oct 23, 2003. 谢志岿,陈红艳. (2003). 城中村:中国背景下的城市化病式. http://www.drcnet.com.cn, Oct 23, 2003.

Xu, F. (2000). *Women migrant workers in China's economic reform*. Basingstoke: Basingstoke: Macmillan.

Yang, X. J. (2013). China's rapid urbanization. *Science (New York, N.Y.), 342*(6156), 310.

Yang, S. & Cao, J. (2004). Handling landless peasants during urbanization, Chinese rural research net, http://www.ccrs.org.cn, Sept 19, 2004.杨盛海,曹金波. (2004). 城市化进程中的失地农民问题对策探析, 中国农村研究网, http://www.ccrs.org.cn, Sept 19, 2004.

Ye, X., Xu, X., Lee, J., Zhu, X., & Wu, L. (2015). Space–time interaction of residential burglaries in Wuhan, China. *Applied Geography, 60*, 210–216.

Yen, C. (1934). Crime in relation to social change in China. *American Journal of Sociology, 40*(3), 298–308.

Zeitler, A. (2005). *Between Russia and China—central Asia's transition experience* Institut für Ost- und Südosteuropaforschung (Institute for East and South-East European Studies).

Zhan, X. (2014). Effect of migration on children's Self-esteem in rural China. *China and World Economy, 22*(4), 83.

Zhang, J., Ma, J., Jia, C., Sun, J., Guo, X., Xu, A., & Li, W. (2010). Economic growth and suicide rate changes: A case in China from 1982 to 2005. *European Psychiatry, 25*(3), 159–163.

Zhang, L., Messner, S. F., & Liu, J. (2007). A multilevel analysis of the risk of household burglary in the city of tianjin, China. *The British Journal of Criminology, 47*(6), 918–937.

Zhao, S. L. (2008). Anomie theory and crime in a transitional China (1978–). *International Criminal Justice Review, 18*(2), 137–157.

Zheng, X. (2009). Africans in Guangzhou increase 30–40 % annually, Southern Weekly, Aug 17, 2009. 郑璇. (2009). 广州非洲人每年以30 %至40 %速度递增,《南都周刊》2009年08月17日.

Zhou, Y. (1999). *Urban geography*. Beijing: Commercial Press. 周一星. (1999). 《城市地理学》. 北京:商务印书馆.

Zhou, L. (2004). New contemporary empirical criminology. Beijing: People's Court Publishing House. 周路. (2004). 《. 当代实证犯罪学新编》, 北京: 人民法院出版社.

Zhou, Z. (2014). Towards collaborative approach? Investigating the regeneration of urban village in Guangzhou, China. *Habitat International, 44*, 297–305.

Zhu, Y., Xue, B., & Wang, D. (2006) Disputes on Guangzhou's intention to raise barriers of foreign workers' admission, Information Times, Dec 18, 2006. 祝勇,薛冰,王道斌, (2006). 广州拟抬高外来人员进入门坎引争议,《信息时报》2006年12月18日.

Chapter 2
Making Sense of Social Disorganization

Crime is a common social phenomenon existing for thousands of years. Due to different political and economic system, national tradition, and cultural background, crime presents various patterns in different countries. Rapid social transition accompanying economic growth and system transformation make crime a serious social problem. Social transition affects social life in all directions and induces social disorganization in every respect. Its influence to commit crime proves easy to cause a power vacuum in social institutional change, and negatively affect on crime prevention and social control; it tends to produce negative psychological phenomena such as anomie, stress, resentment, and confusion due to disorganization and reconstruction of social order and social norms, which result in frequent anomie and deviant behavior (Zhou 2004). Altogether, crime is natural product of rapid social transition (Zhou and Cao 2007). A study on the relationship between social disorganization and crime in China has irreplaceable significance to clearly understand criminal phenomenon in periods China's social transformation. Proper crime prevention and control measures could be made through a deep study on the influences of various factors of social disorganization on crime. Thus criminal legislation could be improved.

Although social disorganization theory is one of the earliest developed sociological theories in modern Western, "social disorganization," the basic concept of social disorganization theory is still to be one of the few sociological terms with "the most confusing and most indistinct definitions" (Cohen 1959). This book creatively understands "social disorganization" on two levels: spatial structural disorganization and social structural disorganization. Because of this, the social disorganization theory will be re-annotated and step forward in a much clearer form of conceptualization.

H. Xiong, *Urban Crime and Social Disorganization in China*,
DOI 10.1007/978-981-287-859-5_2

2.1 Economic, Modernization and Crime

2.1.1 Modernization and Crime

Research on relationships between crime and modernization was first started by French sociologist Emile Durkheim. In 1893, Durkheim analyzed the social changes process relevant to industrialization in his famous book "The Division of labor in Society" (Durkheim 1964). Social transition was the process that "mechanical" society developed to "organic" society. When the society developed to its organic form, social morbid condition which Durkheim called "anomie" will occur. "Anomie" will lead to social pathology, including crime. Durkheim considered that crime was a "normal" social phenomenon in mechanical society and advanced the viewpoint that "crime was normal" in his second major works "Rules of the Sociological Method" (Durkheim 1964). He believed that crime is "bound up with the fundamental conditions of all social life" and serves a social function (Durkheim 1964). Subsequently, Durkheim popularized the concept of anomie in his most famous work "Suicide" (Durkheim 1951). Durkheim's anomie theory was later used as theoretical basis to explain crime and other various deviant behaviors (Clinard 1964). Durkheim's viewpoints are so broad and profound that he was called one of the main sociologists who were most famous and most difficult to interpret and comprehend (LaCapra 2001). Durkheim's famous argument on modernization and crime was that when mechanical society turned to organic society in modernization, the purpose of punishment turned from repression to recovery. There will be a "functional" law widely used to regulate emerging interactions in organic society; a number of deviant behaviors will increase in organic society in rapid social transitions.

Many criminological theories were formed on basis of Durkheim's perspectives on the relationship between crime and modernization in recent years. It can be said that basic crime patterns in modern society can only be explained by some criminal theories that use modernization as the framework (Vold 1998). Shelley (1981) reviews multiple studies relating to relationships between crime and modernization, and found that crime patterns experienced in modernization would also appear in developing countries. Furthermore, many researches were contrary with Durkheim's predictions about relationships between modernization and crime. Durkheim believed that crime was stable, while the premodern society was characterized by a high and crime rate (Vold 1998). Violent crime rate experienced a long-term reduction in the modernization process, which was also not predicted by Durkheim's theory (Messner 1982). Short periods of growth of violent crime rates was observed in long-term reducing trends and appeared in the early stages of urbanization and modernization. Some scholars attributed short periods of the growth of violent crime rates to war and adolescent population growth, rather than Durkheim's rural cultural collapse (Gurr 1979, 1981).

2.1.2 Economic and Crime

Theories about relations between economic conditions and crime should be traced back to ancient societies. There is an enormous amount of research on the relations between economic conditions and crime since the modern times. In the early 1800s, attempts were made by Guerry and Quetelet to demonstrate the relationship between these two phenomena as soon as national crime statistics were available in France (Beirne 1993). Grerry found that the wealthiest regions of France had more property crime but less violent crime. He concluded that the higher levels of property crime were caused by opportunity; there were more things to steal in the wealthy provinces. Quetelet found a similar pattern and also suggested that opportunity might be a factor; however, he also pointed out that the great inequality between poverty and wealth in the more developed provinces would influence crime rates. Inequality could generate resentment among the poor, whereas in contrast, poor areas tended to have less inequality and less resentment because everyone was in the same economic bracket.

There are no unified conclusions about relationships between crime and economy despite the ongoing research and analysis (Cornwell and Trumbull 1994; Crutchfield 1989; Grant and Martinez 1997; Loftin and McDowall 1982; MacDonald 2002; Machin and Meghir 2004; Merlo 2004; Pudney et al. 2000; Samara 2005; Wong 1995).

Since that time, hundreds of studies have been published that extend back over a period of almost 200 years. These have often given complicated and apparently contradictory results. Now I will demonstrate the important discussions on the following theoretical problems: the relationship between crime and the business cycle, relationships between crime and poverty and concentrated poverty, relationships between crime and unemployment. Theoretical studies about relationships between economic conditions and crime are focused on these areas.

Relationships between crime and business cycles Numerous studies have been done on the relationship between crime and the business cycle. The thinking was that there should be more crime during times of economic downturns with the increase of impoverished people, and that there would be less crime during times of economic expansions (Vold 1979). Most of these studies, however, find that the general crime rate does not increase during economic recessions and depressions (Long and Witte 1981). Some studies even find the opposite situation—that crime actually decreases during such periods (Allen 1996). There is also research that dissects the relationships between economic expansion and crime and maintains that economic expansion does not necessarily lead to crime reduction (Lafree 1998). As far as the United States is concerned, economic expansion in the 1960s resulted in a rise in crime, while crime rates were reduced in the 1990s (Blumstein and Wallman 2006).

Relationships between crime and poverty/concentrated poverty Some researchers hold the opinion that there is no relationship between the poor population and crime (Cho 1974). It has been found that the percentage of people below the poverty line in the forty-nine largest cities of the United States was not associated with any of the seven index crimes reported by the FBI. Jacobs (1981) reached a similar conclusion with respect to the crimes of burglary, robbery, and grand larceny. In contrast, hrlich found that there was a positive relationship between state property crime rates for 1940, 1950, 1960 and the percentage of households receiving less than half of the median income (Ehrlich 1974). Loftin and Hill created an index of "structural poverty" including measures of infant mortality, low education, and one-parent families. These findings resulted in a very strong correlation between this measure and the state of homicide rates (Loftin and Hill 1974).

Although poverty or unemployment may not be a direct cause of crime, areas that are the most deteriorated, even within the context of inner-city poverty, seem to have much higher crime rates than more stable lower-class environments (Massey 1996). William Julius Wilson describes how working- and middle-class families flee inner-city poverty areas, resulting in a concentration effect, in which elements of the most disadvantaged population are consolidated in urban ghettos. Urban areas marked by concentrated poverty become isolated and insulated from the social mainstream and more prone to criminal activity, violence, and homicide. Lee found that the degree of poverty concentration was more important than overall poverty rates on murder (Lee 2000). Some scholars examined the relationship between economic inequality and crime, and supposed that economic inequality is an important factor resulting in violent crime (Harer and Steffensmeier 1992). Takeuchi et al. (1991) studied the influence of family economic pressure on children's emotion and behavior.

Relationships between crime and economic inequality/relative deprivation There is ample evidence that neighborhood-level income inequality is a significant predictor of neighborhood crime rates. Sharp divisions between the rich and poor create an atmosphere of envy and mistrust that may lead to violence and aggression. Generalized feelings of relative deprivation are precursors to high crime rates. According to this view, lower-class people might feel both deprived and embittered when they compare their life circumstances to those of the more affluent. The constant frustration that results from these feelings of inadequacy produces pent-up aggression and hostility, and leads to violence and crime. According to the relative deprivation theory, if income inequality widens, crime rates may spiral upward even as the size of the indigent population is in decline. Relative deprivation is truly relative. Even the most affluent Americans may feel deprived if they fail to achieve their lofty and unlimited goals, and they may use illegal means to deal with their feeling of deprivation. The relative deprivation model is important because it helps explain the ambiguous association between crime and the economy. During a recession, crime rates may fall because everyone is suffering, and consequently there are relatively few of relative deprivation.

Relationships between crime and unemployment Many people believe that unemployment causes crime (Berk et al. 1980), then crime should increase when unemployment is high and decrease when unemployment is low (Glaser and Rice 1959).

This popular view presumably is based on the assumption that unemployment causes poverty, and then poverty causes crime. Consider first the studies, a study by Glaser and Rice (1959) which focused on relationship between unemployment and juvenile delinquency found that delinquency is inversely related to unemployment; that is delinquency is high when unemployment is low and vice versa. Glaser and Rice suggested that this might be because in times of unemployment parents are more available to their children. Wright et al. (1997) examined part-time students and found that part-time jobs would increase crime risk of school boys. However, Singell and Fleischer (1967) concluded that delinquency is directly related to unemployment, and that 1 % increase in unemployment results in an approximate 15 % increase in delinquency. Ehrlich (1974) found that unemployment had no effect on the criminality of urban males in the age group 14–24. Danser and Laub (1980) used victimization data rather than official police statistics and concluded that there was no relationship between juvenile delinquency and juvenile unemployment rates, even within specific age, sex, and racial groups. Calvin, in contrast, argues there is a close relationship between delinquency and juvenile unemployment and crime for black youths, and maintains that those who argue against this point are using incorrect data or faulty interpretations.

There have been contradictory findings on the question of the relationship between unemployment and adult crime. Many researchers believe that there are no relationships between unemployment and crime. Nagel found a strong correlation between crime rates and unemployment rates when he ranked each of the fifty states on those two measures. Brenner concluded that a sustained 1 % increase in unemployment results in a 5.7 % increase in murder on the basis of a study of national crime and unemployment statistics from 1940 to 1973. Berk and his colleagues studied programs that provide unemployment benefits to released prisoners, and concluded that unemployment and poverty do cause crime for ex-offenders (Berk et al. 1980). In contrast, a number of other authors have concluded that there is either no relationship between unemployment and crime or that the relationship is insignificant (Jacobs 1981).

These inconsistent and contradictory results continue to be generated by extensive and improved research (Nagel 1981). Freeman reviewed eighteen of these studies and concluded that higher unemployment rates is associated with higher crime rates, but that the relation is weak and generally insignificant. However, Chiricos (1987) reviewed sixty-three studies of crime and unemployment, and concluded that the relationship between unemployment and crime is positive and frequently significant, especially for property crime, and that this effect was especially strong after 1970. Chiricos also argued that the positive relation between crime and unemployment is more likely to be found when smaller units are examined rather than larger units, and that economic conditions in larger units often have little impact on the extent of poverty and deprivation in particular areas (Land et al. 1990).

In addition to these studies on the relationship between crime rate and unemployment rate, there are some studies that examine particular aspects of unemployment. For example, White (1999) examined the impact of job reduction on crime rates and found that reduction of manufacturing jobs affected the increase of financial crime via poverty but that unemployment had no affect on violent crimes. Shihadeh and Ousey (1998) found that the reduction in low-skill jobs led to increased poverty and resulted in increased violent crimes. Sampson (1987) examined unemployed and divorced families' effects on violence crimes by the Blacks. Shihadeh and Ousey (1998) examined the effect of black social isolation on the rates of black urban violence. Steffensmeier (1980) reviewed and assessed sex differences in patterns of adult crime. Wang and Minor (2002) reviewed relationship between employment access and crime patterns in Cleveland.

2.2 Urban Spatial Disorganization and Crime

Research on the relation between urban spatial structure and crime began in 1830s by the ecological Chicago School (Loukaitou-Sideris et al. 2001). After factor analysis in the 1950s and 60s (Lownan 1986) and due to increase of map drawing, computer software and other technical requirements, a pure study of crime from a spatial structure standpoint is still remains a subordinate area of focus for criminologists and sociologists. The geography of crime becomes a branch of geography to study the spatial distribution of crime and the relationship between crime and spacial environment (Herbert 1982).

With criminal quantitative aspects, Harries (2006) empirical analysis of 97,800 crimes in Baltimore was used to re-quantify crime density combined with residential and commercial land. Regarding crime prevention, Herbert and Harries (1986) studied the urban crime prevention of the United States and the United Kingdom, and concluded that local defense measures may be more effective than pure policing measures, such as the neighborhood watch and community surveillance. Someone examined replacement relation between cell behavior and street prostitution in Birmingham and Bradford, and supported that "not-in-my-back-yard" reflected composite anxiety to commercial pornography such as prostitution. They pointed out that mechanically expelling prostitution did not solve any problems (Hubbard 1998).

In regards to the relationships between urban space and crime, most studies before 1990 had been focused on crime patterns, crime types, criminals and victims, and spatial distributions (Pyle 1976; Herbert 1977; Williams 1985; Lowman 1986; Maltz 1976; Blau and Blau 1982). After 1990 however, scholars' study interest turned to the structural mechanism of crime (environment, society and background) and various types of crime in the discussion of cultural connotation (Fyfe 1991; Pawson and Banks 1993; Pain 1997; Shihadeh and Flynn 1996; Coughlin and Venkatesh 2003; Liu et al. 2009; Zhang et al. 2007a, b, 2009a, b)

Regarding crime culture, Mcllwaine (1999) analyzed the relationship between crime and development as well as various types of criminal culture. A new research trend of criminal geography has now emerged and involves the combination of the geography of crime with gender research, specifically research on the female fear of violent crimes. Theoretical papers and writings about criminal geography are a relatively rare occurrence in China (Zhang et al. 2009a, b). Main researches include Sun and Wei's (2004, 2006) theoretical induction on geography of crime, as well as Wang's (1988) overview on the western theories about criminal geography. In 1988, Wang (1988) began to introduce criminal geographical studies of a foreign city. In his study, he provided an in-depth analysis of a series of problems such as: the influence of the urban spatial environment to urban crime, comprehensive concepts on urban crime causes, nonpublic spatial blind areas of urban crime, public spatial blind areas of urban crime, marginal spatial blind areas of urban crime, the relationships between city development and urban crimes, and crime prevention effects of urban planning and design. He then put forward urban spatial crime prevention measures as Mao and Dai (2006) used these findings to analysis the relationships between urban spatial environment and crime. However, the domestic research mainly stopped at the summary of foreign theory about the geography of crime, and there was no development or innovation of their own that took place. Due to the lack of empirical data in a specific research study (Mao and Dai 2006), the operability of this theory has been questioned.

There is a striking group of theories about relationships between urban spatial structure disorganization, and crime that some basic concepts were originally created in other disciplines. For example, concepts of "invasion" and "replacing" in early criminal ecology theory, originated from botany, which describe that the process of invasion and succession by new residents in the vegetable kingdom is as same as it in human habitation. This process reflected in urban social space was also a social disorganization process (Park 1952, 1967, 1988). Field theory is one theory of geography of crime that uses the concept of "field" from physics to illustrate the formation principle, spatial structure, system function and classification of crime (Sun and Wei 2006). In addition, Chen et al. (2003) also draws some of the basic concepts from the environmental behavior theory to research environmental influences of crime in urban edge district.

A Study on spatial distribution of urban crime can be specifically divided into three levels macro, middle, and micro level.

Macro level research on spatial distribution of crime uses countries or even continents as the study units. For example, some research compares current crime status between developing and developed countries, and discusses the relationship between the level of development of the country and their crime. This leads researchers to believe that the crime rate in developed countries has an overall trend of increase, while crime rates in developing countries were generally elevated along with the rapid industrialization and development (Sun and Wei 2004).

Middle level research on spatial distribution of crime uses province, state, or city groups as research units. For example, Nelson et al.'s (2001) study on spatiotemporal characteristics of violent crime in British urban center; Sun's (2006) review of Chinese criminal history since the founding of the PRC, and analysis of regional difference of crime was based on 31 provincial level administrative regions, 9 economic regions, and 3 economic zones; Shigeru's (1988) study of relationship between Japanese urban environment and crime, and his analysis of the problems between citizens awareness; Newman and Kenworthy's (1999) concept of "Defensible Space" on the basis of study on urban crime which believed that material spatial environmental improvement could reduce crime; Liang's (1993) opinion on distribution and interval difference of urban crime phenomenon in province Gansu in China, revealing geographical distribution and regional differences of criminal phenomenon; Doeksen (1997) studied suburban streets in New Zealand and supported that people's attachment and public responsibility to urban public space could enhance social control and thereby reduce crime in the city; Xing (2006) researched on public security prevention and control system of northwest cities in China based on the "defensible space" theory. Research on a micro level uses a single city as the research object and focuses on criminal internal occurrence and distribution in a single city.

Research on a micro level using a single city as research object are common. For example, Cheng and Ma (1997) used the concept of location quotient to study criminal spatiotemporal characteristics and distribution regulations in Beijing city, and concludes that Beijing city and the spatial distributions of crime each in location are different; Mao and Dai's (2006) discussed characteristics of urban crime, temporal and spatial distribution of crime, and the relationship between crime and environment on the basis of study of urban crime mechanism and criminal environment types in Shanghai city; Du (1997) had a different approach and studied criminal geographic spatial distribution of the Canadian city of Edmonton and insisted that there were existing crime in areas within the city; Schweitzer et al. (1999) selected 44 residential areas in Lansing city of Michigan in the United States to study residential environment's effects on crime and fear; Ackerman and Murray (2004) studied crime spatial forming patterns of Lima city, Ohio, the United States of America, and pointed out the "problematic plot" in communities; Luymes and Tamminga (1995) studied the relationship between urban avenue and urban crime, and put forward to planning and design of "Green Boulevard"; Wagner (1997) found that the traffic mode of the city will play a certain role on the city's crime prevention planning; Loukaitou-Sideris et al. (2001) studied the influence of bus station crime and found that environmental factors could affect the number of people who take the bus; Ichniowski and Preston (1989) focused on the relationship between the city structure and organized crime in New York; Guan (2002) viewed on how to prevent the crime in public space from the point of city planning; Jiang (2002) studied the question of urban residential security planning; Du and Tang (1995) studied the mathematical model of the urban location choice and foreign travel problems relevant to urban crime; Weng and Pan (2003) studied the crime prevention theory from city planning; Xu (2003) reviewed nearly 30 years of crime prevention theories from environmental design. Liu (2006) discussed questions about urban crime and corresponding settlements from the perspective of city planning, particularly preventive measures of property crimes in communities. Zhu et al. (2006) discussed the security planning of urban residential space; Chen and Wang (2010) proposed realization of crime prevention by design of sports space in residential area; Liu (2004) proposed the defensible space theory and crime prevention through environmental design; Tang (2005) studied on the city design and crime prevention and control in urban public space.

2.3 Social Disorganization and Crime

Social disorganization theory is mainly used to study the relationship between crime and the community in the West. Social disorganization theory is also considered as theoretical basis of this book. So that detailed analysis on research status of social disorganization theory is necessary. Social disorganization theory is one of the early developed western criminal sociological theories. It goes beyond the previous theories which relate crimes to psychological or biological characteristics and individual choice, and states that the adverse economic class as the primary cause of crime. Social disorganization theory as well as strain theory and cultural deviance theory, is mutually independent but overlap, and it belongs to the social structure theory. Social disorganization theory can also be traced to Durkheim's descriptions on social changes and crime. Durkheim considered that the relationship between high-speed social change and crime increase was caused by social control collapse. Scholars in the department of sociology in the University of Chicago viewed Durkheim's opinions as a theoretical basis to study relationships between crime and high-speed change in a community.

2.3.1 Early Theoretical Point

Park and Burgess's theory of human ecology: Robert Park proposed a parallel between the distribution of plant life in nature and the organization of human life in societies (Warming 1969). Park viewed the city as a kind of "super-organism" that had "organic unity" derived from the symbiotic interrelations of the people who lived within it. These natural areas had an organic unity of their own and played a part in the life of the city as a whole. The process of "invasion, dominance, and succession" in plant ecology can also be seen in human societies. In cities, one cultural or ethnic group may take over an entire neighborhood from another group, beginning with the shift of only one or two residents. Similarly, business or industries may move into and ultimately take over a previously residential neighborhood (Park 1952). Burgess (1923) further explored Park's theory of human ecology as he pointed out that cities do not merely grow at their edges, rather, they have a tendency to expand radically from their center in patterns of concentric circles moving gradually outward. Burgess described these concentric circles as "zones." A city in social change normally has five zones, each of which is growing and thus is gradually moving outward into the territory occupied by the next zone, in a process of invasion, dominance, and succession (Park 1936).

Shaw and McKay's research in the "delinquency areas" of Chicago: Park's theories were used as the basis for a broadly ranging study of the problem of juvenile delinquency in Chicago by Shaw. Shaw designed a special research program to explore the process in which juvenile delinquency deviated the traditions according to theories of human ecology (Finestone 1976). In *Juvenile Delinquency and*

Urban Areas, Shaw and McKay (1942) concluded that delinquency and other social problems are closely related to the process of invasion, dominance, and succession that determines the concentric growth patterns of the city. The "interstitial areas" would be formed when special areas in a city are invaded by new residents, with a variety of social problems that are directly traceable to the rapid shift in population (Shaw and Mckay 1969).

2.3.2 Revitalization of the Theory of Social Disorganization

After a relatively brief period of prominence during the 1950s and 1960s, many criminologists came to view the concept of social disorganization developed by Shaw and McKay as marginal to modern criminological thought, especially after Miller (1962) and others evaluated and argued that Shaw's Chicago Area Project failed to prevent juvenile delinquency. During this period, theories with a social-psychological orientation stressed socialization within the family, school, and peer groups. These ideas dominated the criminological literature of that time period; however, the social disorganization theory is revitalized by area studies conducted by Bursik, Stark, Sampson, and Kornhauser. These modern social ecologists developed a "purer" form of structural theory that emphasizes the association of community deterioration and economic decline to criminality but places less emphasis on value conflict.

Kornhauser's *Community Control*: Kornhauser (1978) broke down the theories of Shaw and McKay into two points—"social disorganization" and "subculture." "Social disorganization's" stance is that disorganized communities unable to maintain effective social control in which neighborhood and institutions have collapsed; juvenile delinquency will emerge. In other words, the "subculture" view is that juvenile delinquency will be gradually supported by shared values of community residents over time. Shaw and McKay believed that "subculture" was more influential than "social disorganization" on youth crime, and the majority of slum juvenile delinquency is the result of subculture. Kornhauser claimed that social disorganization was the main cause to generate these crimes. He outlined a "community control" mode from the theory of Shaw and McKay. The basic point is that, communities with poverty, ethnic heterogeneity and high residential mobility are difficult to maintain normal social relations and public institutions, and hence will have high rates of crime and juvenile delinquency.

Bursik, Webb, and Stark on *residential succession*: Bursik and Webb also believed that social disorganization is the main factor that affects juvenile delinquency in neighborhoods. They tested the concept of residential succession using data on Chicago neighborhoods directly comparable to that of Shaw and McKay (Sampson 1995). They found that the residential succession argument was supported by data from 1940 to 1950. However, after 1950 all neighborhoods undergoing racial change were characterized by high delinquency rates, regardless of their delinquency rates before the change. Bursik and Webb interpret their finding in terms of community stability. To further explain the phenomenon of residential succession,

Stark (1987) presented a formal theory in thirty integrated propositions. These thirty propositions focused on five structural aspects of urban neighborhoods: density, poverty, mixed use, transience, and dilapidation. Stark argues that these five structural characteristics increase moral cynicism among community residents and provide more opportunities to commit crime, increase the motivations to commit crimes, and decrease informal surveillance by which crime in a community is held in check. As a consequence, crime-prone citizens are attracted to the neighborhood, while law-abiding people get out if they have the opportunity to do so. It results in high crime rates that tend to persist even when there is a complete turnover in the population.

Sampson on *collective efficacy*: Sampson (1987, 1995) reviewed recent research on the relation between neighborhoods and crime in an attempt to determine how community structures and cultures create different crime rates. He found that poverty itself is not related to crime. Rather, poverty combined with residential mobility seems to be associated with higher levels of violent crime. Neighborhood rates of family disruption are strongly and consistently related to rates of violence. Neighborhoods with high percentages of African Americans have higher crime rates, but race itself tends to be unrelated when family disruption and poverty are taken into account. Finally, neighborhoods with high population density and high concentrations of individuals who do not live within a family situation tend to have higher rates of crime and violence. Sampson explained this pattern of research findings using the framework of social disorganization. He defined social disorganization as the inability of the community to realize its common values. There may be a variety of reasons that some communities cannot realize their common values, but one reason is the lack of what Coleman calls "social capital"—i.e., networks of relationships among people that facilitate common actions and make possible the achievement of common goals (Coleman 1988). In general, when there are many social relationships among community residents, there is less crime; low social capital would reduce informal social control and this leads to the growth of crime and community disorganization.

Sampson and Groves (1989) found that the existence of juvenile street groups was caused by the community's lack of informal social control to the youth. Sampson, then introduced the term of "collective efficacy" and defined it as the community's ability to maintain order in public places. Sampson believed that only the linkage of community cohesion, mutual trust, and common aspiration can reach collective efficacy. After empirical analysis, Sampson and Raudenbush (1999) inferred that social structural defects and weakened collective efficacy were the positive factor that promotes crime rates. Researchers supporting social disorganization theory prefer to link social disorganization to many other concepts and categories, such as race (Stults and Baumer 2007), social isolation (Shihadeh and Ousey 1998), social capital (Messner et al. 2004), ethnic heterogeneity (Hansmann and Quigley 1982), social injustice (Kelly 2000), and social structure (Liska and Chamlin 1984; Williams and Timberlake 1984). These detailed expositions enrich and strengthen the relative research on the relationship between social disorganization and crime, as well as widen the applied extension of the social disorganization theory as a whole.

2.3.3 Critical Summary on Research Status of the Social Disorganization Theory

(I) There still has been no unified definition on the basic concepts of the social disorganization theory. Many research results are conflicting and inconclusive. For example, there are different understandings about the concept of "social disorganization." Durkheim (1964) believed that the uncertainty and expectations of the future would cause social disorganization; Shaw and McKay thought that quantitative impoverished population, ethnic difference and frequent migration are three major structural causes of community disorganization; Sampson defined social disorganization as a community that has no ability to realize its common values. In relationships between economic status and crime, empirical research on relationships between unemployment and crime caused different or even opposite conclusions. On the study of the relationship between modernization and crime, there has still no uniformed conclusion.

(II) There has also been no certain conclusion about causality of crime and social disorganization. It is generally believed that social disorganization leads to the increasing crime rate. However, I think that there are bilateral relations between social disorganization and crime, namely that social disorganization causes an increase in the crime rate, while the increasing rate of crime would exacerbate social disorganization.

(III) Factors constituting the main body of current research include: informal social control, social connection, social capital, and collective efficacy. Current research emphasizes the relationship between structural factors and community crime, while ignoring the effect of culture on community crime. Previous research reveals that the not only structural factors of the social disorganization theory, but also cultural factors influence on crime should be paid attention to. For example, Shaw and McKay pointed out long ago that subculture was an important component of the community social structure. Previous research concluded that these two factors should act together to community crime, but did not put address the concept of "cultural disorganization." Previous research was also not aware that a disorganized community would be not only be disorganized in the social structure, but also in its culture.

(IV) Research that was focused on the influence of "informal social control" showed less solicitude for the effect of formal social control on community crime.

(V) Most of the research was limited to the influence of various factors within the community on crime and the correlation between various inner factors, while the research ignored the influence of the external environment of the community on community crime.

(VI) As far as research method is concerned, the most research data is collected through questionnaire surveys. And once completed, the quantitative data analysis is compiled using statistical software, while few researchers made qualitative researches through in-depth interviews.

References

Ackerman, W. V. & Murray, A. T. (2004). Assessing spatial patterns of crime in Lima, Ohio. *Cities, 5*(21), 423–437.

Allen, R. C. (1996). Socioeconomic conditions and property crime: A comprehensive review and test of the professional literature. *American Journal of Economics and Sociology, 55*(3), 293–300.

Beirne, P. (1993). *Inventing criminology*. Albany: State University of New York Press.

Berk, R. A., Lenihan, K. J., & Rossi, P. H. (1980). Crime and poverty: Some experimental evidence from ex-offenders. *American Sociological Review, 45*, 766–786.

Blau, J. R., & Blau, P. M. (1982). The cost of inequality: Metropolitan structure and violent crime. *American Sociological Review, 47*(1), 114–129.

Blumstein, A., & Wallman, J. (2006). *The crime drop in America* (Rev. ed.). New York: Cambridge University Press.

Burgess, E. W. (1923). The interdependence of sociology and social work. *Journal of Social Forces, 1*(4), 366–370.

Chen, F., Min, M., & Yin, X. (2003). Environmental impact of urban fringe crime. *City Issue, 112* (2), 45–47. 陈峰云, 闵敏, 殷旭东 (2003). 城市边缘区犯罪问题的环境影响,《城市问题》, 112(2): 45–47.

Chen, Z., & Wang, H. (2010). Crime prevention implementation through residential areas fitness site planning. *Central China Architecture, 28* (1). 陈智君, 王红扬 (2010). 通过居住区体育健身场所规划设计实现犯罪预防,《华中建筑》, 28(1).

Cheng, L., & Ma, L. (1997) Geographical analysis on Beijing urban crime. *Human Geography, 3*, 7–12. 程连生, 马丽. (1997). 北京城市犯罪地理分析.《人文地理》, *3*, 7–12.

Chiricos, T. G. (1987). Rates of crime and unemployment: An analysis of aggregate research evidence. *Social Problems, 34*(2), 187–211.

Cho, Y. H. (1974). *Public policy and urban crime*. Cambridge, MA: Ballinger.

Clinard, M. B. (Ed.). (1964). *Anomie and deviant behaviour*. New York: The Free Press.

Cohen, A. K. (1959). The study of social disorganization and deviant behavior. In Robert K. Merton, et al. (Eds.), *Sociology today*. New York: Basic Books.

Coleman, J. (1988). Social capital in the creation of human capital. *Americal Journal of Sociology, 94*(Supplement), 95–120.

Cornwell, C., & Trumbull, W. (1994). Estimating the economic-model of crime with panel-data. *Review of Economics and Statistics, 76*(2), 360–366.

Coughlin, B. C., & Venkatesh, S. A. (2003). *The urban street gang after 1970.*

Crutchfield, R. D. (1989). Labor stratification and violent crime. *Social Forces, 68*(2), 489–512.

Danser, K. R., J. H. Laub & National Institute for Juvenile Justice and Delinquency Prevention and Criminal Justice Research Center (Eds.) (1980). *Juvenile criminal behavior and its relation to economic conditions*. Washington, D.C.: U.S. Department of Justice, Office of Juvenile Justice and Delinquency Prevention, National Institute for Juvenile Justice and Delinquency Prevention.

Doeksen, H. (1997). Reducing crime and the fear of crime by reclaiming New Zealand's suburban street. *Landscape and Urban Planning, 39*(2), 243–252.

Du, D. (1997). Geographic research on crime problems in Edmonton, Canada. *Human Geography, 6*, 7–12. 杜德斌 (1997). 加拿大爱得蒙顿市犯罪问题的地理研究.《人文地理》, *6*, 7–12.

Du, D., & Tang, J. (1995). Mathematical modeling of urban crime location choice, *Geography, 14*(3), 26–32. 杜德斌, 汤建中 (1995). 城市犯罪区位选择的数学模拟,《地理研究》, *14*(3), 26–32.

Durkheim, É. (1951). In J. A. Spaulding, G. Simpson (Eds.), *Suicide: A study in sociology*. Glencoe, Illinois: Free Press.

Durkheim, É. (1964). In G. Simpson (Ed.), *The division of labor in society*. New York: London; New York: Free Press; London: Collier-Macmillan.

Ehrlich, I. (1974). Participation in illegal activities. In Gary S. Beeker, & W. M. Landers (Eds.), *Essays in the economics of crime and punishment*. New York: Columbia University Press.
Finestone, H. (1976). Tile delinquent and society: The Shaw and McKay Tradition. In James E. Shorted (Ed.), *Delinquency, crime and society* (pp. 23–49). Chicago: University of Chicago Press.
Fyfe, N. (1991). The police, space and society—The geography of policing. *Progress in Human Geography, 15*(3), 249–267.
Glaser, D., & Rice, K. (1959). Crime, age, and employment. *American Sociological Review, 24*(5), 679–686.
Grant, D. S., & Martínez, R. (1997). Crime and the restructuring of the U.S. economy: A reconsideration of the class linkages. *Social Forces, 75*(3), 769–798.
Guan, H. (2002). *Safety city—Public space crime prevention from urban planning. Master's Degree Book*. Taiwan: Institute of Urban Planning, Taipei University. 关华. (2002). 安全城市——从都市计划论预防公共空间犯罪. 硕士学位论文, 中国台湾:台北 大学都市计划研究所.
Gurr, T. R. (1979). On the history of violent crime in Europe and America. In H. D. Graham & T. R. Gurr (Eds.), *Violence in America* (2nd ed.). Beverly Hills, CA: Sage.
Gurr, T. R. (1981). Historical forces in violent crime. In Michael Tonry & Norval Morris (Eds.), *Crime and justice* (Vol. 3, pp. 340–346). Chicago: University of Chicago Press.
Hansmann, H. B., & Quigley, J. M. (1982). Population heterogeneity and the sociogenesis of homicide. *Social Forces, 61*(1), 206–224.
Harer, M. D., & Steffensmeier, D. (1992). The differing effects of economic inequality on black and white rates of violence. *Social Forces, 70*(4), 1035–1054.
Harries, K. (2006). Extreme spatial variations in crime density in Baltimore County, MD. *Geoforum, 37*(3), 404–416.
Herbert, D. (1977). Crime, delinquency and the urban environment. *Progress in Human Geography, 1*(1), 208–239.
Herbert, D. (1982). *The geography of urban crime*. New York: Longman.
Herbert, D., & Harries, K. (1986). Area-based policies for crime prevention. *Applied Geography, 6*(4), 281–295.
Hubbard, P. (1998). Community action and the displacement of street prostitution: Evidence from British cities. *Geoforum, 29*(3), 269–286.
Ichniowski, C., & Preston, A. (1989). The persistence of organized crime in New York City construction: An economic perspective. *Industrial and Labor Relations Review, 42*(4), 549–565.
Jacobs, D. (1981). Inequality and economic crime. *Sociology and Social Research, 66*.
Jiang, Y. (2002). *Planning studies on urban residential security and defense*. Master's Degree Book. Shanghai: Department of Urban Planning, University of Tongji. 江毅. (2002). 城市住区安全防卫规划研究. 硕士学位论文, 上 海:同济大学城市规划系.
Kelly, M. (2000). Inequality and crime. *The Review of Economics and Statistics, 82*(4), 530–539.
Kornhauser, R. R. (1978). *Social sources of delinquency*. Chicago: University of Chicago Press.
LaCapra, D. (2001). In ebrary Inc. (Ed.), *Emile Durkheim electronic resource: Sociologist and philosopher*. Aurora, CO: Davies Group, Publishers.
Lafree, G. (1998). *Losing Legitimacy* (pp. 122–126). Boulder: Westview Co.
Land, K., Mccall, P., & Cohen, L. (1990). Structural covariates of homicide rates—Are there any invariances across time and social space. *American Journal of Sociology, 95*(4), 922–963.
Lee, M. R. (2000). Concentrated poverty, *race, and homicide. Sociological Quarterly, 41*(2), 189–206.
Liang, Z. (1993). Pilot exploring on urban criminal geography—A case study of Gansu Province. *Human Geography, 1*, 73–78. 梁志寇 (1993). 城市刑事犯罪地理初探——以甘肃省为例. 《人文地理》, *1*, 73–78.
Liska, A. E., & Chamlin, M. B. (1984). Social structure and crime control among macrosocial units. *The American Journal of Sociology, 90*(2), 383–395.

Liu, Z. (2004). *Moral China: Grave concern on contemporary Chinese ethical*. Beijing: China Social Sciences Publishing House. 刘智锋. (2004). 《道德中国: 当代中国道德伦理的深重忧思》. 北京: 中国社会科学出版社.

Liu, H. (2006). *Urban residential space planning study based on crime prevention*. Master's Degree Book. Tianjin: Tianjin University. 刘峘 (2006). 基于犯罪预防的城市居住空间规划研究, 硕士学位论文, 天津: 天津大学.

Liu, J., Messner, S., Zhang, L., & Zhuo, Y. (2009). Socio-demographic correlates of fear of crime and the social context of contemporary urban china. *American Journal of Community Psychology, 44*(1), 93–108.

Loftin, C., & Hill, R. H. (1974). Regional subculture and homicide: An examination of the gastil-hackney book. *American Sociological Review, 39*(5), 714–724.

Loftin, C., & McDowall, D. (1982). The police, crime, and economic theory: An assessment. *American Sociological Review, 47*(3), 393–401.

Long, S. K., & Witte, A. D. (1981). Current economic trends: Implications for crime and criminal justice. In Kevin Wright (Ed.), *Crime and criminal justice in a declining economy*. Mass: Oelgeschlager, Gunn and Hain, Cambridge.

Loukaitou-Sideris, A., Liggett, R., Iseki, H., & Thurlow, W. (2001). Measuring the effects of built environment on bus stop crime. *Environment and Planning B: Planning and Design, 28*(2), 255–280.

Lowman, J. (1986). Conceptual issues in the geography of crime: Toward a geography of social control. *Annals of the Association of American Geographers, 76*(1), 81–94.

Luymes, D. T., & Tamminga, K. (1995). Integrating public safety and use into planning urban greenways. *Landscape and Urban Planning, 33*(1), 391–400.

MacDonald, Z. (2002). Official crime statistics: Their use and interpretation. *The Economic Journal, 112*(477, Features), F85–F106.

Machin, S., & Meghir, C. (2004). Crime and economic incentives. *The Journal of Human Resources, 39*(4), 958–979.

Maltz, M. D. (1976). On the estimation of smuggling in a gray market commodity. *Operations Research, 24*(6), 1156–1163.

Mao, Y., & Dai, S. (2006). Spatial distribution and environmental characteristics of crime—A case study of Shanghai. *Journal of Urban Planning, 3*, 85–93. 毛媛媛, 戴慎志. (2006). 犯罪空间分布与环境特征——以上海市为例. 《城市规划学刊》, 3, 85–93.

Massey, D. S. (1996). The age of extremes: Concentrated affluence and poverty in the twenty-first century. *Demography, 33*(4), 395–412.

Mcllwaine C. (1999). Geography and development: Violence and crime as development issues. *Progress in Human Geography, 23*(3), 453–363.

Merlo, A. (2004). Introduction to economic models of crime. *International Economic Review, 45*(3), 677–679.

Messner, S. E. (1982). Societal Development. *Social Equality, and Homicide, Social Forces, 61*, 225–240.

Messner, S. F., Baumer, E., & Rosenfeld, R. (2004). Dimensions of social capital and rates of criminal homicide. *American Sociological Review, 69*(6), 882–903.

Miller, W. B. (1962). The impact of a 'total-community' delinquency control project. *Social Problems, 10*, 168–191.

Nagel, W. G. (1981). A Statement on behalf of a moratorium on prison construction. *Crime and Delinquency, 23*(2), 234–244.

Nelson, A. L., Bromley, R. D. F., & Thomas, C. J. (2001). Identifying micro-spatial and temporal patterns of violent crime and disorder in the British city centre. *Applied Geography, 21*(3), 249–274.

Newman, P., & Kenworthy, J. (1999). *Sustainability and cities: Overcoming automobile dependence*. Washington: Island Press.

Pain, R. H. (1997). Social geographies of women's fear of crime. *Transactions of the Institute of British Geographers, 22*(2), 231–244.

Park, R. E. (1936). Human ecology. *American Journal of Sociology, 42*, 158.
Park, R. E. (1952). *Human communities* (118). Glencoe, IL: The Free Press.
Park, R. E. (1967). In E. W. Burgess, & McKenzie R. D. (Eds.), *The city*. Chicago: University of Chicago Press.
Park, R. E. (1988). In E. W. Burgess (Ed.), *Introduction to the science of sociology*. Chicago, Ill.: University of Chicago Press.
Pawson, E. & Banks, G. (1993). Rape and fear in New Zealand City. *Area, 25*(2), 55–63.
Pudney, S., Deadman, D., & Pyle, D. (2000). The relationship between crime, punishment and economic conditions: Is reliable inference possible when crimes are under-recorded? *Journal of the Royal Statistical Society Series A (Statistics in Society), 163*(1), 81–97.
Pyle, G. F. (1976). Geographic perspectives on crime and the impact of crime legislation. In J. S. Adins (Ed.), *Urban policymaking and metropolitan dynamics* (pp. 257–292). Cambridge, MA: Ballinger.
Samara, T. R. (2005). Youth, Crime and urban renewal in the western cape. *Journal of Southern African Studies, 31*(1), 209–227.
Sampson, R. J. (1987). Urban black violence: The effect of male joblessness and family disruption. *The American Journal of Sociology, 93*(2), 348–382.
Sampson, R. J. (1995). The community. In James Q. Wilson & Joan Petersilia (Eds.), *Crime* (pp. 193–216). San Francisco: ICS Press.
Sampson, R. J., & Groves, W. B. (1989). Community structure and crime. *American Journal of Sociology, 94*, 774–802.
Sampson, R. J., & Raudenbush, S. W. (1999). Systematic social observation of public spaces. *American Journal of Sociology, 105*(3), 603–651.
Schweitzer, J., Kim, J. W., & Mackin, J. (1999). The impact of the built environment on crime and fear of crime in urban neighborhoods. *Journal of Urban Technology, 6*(3), 59–73.
Shaw, C. R. R., & McKay, H. D. (Ed.) (1969). In *Juvenile delinquency and urban areas: A study of rates of delinquency in relation to differential characteristics of local communities in american cities (Rev. ed.)*. Chicago: University of Chicago Press.
Shaw, C. R., & McKay, H. D. (Ed.) (1942). In *Juvenile delinquency and urban areas: A study of rates of delinquents in relation to differential characteristics of local communities in American cities*. Chicago, Ill.: The University of Chicago Press.
Shelley, L. I. (1981). *Crime and modernization: The impact of industrialization and urbanization on crime*. Carbondale: Southern Illinois University Press.
Shigeru (Ed.), Zheng, G., & Xia, J. (translated) (1988). *City and crime*. Beijing: Masses Press. (日) 伊藤滋(编), 郑光林, 夏金池(译), (1988).《城市与犯罪》, 北京: 群众出版社.
Shihadeh, E. S., & Flynn, N. (1996). Segregation and crime: The effect of black social isolation on the rates of black urban violence. *Social Forces, 74*(4), 1325–1352.
Shihadeh, E., & Ousey, G. (1998). Industrial restructuring and violence: The link between entry-level jobs, economic deprivation, and black and white homicide. *Social Forces, 77*(1), 185–206.
Singell, L. (1967). An examination of the empirical relationship between unemployment and juvenile delinquency. *American Journal of Economics and Sociology, 26*(4), 377–386.
Stark, R. (1987). Deviant places: A theory of the ecology of crime. *Criminology, 25*(4), 893–909.
Steffensmeier, D. J. (1980). Sex differences in patterns of adult crime, 1965–77: A review and assessment. *Social Forces, 58*(4), 1080–1108.
Stults, B. J., & Baumer, E. (2007). Racial context and police force size: Evaluating the empirical validity of the minority threat perspective. *The American Journal of Sociology, 113*(2), 507–546.
Sun, F., & Wei, X. (2004). New research progress of criminal geography. *Human Geography, 5*, 60–63. 孙峰华, 魏晓. (2004). 犯罪地理学研究的新进展.《人文地理》, 5, 60—63.
Sun, F., & Wei, X. (2006). Study on Chinese criminal geography. *Journal of Liaoning Normal University (Natural Science Edition), 20*(4), 493–495. 孙峰华, 魏晓. (2006). 中国犯罪地理研究.《辽宁师范大学学报(自然科学版)》, *20*(4), 493–495.

Takeuchi, D. T., Williams, D. R., & Adair, R. K. (1991). Economic stress in the family and children's emotional and behavioral problems. *Journal of Marriage and Family, 53*(4), 1031–1041.

Tang, J. (2005). Urban design and urban public spatial crime prevention. *Journal of Central China Architecture, 1*. 汤晋. (2005). 城市设计与城市公共空间犯罪防控, 《华中建筑》 *1*.

Vold, G. B. (1979). In T. J. Bernard (Ed.), *Theoretical criminology* (2nd ed./prepared by Thomas J. Bernard. ed.). New York: Oxford University Press.

Vold, G. B. (1998). In T. J. Bernard, & J. B. Snipes (Eds.), *Theoretical criminology* (4th ed./by George B. Vold, Thomas J. Bernard & Jeffrey B. Snipes. Eds.) Oxford: Oxford University Press.

Wagner, A. E. (1997). A study of traffic pattern modifications in an urban crime prevention program. *Journal of Criminal Justice, 25*(1), 19–30.

Wang, F. (1988). Foreign geography of urban crime. *Human Geography, 3*(1), 76–82. 王发曾. (1988). 国外城市犯罪的地理研究. 《人文地理》, *3*(1), 76–82.

Wang, F., & Minor, W. W. (2002). Where the jobs are: Employment access and crime patterns in cleveland. *Annals of the Association of American Geographers, 92*(3), 435–450.

Warming, E. (1969). Plant communities. In Robert E. Park & Ernest W. Burgess, *Introduction to the science of sociology* (pp. 175–182). Chicago: University of Chicago Press

Weng, L., & Pan, J. (2003). Pilot exploring of urban planning and crime prevention theory. *Journal of Chinese People's Public Security University, 2*(102), 135–140. 翁里, 潘建珍 (2003). 城市规划与防控犯罪之理论初探, 《中国人民公安大学学报》, *2*(102), 135–140.

White, G. (1999). Crime and the decline of manufacturing, 1970–1990. *Justice Quarterly, 16*(1), 81–97.

Williams, N. J. (1985). Crime patterns in Abedeen. *Scottish Geographical Magazine, 101*, 49–59.

Williams, K. R., & Timberlake, M. (1984). Structured inequality, conflict, and control: A cross-national test of the threat hypobook. *Social Forces, 63*(2), 414–432.

Wong, Y. R. (1995). An economic analysis of the crime rate in England and Wales, 1857-92. *Economic, 62*(246), 235–246.

Wright, J. P., Cullen, F., & Williams, N. (1997). Working while in school and delinquent involvement: Implications for social policy. *Crime & Delinquency, 43*(2), 203–221.

Xing, J. (2006). *Research and application of northwest urban public security prevention and control system based on defensible space theory*, Master's Degree Book. Lanzhou: Department of Computer Applications, Lanzhou University. 刑杰. (2006). 基于防卫空间理论的西北城市公共安全防控体系研究与应用, 硕士学位论文, 兰州: 兰州大学计算机应用技术系.

Xu, L. (2003). 30 years study and practice of crime prevention from environmental design. *New Architecture, 6*, 4–7. 徐磊青 (2003). 以环境设计防止犯罪研究与实践30年. 《新建筑》, *6*, 4–7.

Zhang, L., Feng, K., & Li, W. (2009a). Review on current China's criminal geography research. *Ludung University Journal (Natural Science Edition), 25*, 267. 张磊, 冯开禹, 李伟涛. (2009). 当前我国犯罪地理学研究综述,《鲁东大学学报(自然科学版)》, *25*, 267.

Zhang, L., Messner, S. F., & Liu, J. (2007a). A multilevel analysis of the risk of household burglary in the city of Tianjin, China. *The British Journal of Criminology, 47*(6), 918–937.

Zhang, L., Messner, S. F., & Liu, J. (2007b). An exploration of the determinants of reporting crime to the police in the city of Tianjin. *China. Criminology, 45*(4), 959–984.

Zhang, L., Messner, S., Liu, J., & Zhuo, Y. (2009b). Guanxi and fear of crime in contemporary urban China. *British Journal of Criminology, 49*(4), 472–490.

Zhou, L. (2004). *New contemporary empirical criminology*. Beijing: People's Court Publishing House. 周路. (2004).《当代实证犯罪学新编》, 北京: 人民法院出版社.

Zhou, S., & Cao, L. (2007). *Theory and positivism of criminology*. Taipei: Wunan Publishing Company. 周愫娴, 曹立群. (2007).《犯罪学理论及其实证》, 台北: 五南图书出版股份有限公司.

Zhu, Y., Liu, H., & Wang, L. (2006). Approaches of urban residential space planning based on crime prevention. *City*, *5*, 21–23. 朱玉兰, 刘峘, 汪磊 (2006). 基于犯罪预防的城市居住空间规划途径探讨.《城市》, *5*, 21–23.

Chapter 3
Analytical Approach

3.1 Basic Conceptions

Concept selection should be on solidly theoretical and systematic base. Due to limited time and space, coupled with the research purpose of the book, the author does not want to spend too much on relevant concept description. Although the conceptualization is an integral part in this paper, for the above reason, only the very influential definitions are selected as the basic conception, such as the World Bank's definition on social capital, the EU's definition on social exclusion.

3.1.1 Social Disorganization

Social disorganization refers to a state of society characterized by the breakdown of effective social control resulting in a lack of functional integration between groups, conflicting social attitudes, personal maladjustment, and social cohesion. In periods of drastic social changes the old norms gradually collapse, however, new standards are not yet built and certain normal functions are impeded. In addition to this, several standard systems conflict with each other and people lose their behavior criterions, then society subsequently becomes disorganized. Social disorganization is differentiated from social disintegration in many ways. The former refers to the method in which society becomes loose and broken, but remains in its original social structure and social system; the latter refers to that the entire social system where the regulations become damaged, so that the original social order cannot be maintained and continued (Davis 2014; Elliott 1961; Emerick 2013; Emery et al. 2013; Faris 1955; Veling 2015).

H. Xiong, *Urban Crime and Social Disorganization in China*,
DOI 10.1007/978-981-287-859-5_3

3.1.2 Social Justice

The generation of social justice is the important standard difference between human society and animal world governed by law of the jungle. Social fairness is also inevitable outcome of human awareness and consciousness of the society (Clingerman 2011). Problems of justice were first presented by Plato in his famous works "Utopia." Plato emphasized that fairness was essentially harmony, and justice was basically personal and national "Virtue" (Plato 1994). Epicurus put forward the theory of the social contract and considered justice as an equity; essentially the product of people's agreements with each other (Lin 2001). Modern initiation thinkers such as Voltaire, Montesquieu, and Rousseau discussed and researched how to realize social fairness and justice from a variety of aspects (Shank 2014; Rousseau 1947). Saint-Simonian regarded social fairness and justice as important goals for a future ideal society. Although feelings and understandings of fairness and justice are not the same in present times and different social formations, however, its basic connotation is proclaimed from different angles. That is, fairness is the basic embodiment of justice as well as the first virtue of social institutions on the basis of equality allowing the existence of difference (Rawls 1999; Buettner-schmidt and Lobo 2012; Tyler and Van 2013).

Social fairness requires each individual to participate in a social cooperative to realize the equality and unity of rights and duties (Marx and Engels 1980).

Current China's social fairness view is as "equality of opportunity," referring to social member's attitude toward opportunities. The first is that 'person' or factitious obstacle hindering the others' development should be clear; the second is that any privilege for individuals should be abolished; the third is that measures taken by national government to improve people's status should be applied equally to all people (Stoll 2011).

3.1.3 Social Discrimination

The core meaning of social discrimination is unfair and unequal. It can be expressed as a kind of behavior and also can be expressed as a kind of system or attitude (Edwards 1987; Jordens 1992). Attitude, behavior, and system are three latitudes of social discrimination. Accordingly, there are three general types of social disorganization: social prejudice (i.e., attitudinal social discrimination), behavioral discrimination, and institutional discrimination. Social prejudice is a fixed, preoccupied perception and attitude [with a] lack of objective evidence. In social psychology, prejudice mostly refers to a negative and repellent attitude (Hall et al. 2015). Behavioral discrimination refers to differentiated behavior according to functionally unrelated status characteristics (Merton 2000). Institutional discrimination refers to unfair institutional arrangement aiming at a specific social group, which is completely rigid and direct, that results in serious social discrimination (Robin 2001; Sassenberg et al. 2003), such as the apartheid system in the history of the United States or the caste system in India.

3.1.4 Social Capital

Social capital is a sociological concept, which refers to connections within and between social networks. The term is frequently used by different social sciences. In general terms, we could say that social capital is the fruit of social relations, and consists of the expectative benefits derived from the preferential treatment and cooperation between individuals and groups (Putnam 2000). Social capital is the connection among persons, existing in interpersonal relationship. Social capital is similar with material capital and human capital. This kind of connection between individual and others in the organization can bring future earnings. Social capital is often involving with specific organization. Individual social capital within the organization reflects the size of the additional benefits brought by the interpersonal contact in the long run. Social capital can be externally expressed as reputation, popularity, public praise, and so on (Baum and Ziersch 2003; Jenkins 2003; Portes 2014).

3.1.5 Social Order

Social order is a concept generally used in sociology, history, politics, and other social sciences. The harmony of the whole society shows social order; on the contrary, social disharmony shows social conflict. According to Auguste Comte's conception of "order reconstruction," the principle of social order mainly includes the following six items: (1) advocating science and natural laws; (2) expanding fraternity tendency; (3) unity of belief and morality; (4) division and cooperation of social labor; (5) strengthen the government authority and regulation; (6) "social transformation" on the basis of private ownership (Etty 2001; ASA Conference 1987; Bierstedt 1974).

3.1.6 Social Control

Social control means the social process in which the social organization controls the of its members by social norms. The term social control could be understood in both the broad and narrow sense. For social control in the broad sense, it generally refers to control on all social behaviors. Social control in the narrow sense particularly means control on deviant behavior. Social control can coordinate social operations of various relationships among social systems which attempt to make the social systmes in harmony with one another (Boman et al. 2012; Bridges and Myers 1994; Church et al. 2012; Deflem and Ebrary 2010; Deutschmann 1994; Ross 1896, 1901; Warner and Burchfield 2011; Watkins 1975).

3.1.7 Social Isolation

Social isolation is also known as residential segregation, and refers to a lack of contact with members of one's species because of race, religion, occupation, habits, cultural level, or wealth. Residents with similar features live in compact communities, while groups without similar features are separated from each other. Social isolation would produce discrimination or even hostility between isolated social groups (Schwab 1992). Two requirements must be met for residential segregated groups: (1) residential spatial partition, (2) subjects of groups are not in contact with each other, i.e., no social intercourse (Cacioppo et al. 2011).

3.1.8 Social Exclusion

The concept of social exclusion is in a state of fuzziness and uncertainty. The author cites the EU's definition to describe the meaning of "social exclusion." Using the EU as a model, social exclusion includes economic, social, and political aspects. At an economic level, social exclusion refers to unemployed population; be deprived of access to property rights (such as property or credit assets); at a social level, social exclusion refers to an individual losing contact with mainstream society. In the aspect of politics, social exclusion refers to certain types of populations, such as women, racial or religious minority populations, or immigrants, who can be fully or partially deprived of political and human rights (Alvey 2001; Bennett 2014; Byrne 2005; Claypool and Bernstein 2014; Glennerster and Centre for Analysis of Social Exclusion 1999; Li 2004; Tunstall 2011).

3.1.9 Cohesion

Cohesion refers to the degree of cooperation to achieve collective goals among group members. The so-called group refers to a collection of people, including family, friend, collectives, classes, and ethnicities. External performance of cohesion exists in individual behavior based on group target tasks focusing on trust, compliance and obedience (Colic-Peisker and Robertson 2015; Cramm 2012; Gaffikin and Morrissey 2011).

3.1.10 Trust

In Social Sciences, trust is considered as a dependent relationship. Trusted individuals or organizations mean that they seek practical policies, ethics codes, law, and previous promises (Fratcher 1973; Gilchrist 2004; Hardin 2006; Harris 2007; Loyola 1928; Prosen 2011; Richter 2010). Epicurus defined trust as to simplify the interpersonal relationship (Epicurus 1670).

3.1.11 Fear

Fear is a distressing negative sensation induced by a perceived threat. The term fear often refers to a mood. Fear is a strong psychological or physiological reaction surrounded with unpredictable factors. Fear is a psychoactive status of human and biology and a special phenomenon only happening on human and biology (see Baidupedia). What would be discussed in this book is residents' fear of crime (Asencio 2014; Chadee 2013; Farrall 2009; Leahy 1948; MacGill 1921; Mosso 1896).

It was discussed previously that the crime rate will cause large fluctuations in periods of rapid social transition. At the present time, when China is in a critical period of economic system reform and political system reform, crime rates continue to rise. In such a time, a particular city—Guangzhou has been selected because its rate of case-filing per 100,000 people is much higher than the national average. Through this investigation, we can see the spatial distribution characteristics of crime rates in Guangzhou.

The author presents punctuate distribution of crime pattern in urban spatial structures, and consequently reveals diverse and inconstant social disorganization in Guangzhou. Through field investigation, three types of communities in different status of social disorganization are selected to do in-depth interview. A series of indexes in the quantitative research of social disorganization are referred to when designing the interview outline. Data has been collected through an in-depth interview to community residents from economic status (including income and unemployment), marriage and family status, residential mobility and ethnic heterogeneity. The author has also compiled statistics relating to social fairness, social discrimination, social capital, social order, social control, social isolation, social exclusion, community cohesion, residents' trust and fear, residents' perceptions of tradition, morality and belief, as well as language conflicts. Data are then further collected to examine these factors in different types of communities to analyze the effects of these factors on social disorganization to put forward for the prevention and control strategy of community public security.

Theoretical framework is shown in Fig. 3.1.

Research construct is shown in Fig. 3.2.

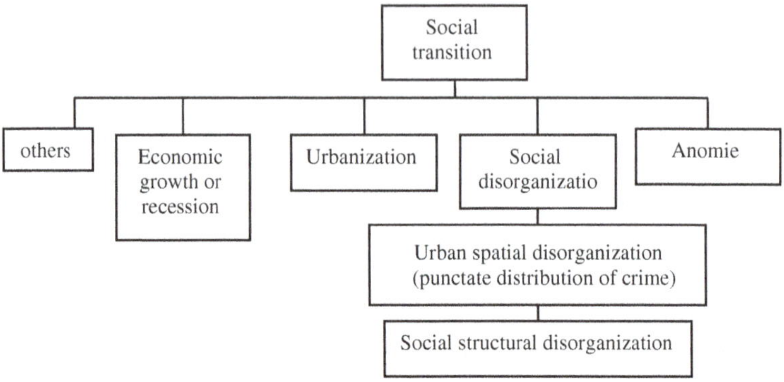

Fig. 3.1 Research framework chart

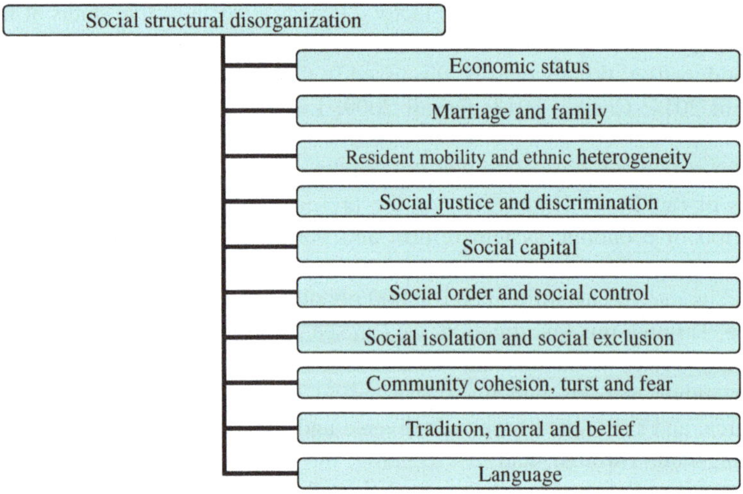

Fig. 3.2 Research construct chart

3.2 Research Methods

As combinations of macroscopic analysis and a case study of qualitative research methods will be used in this book, they will be supplemented by quantitative analysis. The background material enumerated above is a macroscopic description, while the factual analysis process is very complex and difficult. The author will mainly utilize gathered information to do quantitative studies in analysis of relations between urban spatial structural disorganization and crime. At the same time in-depth interviews will be used to study related factors to social disorganization, such as poverty, culture, inequality, fear, and community cohesion. The main research methods in this book are literary analysis, secondary data analysis, fieldwork, and in-depth interviews. Guangzhou will be selected as the research site because the author thinks Guangzhou is the most indicative city of social transformation in contemporary China.

There are three general data collecting methods in criminological research: official data usage, survey, and self-report. For this book, there is no opportunity to get official data as it is state-level secret. And for limited time, fund, and human capital, survey is not considered. For the same reason, self-reports of victim are also hard to get. Criminal data on district level and street level used in this book cannot be accumulated from usual channels, so that news gathering methods can only be used to collect case data. Whether the punctate distribution or criminal population density distributions are accurate in this book is not important, and making them clear is not the purpose of this research. In this book, to be aware of the existence of a punctate distribution is enough. In a word, the impact of data biases in the result is relatively limited.

The reason the author choosing an in-depth interview as the further research method is to forward the analysis and compare the interior character of communities with different crime rates, social disorganization status, and spatial distribution characteristics of urban crime. It is well known that quantitative research is to study the causality between phenomena through digital data. It is an accurate measurement that can be achieved and the problems and phenomena can be described objectively through digital research. Quantitative research uses statistical methods to analyze data and avoids research bias through controlling groups. Quantitative research is used widely in current western criminology, particularly in the related study of social disorganization. In qualitative research the researcher uses subjective information of research objects and includes this in data analysis by entering the situation to find out the common characteristics and connotation in different levels during human life. The results are reported in text description. Qualitative research can provide research methods to special groups from another perspective. It can also explain some problems and phenomena which quantitative research cannot explain. Therefore, according to the different research purpose the author can choose different research methods, multimethod research is imperative in this book.

The purpose of this study is to prove the following two points. One is to find the difference of urban crime distribution and social structural disorganization between Chinese city and western cities; the other is to discuss specific patterns of social disorganization and relationship between social disorganization and crime in different communities. For the purpose of this book, the author chooses quantitative research methods to obtain spatial distribution characteristics through the location of the density of collected cases in GIS maps. In addition to this, the author also chooses qualitative research method to find special character and connotation of social disorganization in different communities. The advantage of an in-depth interview is that: it is very easy and convenient, the data can be collected for special purposes, the two parties can influence and react upon one other, and the interview can be promoted step by step on schedule. The defect of in-depth interview is that it is only a small sample of the actual data, the result of interview is hard to quantize, and there is the inability to control various biases from the subject such as the character, expression and attitude, and communication style.

Speaking concretely, all social deviant cases (not limited to crimes in sense of criminal law, including social deviations such as accident fire, suicide, and safety misadventure) reported by Southern Metropolis Daily (SMD) from January 1 to December 31, 2008 in Guangzhou city are collected first through news gathering methods. Then these cases will be arranged to excel forms according to special types. By using the techniques of GIS, cases are located into GIS maps to calculate the number and density of regional case-filing in each district and street. Specific areas are confirmed through analysis of spatial distribution characteristics of deviant cases. Rate analysis of case-filing per 10,000 people examines the relationship between population, environment, and crime distribution from the perspective of population density. The two kinds of analyses study the spatial characteristics of crime from different angles.

About case classification please see the Appendix A.

About case number on level of street please see the Appendix B.

About population, area, and density of case please see the Appendix C.

Then residential data about social disorganization are collected by qualitative research method through in-depth interviews mainly based on particularity of the study. Researchers can in large, grasp the general characters of social disorganization and crime through quantitative research from which spatial distribution of crime cases can be drawn. Qualitative research methods are a new way for the author to explore the problem of social disorganization, aiming at detecting the experience of individual, concerning the understanding of their world—its advantage lies in that through a microcosmic case analysis we can understand interrelations between persons and persons, persons and groups, or persons with a cultural, political, and economic mechanism (Xiong 2001).

In qualitative research, this study takes three types of communities in Guangzhou city as fieldwork sites, as well as selects certain individuals from each community as an investigation object. The main reason is that the author is much more familiar with the three districts, two of which the author once lived in, one of which the author did not live in but often went to visit. In this investigation the author got strong help from the three neighborhood committees, which allows the investigation to be carried out smoothly.

Information of interviewee is as follows:

Sample selection: non-random sampling, stratified sampling.

Communities in Guangzhou are divided into three categories according to social disorganization degree: social disorganized community, community in social disorganization, and community without social disorganization. Then one community among each typical community is chosen as observed field. They are S village, T cell, and Q cell respectively. Then interview objects are received through a method of non-random sampling. In the sampling process, I try to cover the different age groups (the old, middle-aged, and young), different social status (the upper, middle, and low), various residential status (settled or flowing), various marriage and family status (single, married, separated, or divorced), and as many job types as possible and so on.

There are 28 samples selected (11 from Village S, 13 from Community T, and 4 from Community Q).

From the viewpoint of age, there are 9 samples in the age stage of 17–30, 16 samples in the age stage of 30–55, and 3 samples are above 55 years old;

From the residential status, 15 samples are settled and 13 samples are flowing;

From the marriage and family status, 10 samples are unmarried, 13 samples are married, 2 samples are in separated status, 2 samples are divorced in 2, and 1 sample is remarried;

From the job type, there are 4 migrant workers, 5 state-owned enterprise and institution personnel, 2 private enterprise owners, 1 college teacher, 7 private employees, 3 professionals, 3 service personnel (nurses, security, salespersons), 2 retired workers and 1 unemployed person.

Questions in interview outline are in strict correspondence of independent variables related to social disorganization. Researchers usually use survey method to collect data when engaged in the study of crime and social disorganization. Because of this, there have been developed systemic measurements for the term. In a literary review, indices of social disorganization as dependent variabilities include: the rate of self-residence, the rate of unemployment, the rate of household with more than one person living in a room, resident stability, heterogeneity, community cohesion, disorder, fear, trust, disrupt family. The author added some new terms as index of social disorganization, such as social exclusion and social segregation, tradition, morals, and language. The questions in the interview outline are all formed on the basis of former survey question. For example, to examine formal social control in community, the following three questions are used in the interview outline.

36, Q: Is there any police station in your community?

37, Q: Are there any other judicial organs or administrative organs in or around your community?

38, Q: Can you often see the police in your community?

The author chooses some of these indices as questions for in-depth interview.

There are 66 questions in outline 1. Questions 1–9 are index of personal status, Questions 10–12 are index of employment and unemployment, Questions 13–16 are index of residential status, Question 17 is index of marriage and family status, Questions 18–19 are index of resident stability, Questions 20–23 are index of heterogeneity. Question 24 is index of social justice. Questions 25–29 are index of social capital. Questions 30–35 are index of social order. Questions 36–40 are index of social control. Questions 41–42 are index of social segregation. Questions 43–48 are index of social exclusion. Questions 49–53 are index of fear. Questions 54–55 are index of community cohesion. Questions 56–59 are index of trust. Question 60 is index of tradition. Question 61 is index of moral. Question 62 is index of belief. Questions 63–66 are index of language.

There are 32 questions in Outline 2. Question 1 is index of personal status, Question 2 is index of employment and unemployment, Question 3 is index of residential status, Question 4 is index of marriage and family status, Question 5 is index of resident stability, Question 6 is index of heterogeneity. Question 7 is index of social justice. Question 8 is index of social capital. Question 9 is index of social order. Questions 10–11 are index of social control. Question 12 is index of social segregation. Question 13 is index of social exclusion. Questions 14–16 are index of social discrimination. Questions 17–19 are index of fear. Questions 20–21 are index of community cohesion. Questions 22–25 are index of trust. Question 26 is index of tradition. Question 27 is index of moral. Question 28 is index of belief. Question 29 is index of language. Question 30 is index of lifestyle. Question 31 is about attitude to social disorganization in current China. Question 32 is suggestion.

Outline I is designed in strict accordance with the affecting factors of social disorganization on crime defined by the author. And there are a total of 66 questions in the interview outline, which are strictly corresponding to the affecting factors. As a result, the interview process encountered two devastating obstacles. First, the questionnaire is too long and filled with too many problems. Almost all the interviewees showed signs of fatigue and impatience after being asked 30 questions. Some of them agreed to continue but became perfunctory. Some made an excuse to leave and some explicitly refused to continue to answer any further questions. Second, the question design is too mechanical and specialized, so that the answers are often extremely simple, and difficult to go expand on. Thus, the interview is difficult to continue. Even if continued, the quality of it is not high, and is difficult to meet the author's purpose of the book writing. Because of this, the author designed a second questionnaire. The number of questions is limited to about thirty, and the questions are designed to let the interviewees express their own thoughts, thus the interviews go smoothly.

Observation frequency:
Village S: a field dwelling for a week;
Community T: 10 times, each for about 1 h;
Community Q: 1 time for about 1 h.

Interview type:
Face-to-face interview
Interview outline 1 please see Appendix D.
Interview outline 2 please see Appendix E.
Example of interview record please see Appendix F.
Interview analysis process please see Appendix G.

References

Alvey, S. (2001). In U. Brown & Scottish Poverty Information Unit and Lothian Anti-Poverty Alliance (Eds.), *Social exclusion*. Glasgow: Scottish Poverty Information Unit.

ASA Conference, Migrants, Workers, and the Social Order 1986, University of Kent. (1987). In J. S. Eades (Ed.), *Migrants, workers, and the social order*. London, New York: Tavistock.

Asencio, E. K. (2014). Self-esteem, the fear of crime, and the decision to protect oneself from victimization. *Sociological Forum, 29*(3), 587.

Baum, F. E., & Ziersch, A. M. (2003). Social capital. *Journal of Epidemiology and Community Health (1979–), 57*(5), 320–323.

Bennett, M. (2014). Intergroup social exclusion in childhood: Forms, norms, context, and social identity. *Journal of Social Issues, 70*(1), 183.

Bierstedt, R. (1974). *The social order* (4th ed.). New York: McGraw-Hill.

Boman, J. H. IV, Krohn, M. D., Gibson, C. L., & Stogner, J. M. (2012). Investigating friendship quality: An exploration of self-control and social control theories' friendship hypotheses. *Journal of Youth and Adolescence, 41*(11), 1526–1540.

Bridges, G. S., & Myers, M. A. (1994). *Inequality, crime, and social control*. Boulder, Colo, Oxford: Westview.

Buettner-schmidt, K., & Lobo, M. L. (2012). Social justice: A concept analysis. *Journal of Advanced Nursing, 68*(4), 948–958.

Byrne, D. (2005). In I. Ebrary (Ed.), *Social exclusion electronic resource* (2nd ed.). Maidenhead, England: Open University Press.

Cacioppo, J. T., Hawkley, L. C., Norman, G. J., & Berntson, G. G. (2011). Social isolation. *Annals of the New York Academy of Sciences, 12311*(1), 17–22.

Chadee, D. (2013). Predictors of fear of crime: General fear versus perceived risk. *Journal of Applied Social Psychology, 43*(9), 1896.

Church, W. T., Jaggers, J. W., & Taylor, J. K. (2012). Neighborhood, poverty, and negative behavior: An examination of differential association and social control theory. *Children and Youth Services Review, 34*(5), 1035–1041.

Claypool, H. M., & Bernstein, M. J. (2014). Social exclusion and stereotyping: Why and when exclusion fosters individuation of others. *Journal of Personality and Social Psychology, 106*(4), 571.

Clingerman, E. (2011). Social justice. *Journal of Transcultural Nursing, 22*(4), 334–341.

Colic-Peisker, V., & Robertson, S. (2015). Social change and community cohesion: An ethnographic study of two Melbourne suburbs. *Ethnic and Racial Studies, 38*(1), 75–91.

Cramm, J. M. (2012). Relationships between frailty, neighborhood security, social cohesion and sense of belonging among community-dwelling older people. *Geriatrics and Gerontology International, 13*(3), 759.

Davis, J. (2014). Beyond neighborhoods and crime: Expanding the scope of social disorganization to explain occupational deviance. *Sociological Inquiry, 85*(2), 262.

Deflem, M., & Ebrary, I. (2010). *Popular culture, crime and social control* (1st ed.). Bingley: Emerald.

Deutschmann, L. B. (1994). *Deviance and social control*. Scarborough, Ont: Nelson Canada.

Edwards, J. (1987). *Positive discrimination, social justice, and social policy: Moral scrutiny of a policy practice*. London, New York: Tavistock (New York: in association with Methuen).

Elliott, M. A. (1961). In F. E. Merrill (Ed.), *Social disorganization* (4th ed.). New York: Harper.

Emerick, N. A. (2013). Homicide and social disorganization on the border: Implications for Latino and immigrant populations. *Social Science Quarterly, 95*(2), 360.

Emery, C. R., Trung, H. N., & Wu, S. (2013). Neighborhood informal social control and child maltreatment: A comparison of protective and punitive approaches. *Child Abuse and Neglect*.

Epicurus. (1670). In W. Charleton (Ed.), *Epicurus' morals, electronic resource*. London: Printed for H.H. and are to be sold by Simon Miller at the sign of the Star at the west end of St. Pauls.

Etty, M. (2001). Positivism (Guan, Z., trans.). Beijing: Commercial Press. (法) 马里埃蒂, (2001). 《实证主义》, 管震湖译,北京: 商务印书馆.

Faris, R. E. L. (1955). *Social disorganization* (2nd ed.). New York: Ronald Press Company.

Farrall, S. (2009). In J. Jackson & E. Gray (Eds.), *Social order and the fear of crime in contemporary times*. Oxford: Oxford University Press.

Fratcher, W. F. (1973). In International Association of Legal Science (Ed.), *Trust*. Tübingen, The Hague: J.C.B. Mohr (Paul Siebeck), Mouton.

Gaffikin, F., & Morrissey, M. (2011). Community cohesion and social inclusion: Unravelling a complex relationship. *Urban Studies, 48*(6), 1089–1118.

Gilchrist, A. (2004). In Community Development Foundation (Great Britain) & Runnymede Trust (Eds.), *Community cohesion and community development: Bridges or barricades?* London: Community Development Foundation in association with Runnymede Trust.

Glennerster, H., & Centre for Analysis of, Social Exclusion. (1999). *Poverty, social exclusion and neighbourhood: Studying the area bases of social exclusion*. London: Centre for Analysis of Social Exclusion, London School of Economics and Political Science.

Hall, K. S., Kusunoki, Y., Gatny, H., & Barber, J. (2015). Social discrimination, stress, and risk of unintended pregnancy among young women. *Journal of Adolescent Health, 56*(3), 330–337.

Hardin, R. (2006). *Trust*. Oxford: Polity.

Harris, P. (2007). Trust. *Developmental Science, 10*(1), 135–138.

Jenkins, R. (2003). Social capital. *Lancet, 362*(9393), 1422–1422.

Jordens, A. (1992). *From discrimination to equality: Social welfare benefits and non-british migrants 1947–75* Canberra: Administration, Compliance & Governability Program (ACGP).

Leahy, M. P. (1948). *Fear*. London: Research Books.

Li, B. (2004). In Centre for Analysis of Social Exclusion (Ed.), *Urban social exclusion in transitional China*. London: Centre for Analysis of Social Exclusion, London School of Economics and Political Science.

Lin, N. (2001). In I. Ebrary (Ed.), *Social capital electronic resource: A theory of social structure and action*. Cambridge, UK, New York: Cambridge University Press.

Loyola, M. (1928). *Trust*. London: Sheed and Ward.

MacGill, P. (1921). *Fear!* London: Herbert Jenkins.

Marx, K., & Engels, F. (1980). *Complete works of Marx and Engels* (Vols. 3, 46) (Central Compilation & Translation Bureau, Trans.). Beijing: People's Publishing House. (德) 马克思, 恩格斯着, 中央编译局译, (1980).《马克思恩格斯全集》(第3、46卷) 北京: 人民出版社.

Merton, R. K. (2000). Insiders and outsiders. *American journal of sociology, 78*, 9–27.

Mosso, A. (1896). In E. L. Kiesow (Ed.), *Fear* (Authorised tr. by E. Lough and F. Kiesow. Eds.). Lond. & c.

Plato. (1994). In B. Jowett & I. Ebrary (Eds.), *The republic electronic resource*. South Bend, IN: Infomotions, Inc.

Portes, A. (2014). Downsides of social capital. *Proceedings of the National Academy of Sciences of the United States of America, 111*(52), 18407.

Prosen, A. (2011). Trust. *Geodetski Vestnik, 55*(1), 5–6.

Putnam, R. D. (2000). *Bowling alone: The collapse and revival of American community*. New York: Simon & Schuster.

Rawls, J. (1999). *A theory of justice electronic resource* (Rev. ed.). Cambridge, Massachusetts: Belknap Press of Harvard University Press.

Richter, F. (2010). In A. V. Dijk, M. Beckenbach & N. Gronemeyer (Eds.), *Trust*. Berlin: Theater der Zeit.

Robin, S. (2001). Disparate impact and the quota debates: Law, labor market sociology, and equal employment policies. *Sociological Quarterly, 42*,13–46.

Ross, E. A. (1896). Social control. *American Journal of Sociology, 1*(5), 513–535.

Ross, E. A. (1901). *Social control*. New York: New York & Company.

Rousseau, J. (1947). In C. Frankel (Ed.), *The social contract*. New York: Hafner Publishing Company.

Sassenberg, K., Kessler, T., & Mummendey, A. (2003). Less negative = more positive? Social discrimination as avoidance or approach. *Journal of Experimental Social Psychology, 39*(1), 48–58.

Schwab, W. A. (1992). *The sociology of cities* (pp. 367–376). New Jersey: Simon & Schuster Company.

Shank, G. (2014). Social justice. *Peace Review, 26*(4), 520–524.

Stoll, S. K. (2011). Social justice: An historical and philosophical perspective. *Journal of Physical Education, Recreation and Dance, 82*(8), 36–39.

Tunstall, R. (2011). In Centre for Analysis of Social Exclusion & Suntory and Toyota International Centres for Economics and Related Disciplines (Eds.), *Social housing and social exclusion 2000–2011*. London: Centre for Analysis of Social Exclusion.

Tyler, T. R., & Van, D. T. (2013). *Social justice* (2nd ed.). Oxford: Oxford University Press.

Veling, W. (2015). Social disorganization of neighborhoods and incidence of psychotic disorders: A 7-year first-contact incidence study. *Psychological Medicine, 45*(9), 1789.

Warner, B. D., & Burchfield, K. (2011). Misperceived neighborhood values and informal social control. *Justice Quarterly, 28*(4), 606–630.

Watkins, C. K. (1975). *Social control*. London: Longman.

Xiong, B. (2001). Qualitative research methods discussion: Exploring from gender perspective. *Study on Sociology,* 5. 熊秉纯. (2001). 质性研究方法刍议: 来自社会性别视角的探索. 《社会学研究》, (5).

Chapter 4
Urban Spatial Disorganization and Crime: Punctate Distribution Pattern

Criminal and deviant behavior is one of the prominent manifestations of social disorganization. Study on the spatial distribution features of crime has a direct indicating function for our understanding of social disorganization, especially urban spatial structural disorganization (Chen et al. 2013). In the following analysis, the author will use the collected data about crime, population, and the environment to make a preliminary exploration of spatial distribution characteristics of criminal and deviant behaviors and spatial structural disorganization in Guangzhou City.

4.1 Data Source and Study Scope

4.1.1 Data Source

Criminal data involving this research is mainly rooted in two following parts.

One part of criminal data is from the "Guangzhou Statistic Yearbook 2014" and statistic yearbook of each district of Guangzhou. It is the latest statistical yearbook that can be collected at the beginning of the study, which publicized criminal data in 2013. The number of criminal cases is not reported every year for each district in statistic yearbook, so that the number of criminal cases in some districts is calculated based on official data reported a few years ago. It should be pointed out that there is no data of the number of criminal cases in any year revealed in the Statistical Yearbook 1999–2014 or the "government work report" of Nansha District, so the number of criminal cases of Nansha District is impossible to determine.

Another part of criminal data comes from criminal cases reported in the "Southern Metropolis Daily". Considering that the detailed statistics such as

H. Xiong, *Urban Crime and Social Disorganization in China*,
DOI 10.1007/978-981-287-859-5_4

occurrence time, occurrence place, criminal suspects, victims of crime, and criminal processes can rarely be obtained from public criminal statistic data, news gathering methods were used to collect crime data reported by Southern Metropolis Daily from January 1, 2013 to December 31, 2013. A total of 365 copies of newspapers were reviewed, and 1836 relative reports were collected; 1483 cases were obtained by removing previous reported cases and repeated reported cases. News reports covered most of the published ordinary criminal cases and police offences, so that information biases generated by news filters can be avoided to a certain extent in spite of defective case representation. On one hand, due to the sensitivity of news work, cases not considered as crimes or even police offences by police would be reported by newspapers, so that the cases not included in official data are detailed included in news-gathered data. On the other hand, this paper studies the question of the relationship between crime and social disorganization.

While social disorganization is not only reflected in crimes defined by criminal law, but also reflected in deviant behaviors that are not considered as crimes by criminal law, cases calculated in this book should accurately be deemed criminal and deviant cases (Liu et al. 2014). For example, suicide is always an important embodiment of social anomie and social disorganization as a serious criminal behavior in western criminological research traditions which is not considered to be a crime in Chinese law. It is difficult to find almost any official statistics about suicide in current China. However in news coverage, especially in city as Guangzhou with much more developed media concerning people's livelihood, suicide events are elaborated by newspapers, which expose the superiority of news versus official information. Case statistics are divided into several items including occurrence time (year and month), special districts crimes, particular locations, types of crime, gender, age and the hometown of criminals (Ye et al. 2015; Cheung 2013; Baum 1996). Then these cases are organized into maps according to occurrence site. 1392 cases are located in districts, 1352 cases are located in the streets, while 40 cases cannot be located on maps which as they just indicate the occurrence in Guangzhou City.

It must be pointed out that using news gathering methods to collect data is not created by the author. External research is very difficult for this book as criminal information is treated as state secret in China. It may be easier to get public data from provinces or cities, as it is difficult to get district-level public data, and even more difficult to get street-level public data. In previous studies, there are two papers required to assess this street-level data: Cheng and Ma's (1997) "Criminal geographic analysis of Beijing City" which discusses crime characteristics and temporal-spatial distribution in Beijing city, however, the book did not indicate the data source; Mao and Dai's (2006) "crime spatial distribution and environmental characteristics—a case study of Shanghai city" also lacking the location of criminal cases to each streets in Shanghai city. It does, however, include "the detailed statistics such as occurrence time, occurrence place, criminal suspects, victims of crimes, the criminal process could be rarely obtained from public criminal statistic data, as news gathering methods are used to collect crime data". Although their paper is a production of a doctoral program specially supported by research funds afforded by the Ministry of Education, these news gathering method provide various disadvantages as the authors still chose news gathering methods to collect the case data needed in research. In this book, the author is facing the same dilemma.

Demographic statistics, social statistics, and environmental statistics come mainly from the annual "Statistic Yearbook of Guangzhou" (2000–2013), (Guangzhou Bureau of Statistics 2001, 2002, 2003, 2004, 2005, 2006, 2007, 2008, 2009, 2010, 2012, 2013, 2014) "Guangzhou Yearbook 2000–2013", "Guangzhou statistic yearbook 2000–2013" of each District in Guangzhou, "2000 Bulletin of Major Information of The 5th Census of Guangzhou", and "2010 Bulletin of Major Information of the 6th Census of Guangzhou".

4.1.2 Research Scope

The geographical scope of this study is the regional space of each of the districts governed administratively by Guangzhou city (not including 2 county-class-cities of Zengcheng and Conghua), including 10 districts: Yuexiu District, Haizhu District, Liwan District, Tianhe District, Baiyun District, Huangpu District, Panyu District, Huadu District, Nansha District, Luogang District. 119 street offices and 24 towns that are set as subdistrict units.

Criminal statistics are used for different levels of analysis according to their different sources and statistic status. The total number of criminal case-filing in "Guangzhou Statistic Yearbook" is used in analysis on district level. Materials from South Metropolitan Daily could be located into each district and street to be used in analysis on district level and street level. They are: theft, murder, robbery, fraud, intentional injury, traffic accident, extortion, suicide, safety misadventure, fortuitous event, fire, and drug-related crime. The reason that these 12 types of crimes were selected is: first, these crimes would greatly impact public social psychology, weaken residents 'sense of security, and increase degree of fear. Furthermore, these crimes are often closely related with urban spatial environment while features of urban spatial environment often become the latent causes of these crimes, such as the Haizhu Bridge in Guangzhou, once called "the most famous bridge in China" by the media. There were more than 40 jumped off the bridge incident in a month on Haizhu Bridge which became the focus of public outcry. There are specific reasons relevant to the geographical and social environment why these people chose Haizhu Bridge as suicide site. When we study these kinds of crimes, we can produce a clearer analysis. In addition, these kinds of crimes are generally committed in public, and therefore attract the attention of the media. Full coverage will often occur made by the media in first time as soon as the occurrence of these types of cases, so that the number of these 12 types of cases reported would be more close to the actual one compared with other types of cases, especially some private cases (such as adultery, bigamy, forcible rape, corruption, bribery, and others). Thus, choosing these categories of cases of research objectives can minimize the insufficiencies of nonrandom sampling to ensure that the research is carried on accurately.

4.2 Spatial Distribution Characteristics of Crime

I will first study the spatial distribution characteristics of crime in Guangzhou. By using the techniques of GIS, cases are located into GIS maps to calculate the number and density of regional case-filing in each district and street. "Hot areas" and "Hot spots" are confirmed through the analysis of spatial distribution characteristics of deviant cases. Rate analysis of case-filings per 10,000 people examines the relationship between population, environment and crime distribution from the perspective of population density. These two kinds of analysis study the spatial characteristics of crime from different angles.

The quantitative distribution of criminal cases in each district according to criminal statistic analysis is as follows:

There is more case numbers in northern districts while less case number in southern districts, with the highest case filings in the city center of Guangzhou.

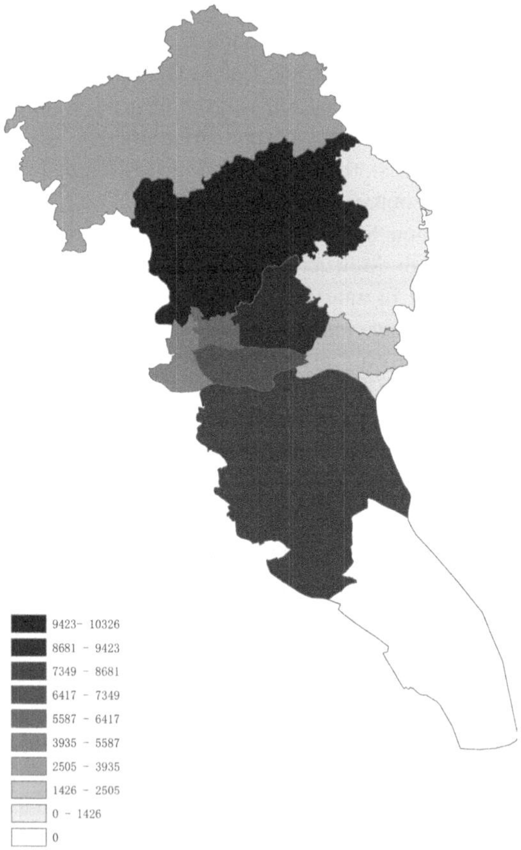

Fig. 4.1 Total number of regional criminal case-filing

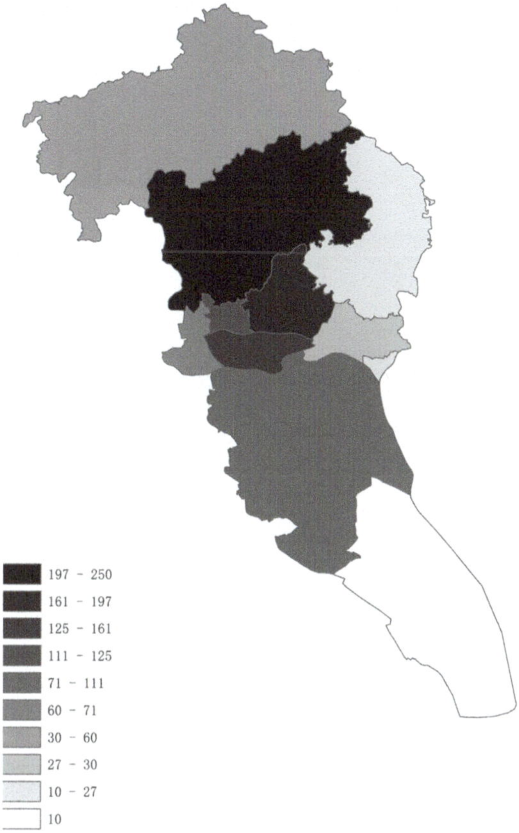

Fig. 4.2 Total number of regional case-filing reported by SMD

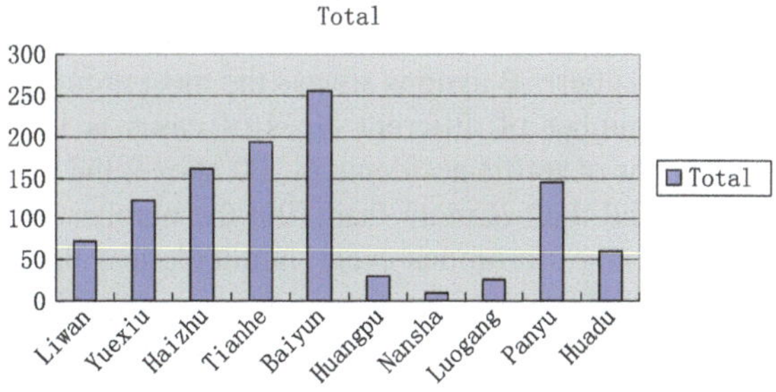

Fig. 4.3 Regional distribution of cases reported by SMD

The total number of cases in the Baiyun District is much higher than that of other districts in Guangzhou (Figs. 4.1 and 4.2).

SMD case materials display:

1. District distributions of different types of cases are largely dissimilar (Fig. 4.3). District Baiyun is still the area with the largest case amount, followed by the three districts of Yuexiu, Tianhe and Haizhu. Case amount in Huangpu, Luogang and Nansha are significantly lower. The number of homicide cases in

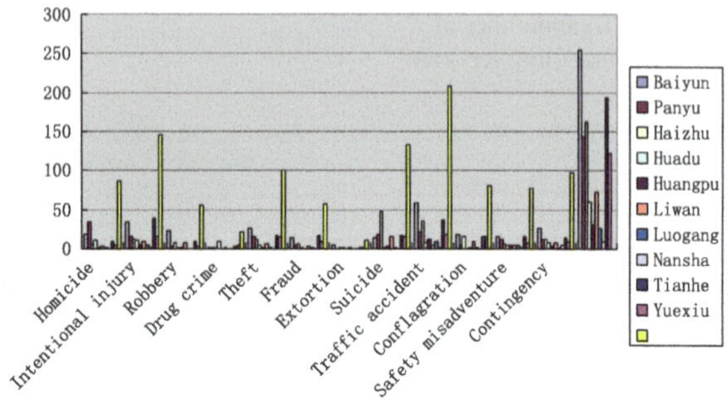

Fig. 4.4 Regional distribution of various types of cases reported by SMD

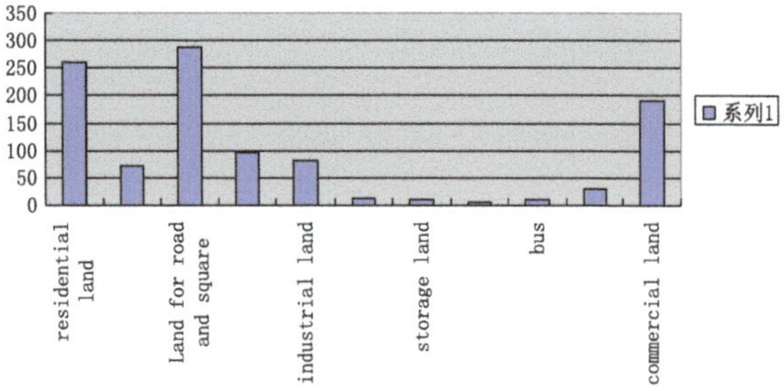

Fig. 4.5 Distribution of various types of cases occurred in different lands reported by SMD

Panyu, Baiyun and Huadu is significantly higher than which in the other districts. The number of intentional injury cases in Tianhe and Baiyun is significantly higher than which in the other districts. The number of robbery cases in Baiyun is significantly prominent. The number of suicide cases in Haizhu is significantly prominent, which should thank to "the most famous bridge"—Haizhu Bridge in its jurisdiction. The number of drug-related crime cases in Huadu is significantly prominent. Overall it is higher in hypo-central areas than in the suburb. Baiyun is always the most prominent area.

2. The number of different types of cases is largely dissimilar (Fig. 4.4). The number of traffic accidents is 200 above; the number of intentional injury, suicide and theft is more than 100; the number of other cases is below 100 with much more fortuitous event, homicide and fire more than 80; number of drug cases and extortion are fewest, respectively 23 and 12. High incidences of malicious mischief, theft and murder cases will largely damage the citizen's rights, physical and property rights, and greatly affect the residential security as the fear of crime is ever generated.
3. Case quantities and types in lands of different natures vary greatly (Fig. 4.5). Roads and squares, residential land and commercial land are high occurring areas with respectively 291, 257 and 192 cases occurring in, much higher than that in lands of other natures. Green land and storage land have fewer cases. There are 10 cases on the bus, which are all pick-pocketing pick-pocket case. Occurrence in municipal facilities is the minimum with just 5 cases. Suicide is one of most frequent cases in residential land with a number of 58. And then is

theft, accidents, homicide and safety misadventure, respectively with number of 39, 28, 25 and 23.

In residential areas, there are 115 cases that occurred in the urban-village rental housing. Traffic accidents are also very frequent with a number of 120 cases. And then there is intentional injury, suicide and robbery respectively with number of 52, 40 and 21. Intentional injury, fraud and theft are more frequent in commercial areas (including hotels, shopping malls, supermarkets and others) respectively with a number of 48, 31 and 28.

4.3 Spatial Density Distribution Characteristics of Criminal Cases

The purpose of spatial density analysis of criminal cases is to study the spatial agglomeration characteristics of criminal cases.

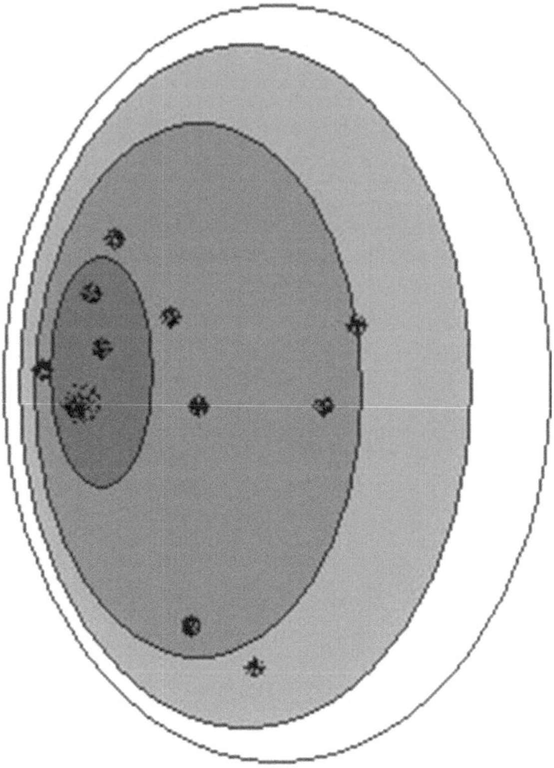

Fig. 4.6 *Circle* pattern of cases reported by SMD

4.3.1 Layered-Circle Structure

As far as spatial distribution of all criminal cases in every district is concerned, spatial density distribution of criminal cases shows a layered-circle structure (Fig. 4.6): core zone, central urban area, suburban area and exurb area. Criminal density decreases as the distance increases gradually from the core area to the suburbs. Case spatial aggregation degree in core areas and central urban areas are much higher than it in peripheral areas. The case spatial density of Yuexiu District is highest with 3.71/km^2, which is far higher than other area, followed by Tianhe, Haizhu and Liwan District with more than 1.00/km^2. Huangpu, Baiyun and Panyu District follow with a perimeter of 0.32/km^2, then Huadu and the Luogang District with 0.06/km^2 around. The lowest cases spatial density is in Nansha District with 0.03/km^2. It is visible that case spatial aggregation degree in core areas and central urban areas are much higher than it in peripheral area. These cases seriously impact public security such as murder, intentional injury, robbery, and theft (Fig. 4.7). This layered-circle structure distribution pattern is related to the high concentration of property, population and crime target in city center.

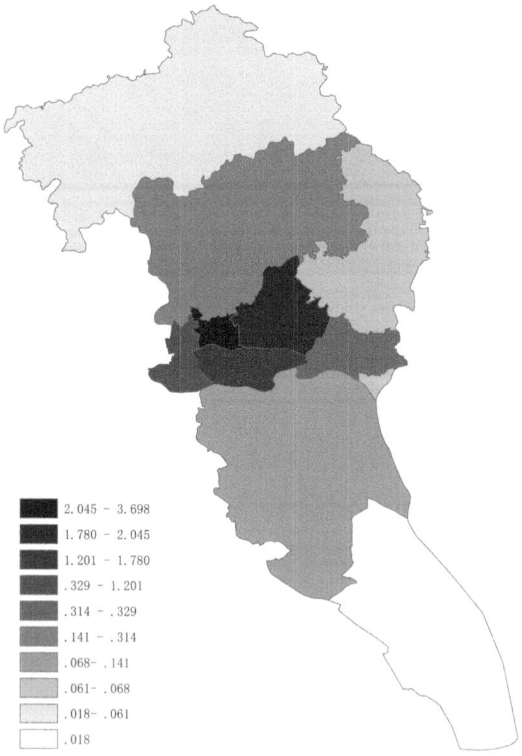

Fig. 4.7 Regional spatial density distribution of cases reported by SMD

Spatial density distributions of cases reported by SMD reveals that gradient layered-circle pattern is more obvious with gradually decreased spatial density from urban central areas such as Yuexiu and Tianhe to outside areas. The street with the highest case density is Beijing street of Yuexiu District at a level of 19.64/km^2 (Fig. 4.7).

4.3.2 Hot Spots

The layered-circle structure is not equal gradient with hot spots (Fig. 4.6). In this figure, the darker shading means a higher case density. Hot spots are sites with more case occurrence or long-term security issues. Hot spots in urban centers are often in commercial areas and old residential areas or train stations, bus stations and other crowded places, such as Beijing Street and Liuhua Street. Streets with highest Case spatial density are Beijing street, Binjiang street and Liuhua street

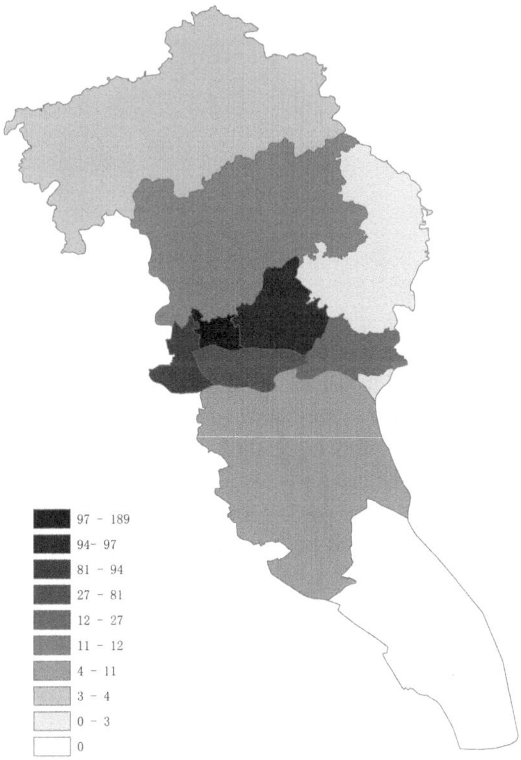

Fig. 4.8 Regional spatial density distribution of criminal cases

Fig. 4.9 Spatial density distribution of cases reported by SMD by level of street

in turn, with spatial density of 19.72, 14.63 and 11.84/km^2 (Figs. 4.8, 4.9, 4.10 and 4.11).

Hot spots in urban centers are mainly concentrated in the old part of the city. Beijing Street in the Yuexiu District is an example of this as it is the main commercial area with more theft and fire cases than other districts. Liuhua Street in the Yuexiu District is also a hot spot as it houses several traffic stations such as Guangzhou Railway Station, Guangdong Province Bus Passenger Terminal, Guangzhou City Bus Passenger Terminal, Liuhua Bus Passenger Terminal, Baima Bus Passenger Terminal, and has an average floating population of more than 100,000 people passing through every day. In addition to this, there are several shopping malls and clothes wholesale markets in Liuhua streets such as Tianma Building, Baima commercial complex, Liuhua clothes plaza, kapok BBK shopping mall where high incidents of crime would occur.

The Haizhu Bridge is the main reason for the higher case spatial density of the Binjiang Street in the Haizhu District. There were 18 suicides in 2013 on Haizhu Bridge, which greatly increases the case spatial density of Binjiang

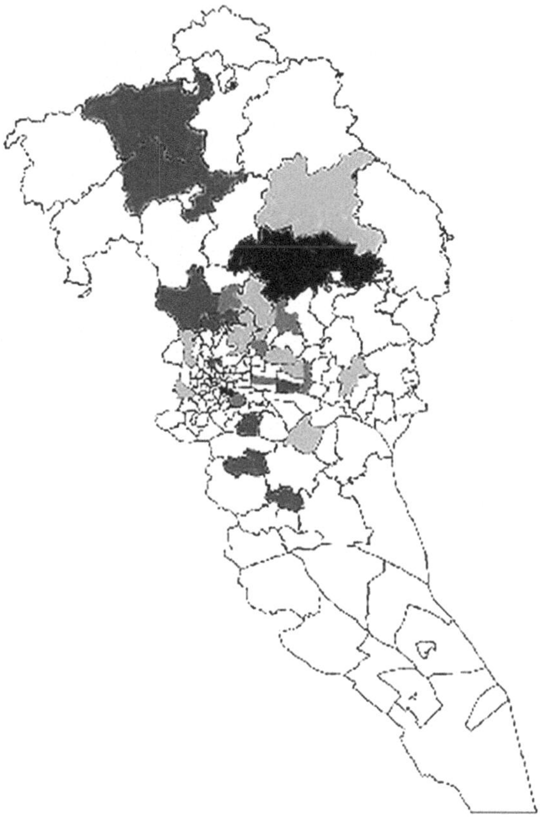

Fig. 4.10 Absolute quantity distribution of cases reported by SMD by level of street

Street. Hot spots in the suburbs are mainly concentrated in highly urbanized areas, which are local commercial centers where a large number of industrial plants and a mass of migrant workers are located. Theft and fraud rates are very high in Xiaoguwei Street where University City is located and college dormitories are concentrated.

4.4 Demographic Density Characteristics of Criminal Cases

The purpose of demographic density analysis of criminal cases is studying the spatial distribution status of the demographic density of criminal cases.

Analysis of the demographic density distributions of cases reported by SMD also indicate that spatial density distribution of criminal cases shows a layered-circle structure. In the layered-circle structure figure of demographic criminal density,

Fig. 4.11 Spatial density distribution of cases reported by SMD

the suburb district Baiyun becomes the center as it has the highest case-filing rate per 100,000 people; the next is District Yuexiu, Haizhu and Tianhe in central urban areas; then in turn is Luogang, Panyu, Liwan, Huadu and Nansha, and further spreading outwards. In general, the demographic density distributions of cases are almost the same as spatial density distributions. It describes that feature of case density distribution is significant and related to environmental factors. Both show the layered-circle structure with hot spots and reveal the decrease in number as the distances increase gradually from the core area outward (Figs. 4.12, 4.13 and 4.14).

4.5 Research Limitations and Sensitive Tests

The main research defect of this book involves the collected data. Officially public criminal data is only the total number of criminal cases and police offences every year. Only Haizhu, Yuexiu, Tianhe, and Liwan declare their criminal case-filing number as administrative units of the district. As far as the Baiyun district goes with "the highest criminal case-filling number", its actual criminal case-filling

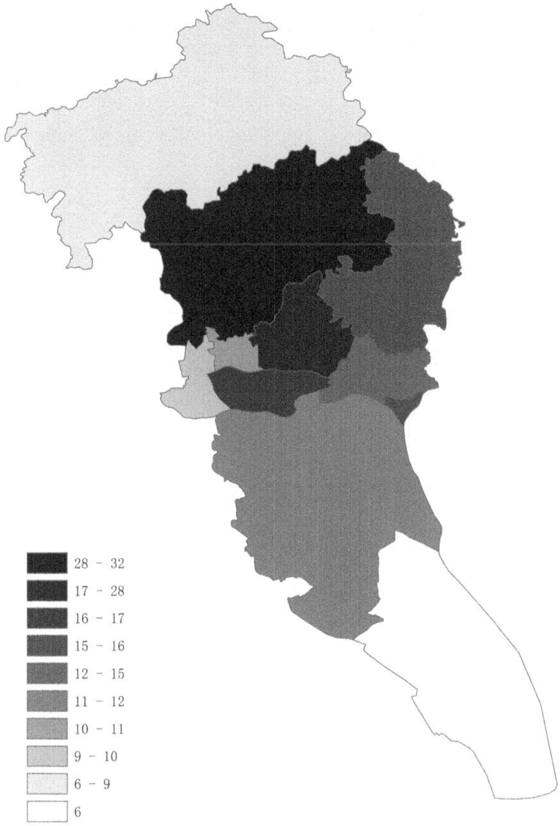

Fig. 4.12 Demographic density distribution of cases reported by SMD

number cannot be obtained. Because of this, the case density map cannot be made according to official criminal data at the level of district. Criminal data on street level is more difficult to get from official channel. Therefore, research can be continued only through news gathering methods.

1. News gathering method can reflect the realistic regulations to a certainty.

Research shortcomings in data, the author try to adopt various methods to make the conclusion reflect the realistic regulations to a certain extent:

News reports were in long duration, and covered most of published ordinary criminal cases and police offences, so that information bias generated by news filter can be avoided in a certain extent in spite of defective case representation. On one hand, due to the sensitivity of news work, cases not considered as crimes or even police offences by police would be reported by newspapers, so that the cases not included in official data are detailed included in news-gathered data. However, this paper focuses on the question of the relationship between crime and social disorganization. Social disorganization is not only reflected in crimes defined by criminal law, band can be reflected in deviant behaviors that are not considered as

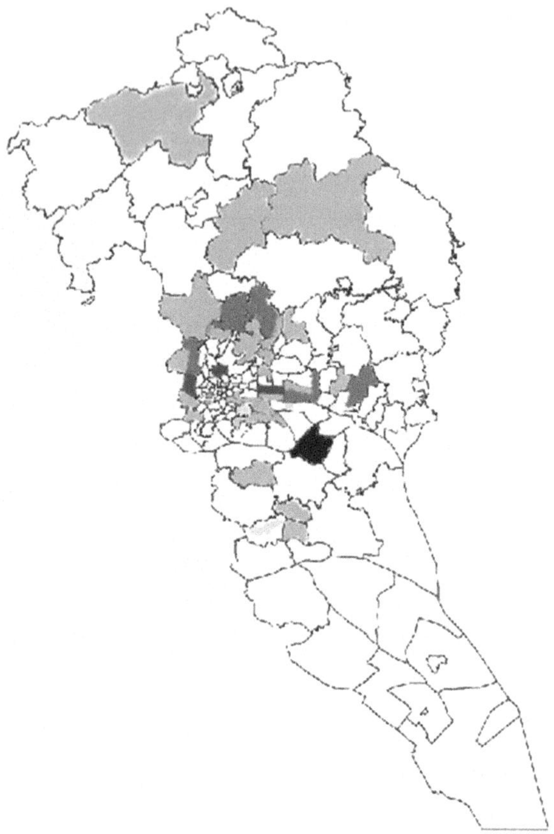

Fig. 4.13 Demographic density distribution of cases reported by SMD by level of street

crimes by criminal law, and the cases calculated in this book should accurately be deemed "criminal and deviant cases".

For example, suicide is always an important reflection of social anomie and social disorganization as serious criminal behavior in western criminological research traditions which is not considered to be a crime in Chinese law. It is difficult to find almost any official statistics about suicide in current China. However in news coverage, especially in city as Guangzhou with a more developed media circuit concerning people's livelihood, suicide events are expressed through the media.

Public offering newspapers in Guangzhou are mainly South Daily (underline or place quotations around the names so people understand it is a company), Guangzhou Daily, Southern Metropolis Daily, Yangcheng Evening News, the Information Times and the Xinkuaibao Daily. Therefore, South Daily is the official newspaper of provincial Party committee, while Guangzhou daily is the organ of Guangzhou municipal Party committee. Due to the rich political biases of these

Fig. 4.14 Punctate demographic density distribution of cases reported by SMD

two newspapers, they clearly maintain their propaganda and agenda and rarely report negative cases. Because of this, the two newspapers are not considered when choosing authentic news gathering sources. While the Southern Metropolis Daily, Yangcheng Evening News, Information Times and the Xinkuaibao Daily are comprehensive dailies geared to the needs of reading public. Therefore the Southern Metropolis Daily is the quarto paper with the largest circulation in Guangdong Province. In order to maintain an objective point of view, the author collected and compared cases that were reported on these newspapers on March 21, 2011. The number of cases reported by Yangcheng Evening News is 0; the number of cases reported by Xinkuaibao Daily is 1; the number of cases reported by Information Times is 0; the number of cases reported by Southern Metropolis Daily is 2 which were one safety accident and one intentional injury case. Because of this, it is visible that the Southern Metropolis Daily reports cases in a much wider scope.

In addition, news published one year ago cannot be viewed online in the other three newspapers except SMD. It will obviously take more time to review the information from traditional paper newspapers. So the author can only choose SMD as the news gathering source due to the limited time.

2. Confirmation of Demographic Occupation distribution feature to density distributions feature of cases reported by SMD.

Analysis results of spatial feature of demographic occupation distribution by Zhou et al. in 2006 are used to support the rationality of spatial distributions features of cases reported by SMD. Zhou et al. (2006) use the "Ward Method" of cluster analysis and load values of four principle factors such as the educational level, develop degree of commerce and service, agricultural population proportion, and gender differentiation degree, to divide the 95 streets and towns in Guangzhou city into 6 occupation zones. These zones are: the commerce and service concentrated zone; the office occupation zone; the technology and education occupation zone; the mixing occupation zone; the industrial production zone; and the agricultural production zone. Zhou et al. (2006) believes that there are obvious spatial distribution variances of occupation structure in Guangzhou city, and this constructs spatial patterns of the demographic occupational structure of Guangzhou city. Commerce and service concentrated zones are mainly located in old towns with a high population density with old demosociographic structure and low education degree. These are the earliest developed regions in the history of Guangzhou and are located in the Liwan District, southern Yuexiu District and northwest of Haizhu District.

Office occupation zones are mainly distributed in north and east of old city of Guangzhou, including Dongshan District, Yuexiu District and northwest of the Haizhu District. Professional and technical personnel, service personnel, national and party cadres are much more common in this type of occupational zone with moderate occupation density.

People in technology industry and educational occupation zones are extremely well educated with a larger proportion of office staff and technical staff, most of whom are young males. This type of occupational zone is highly concentrated with colleges and universities and scientific research organizations. These zones are gathered around Wushan Street and the Tianhe District.

Extraneous population is mostly gathered in mixed occupational zones with a larger proportion of young males of lower education. Mixed occupational zones are mainly situated at the edge of new urban districts such as Tianhe, Baiyun, Liwan, and Haizhu. Second and third industry accounts for a large proportion in this type of occupational zones, which are suburban industrial zones with slightly agricultural compositions.

Industrial production zones lie in the periphery of the suburban areas of Guangzhou City including the District of Huangpu and Panyu. Young extraneous population is gathered here with an average educational background of junior

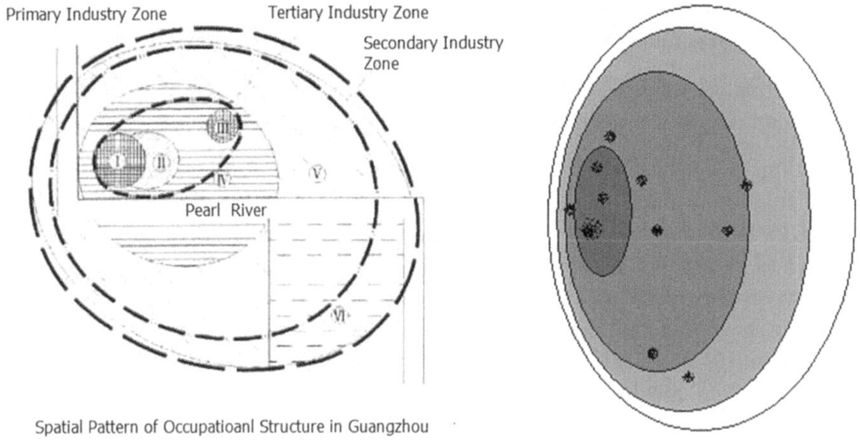

Fig. 4.15 Comparison between spatial pattern of occupational structure and *circle* pattern of cases reported by SMD

middle school. Large population proportions are lower-skilled workers engaged in manufacturing and construction industry with a low gender ratio and high population proportion in second industry. This type of occupational zone is in new developed areas during a large-scale construction period. The proportion of first industry is high in agricultural production zones with relatively more females engaged in agricultural actives. Adolescent population proportions are high with low education level. Population density in this area is relatively lower. This type of occupational zones are scattered throughout the Panyu District and the outskirts of Guangzhou (Sun et al. 2013).

Occupation distribution features can basically confirm cases spatial distribution characteristics reported by SMD. Demographic occupation distribution features are basically layered-circle structures, coinciding with cases spatial distribution characteristics reported by SMD (Fig. 4.6). Theft, robbery and fire cases occur more in commerce and service industry concentrated zones such as Yuexiu, Liwan and other regions, as they are in the old city and are commercial centers which belong to the high incidence areas. Tianhe, Baiyun, Haizhu are mixed occupation zones also belong to the high incidence areas for massive extraneous population and have a high proportion of young males. Industrial production zones lying in the periphery of suburban areas of Guangzhou City, such as areas near the urban zones in Panyu and Huangpu, are high incidence areas too, where young extraneous population is involved in manufacturing and construction industry (Fig. 4.15).

3. Confirmation of density distribution feature of cases reported by SMD through migrant population distribution feature.

According to Census Data 2000 of Guangdong Province, the total number of floating population reached 4,281,800 in 2000 in Guangzhou City. Therefore, the number of local floating population amounts to 968,900, while 22.63 % of the total number of extraneous floating population amounts to 3,312,900. Among them is the inner-provincial influx population which amounts to 1,162,900 persons, which is 27.16 % of the total floating population; the outer-provincial influx population amount to 2,150,000 persons, which is 50.21 % of the total floating population. The data concludes that the outer-provincial influx population is the main body of floating population in Guangzhou. Source distribution of outer-provincial influx population is as the following: 630,400 persons from Hunan, accounting for 29.32 % of outer-provincial influx population; 378,300 persons from Sichuan, accounting for 17.59 % of outer-provincial influx population; 267,100 persons from Guangxi, accounting for 12.43 % of outer-provincial influx population; 235,000 persons from Jiangxi, accounting for 10.93 % of outer-provincial influx population; 193,200 persons from Hubei, accounting for 8.98 % of outer-provincial influx population. This trend continues with 119,500 persons from Henan, accounting for 5.56 % of outer-provincial influx population; 68,000 persons from Guizhou, accounting for 3.16 % of outer-provincial influx population; and 258,500 persons from the other 23 provinces, autonomous regions, municipalities directly under the Central Government accounting for 12.02 % of outer-provincial influx population. It is obvious that the outer-provincial influx population is mainly from impoverished Midwest areas of China such as Hunan, Sichuan and Guangxi.

The distribution patterns of 4,281,800 of the floating population of Guangzhou is 3,509,500 people into the urban area, accounting for 81.96 %; 383,700 people into towns and 388,600 people into villages. It is visible that the floating population of Guangzhou prefers bustling urban areas more than towns and rural villages. From the age structure framework, the floating population in Guangzhou is mainly young adults. The number of young floating population of age groups 15–34 reaches 2,479,800, and accounts for 78.85 % of the total number of

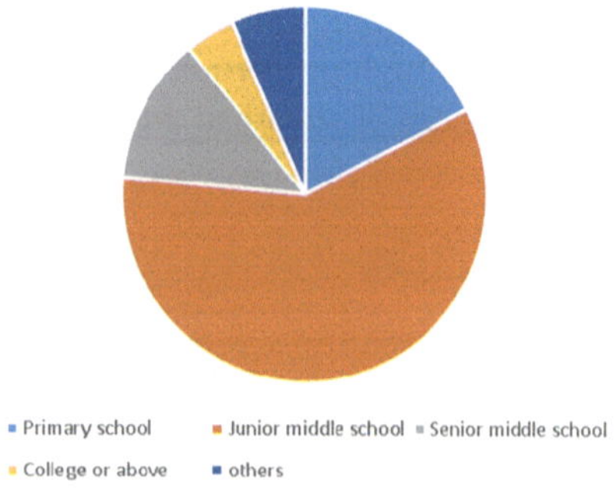

Fig. 4.16 Floating population percentages on education level

floating population. From the angle of the gender ratio, the number of males is 1,796,800 and female is 1,516,100, with gender ratio of 1.185. This reveals that the male young rural migrant workers are the main body of floating population. From the aspect of education, the total number of extraneous population aged 6 and over reaches 3,174,900. Therefore, the number of the population with an education degree of junior middle school is up to 1,870,300, accounting for 58.91 %; the number of population with education degree of primary school accounts for 17.52 % of the totals; the number of population with education degree of senior middle school accounts for 12.67 %. The number of the population with education degrees from primary school and junior middle school amount to 2,426,600 people, occupying 76.43 %; the percentage of the population with education degree of college graduated or above account for only 4.35 %. It supposes that most floating population in Guangzhou is in the low educational level of the country's status quo (Yao et al. 2010; Liu 2005, 2006; Cheong and Wu 2015; Curran 1998; Jian 1996) (Fig. 4.16).

A conclusion can be drawn from the above characteristic analysis about floating population that migrants into Guangzhou are mostly young males from Hunan, Sichuan, Guangxi and other western impoverished areas and graduated from primary and junior high school that choose to migrate into the urban areas.

Let's examine the spatial distribution of floating population. According to the fifth census data, the floating population in Guangzhou is mainly distributed in

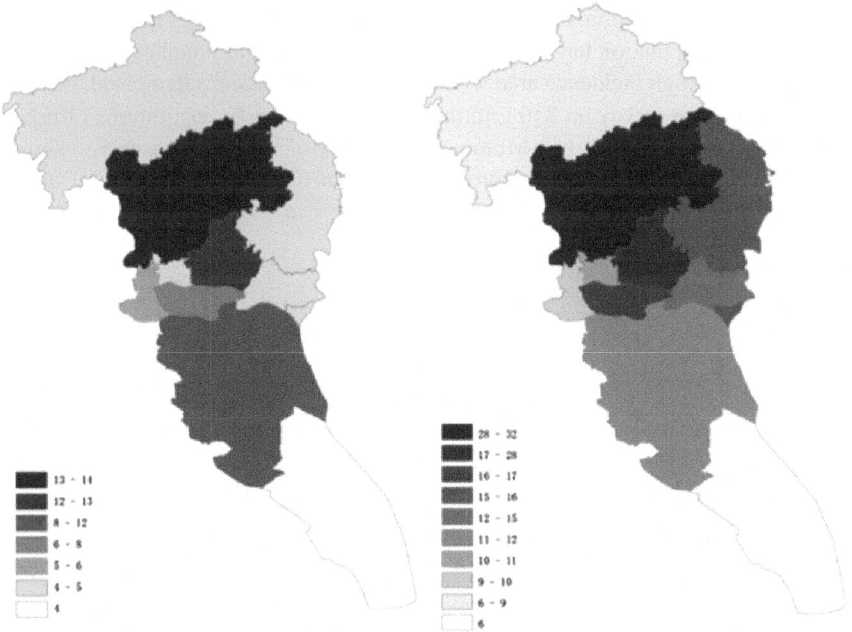

Fig. 4.17 Comparison between spatial density distribution of floating population and demographic density distribution of cases reported by SMD

Panyu, Baiyun, Tianhe and Haizhu (Fig. 4.14). From the perspective of the proportion of the floating population, growth of floating population in Baiyun and Panyu is prominent, and spatial distribution of floating population shows a suburb trend. Floating population concentrated streets are either administrative or economic center of suburb. For example, Shiqiao and Xinhua are administrative and economic centers of the respective districts; Shijing, and Tonghe are industrial centers of their districts. Streets concentrated by the floating population are either plant gathering areas in new urban areas and suburb or villages-in-city in old urban areas. For example, Huangshi, Xinshi, Shahe and Songzhou are plant gathering areas (agricultural?), while Xiancun, Yuancun, Jingtai and Sanyuanli are villages-in-city. Generally speaking, the floating population constructs the main body of criminals in Guangzhou (Jiang et al. 2013) (Fig. 4.17).

Let's compare spatial density distribution of floating population with demographic density distributions of cases reported by SMD and it will be found that both of them are dovetailed reciprocally. The Baiyun District has the highest floating population density as well as the highest demographic density of cases reported by SMD; Tianhe District has the floating population density ranked second as well as the second high demographic density of cases reported by SMD.

4. Confirmation of arc-belt distribution feature of urban villages and crimes to density distributions feature of cases reported by SMD.

Villages in city have long been regarded as urban public security black spots. "Villages in city concentrate cheap rental housings intensively, and become low-income floating population's first choice to live in. In some villages in city the number of floating population has generally exceeded the resident population, and these places are often high incidence area with complex social order." (Jiang et al. 2013).

According to a survey on 850 criminal floating persons by institutions of urban management of the Guangzhou Municipal Academy of Social Sciences also shows that about 78.9 % of the investigators come from the poor western rural areas. They are approximately (77.5 %) living in villages in city and rental housing in

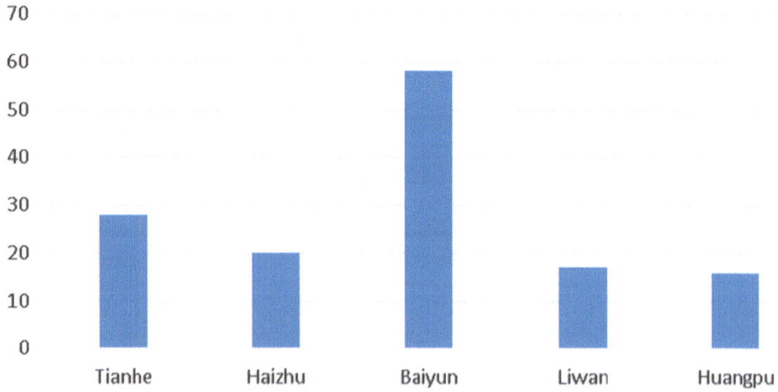

Fig. 4.18 Number of urban-villages in old districts in Guangzhou

rural-urban fringe zones in Guangzhou, while 69.7 % of the respondents are of the view that "villages in city" are good burrowing places for them (Huang 2008).

There are 139 villages in city distributed in 5 old urban districts. They are: Tianhe District (28), Haizhu District (20), Baiyun District (58), Liwan District (17), Huangpu District (16) (Fig. 4.18).

Tianhe District	Longdong, Shipai, Xinshi, Kangle, Xiancun, Chengjiecun, Tancun, Kemulang, Liedecun, Shangshe, Tangdong, etc.
Haizhu District	Wufeng, Ruibao, Chigang, Datang, Shixi, Lijiao, Kanglecun, Lujiangcun, etc.
Baiyun District	Tangxiacun, Tangxicun, Keziling, Songbaicun, Sanyuanli, Yaotaicun, Yongtaicun, Chentiancun, Jiangxiacun, Shayongcun, Jinxicun, Meihuayuan, etc.
Liwan District	Dongjiaonan, Kuipengzhou, Longxizhong, Longxixi, Longxinan, Bujiao, Zengjiao, Haibei, Dongshi, Donglian, Xipu, Luochongwei, Jiaokou, etc.
Huangpu District	Huangcun, Qianjincun, Huanxicun, Shixicun, Zhucun, Xiaoxintang, Mubei, Lingtang, Lianxi, Tancun, etc.

By the end of 2003, there were about 300,000 permanent residents living in urban-villages. In addition to this, the extraneous temporary resident population was more than 1,000,000 in villages in city (Guangzhou Statistic Bureau 2011).

Some of these villages-in-city are just high occurrence spots according to cases reported by the SMD, such as XianCun, YuanCun, ChiGang, TangXi, SanYuanLi, JiangXia, JingXi, LuoChongWei, and ZhuCun. When we look at the high criminal occurrence areas provided by the Guangzhou police, the most crime in centralized areas are residential areas, main roads and commercial areas. From the map, the two north and south crime arc-belts are already basically formed and almost join together. Specifically, the northern crime belt includes Liuhua in the Yuexiu district, Shijing and Songzhou in the Baiyun district, Shipai, Tangxia and Tianhenan in the Tianhe district. Instable areas include Xiancun in the Tianhe district and Dengfeng in theYuexiu district. The south crime belt includes Shiweitang in the Liwan district, Shiqiao and Shiqi in the Panyu district, Fengyang and Ruibao in the Haizhu district. These sites are consistent with crime black spots according to cases reported by SMD.

From the above, no matter from perspective of demographic occupation distribution feature, migrant population distribution feature or arc-belt distribution feature of villages-in-city and crimes, the layered-circle structure and high occurrence spots relevant to crime are consistent with criminal density characteristics according to the cases reported by SMD. Therefore, criminal density characteristics according to the cases reported by SMD can be used as references to a certain extent.

Although the collected samples are limited in number, and can only reflect real regulations to a certain extent, the comprehensiveness and accuracy need to be improved, especially considering the questionable reliability. The purpose of the author's study is to illustrate criminal cases in Guangzhou City that are dot-distributed in irregular layered-circles. Taking into account the specific spot location and exact criminal population density distribution, the lack of sampling data which this book is based on may be less accurate. After all, data collected through news gathering methods produces data neither the total crime number, nor with high accuracy as it involves random sampling. However, whether the punctate distribution positions or criminal population density distributions are accurate in this book is not very important, and making them clear is not the purpose of this research. In this book, to be aware of the existence of a punctate distribution is sufficient.

The reason this is primary is that we need to ensure the research is to be carried on in the circumstances that accurately portray criminal materials that were previously unavailable, as well as to afford a kind of research method to develop spatial criminology in China. Second, as long as crime distribution in Guangzhou shows a punctate pattern, we need to recognize high occurrence spots of crime as well as areas with relatively good social safety. Considering that crime is a significant source of social disorganization, the author focus on three different types of communities based on this opinion. This book tries to reveal a concrete status of social disorganization in different communities through an in-depth interview with residents in different types of communities.

References

Baum, R. (1996). China after Deng: Ten scenarios in search of reality*. *The China Quarterly, 145*, 153–175.

Chen, P., Yuan, H., & Li, D. (2013). Space-time analysis of burglary in Beijing. *Security Journal, 26*(1), 1–15.

Cheng, L., & Ma, L. (1997). Geographical analysis on Beijing urban crime. *Human Geography, 3*, 7–12. 程连生, 马丽. (1997). 北京城市犯罪地理分析.《人文地理》, 3: 7–12.

Cheong, T. S., & Wu, Y. (2015). Crime rates and inequality: A study of crime in contemporary China. *Journal of the Asia Pacific Economy, 20*(2), 202–223.

Cheung, N. W. T. (2013). Rural-to-urban migrant adolescents in Guangzhou, China: Psychological health, victimization, and local and trans-local ties. *Social Science & Medicine, 93*, 121. (1982).

Curran, D. J. (1998). Economic reform, the floating population, and crime: The transformation of social control in China. *Journal of Contemporary Criminal Justice, 14*(3), 262–280.

Guangzhou Bureau of Statistics. (2001). *Guangzhou statistics yearbook 2000*. Beijing: China Statistics Press. 广州市统计局, (2001).《广州统计年鉴2000》. 北京: 中国统计出版社.

Guangzhou Bureau of Statistics. (2002). *Guangzhou statistics yearbook 2001*. Beijing: China Statistics Press. 广州市统计局, (2002).《广州统计年鉴2001》. 北京: 中国统计出版社.

Guangzhou Bureau of Statistics. (2003). *Guangzhou statistics yearbook 2002*. Beijing: China Statistics Press. 广州市统计局, (2003).《广州统计年鉴2002》. 北京: 中国统计出版社.

Guangzhou Bureau of Statistics. (2004). *Guangzhou statistics yearbook 2003*. Beijing: China Statistics Press. 广州市统计局, (2004). 《广州统计年鉴2003》. 北京: 中国统计出版社.

Guangzhou Bureau of Statistics. (2005). *Guangzhou statistics yearbook 2004*. Beijing: China Statistics Press. 广州市统计局, (2005).《广州统计年鉴2004》. 北京: 中国统计出版社.

Guangzhou Bureau of Statistics. (2006). *Guangzhou statistics yearbook 2005*. Beijing: China Statistics Press. 广州市统计局, (2006).《广州统计年鉴2005》. 北京: 中国统计出版社.

Guangzhou Bureau of Statistics. (2007). *Guangzhou statistics yearbook 2006*. Beijing: China Statistics Press. 广州市统计局, (2007).《广州统计年鉴2006》. 北京: 中国统计出版社.

Guangzhou Bureau of Statistics. (2008). *Guangzhou statistics yearbook 2007*. Beijing: China Statistics Press. 广州市统计局, (2008).《广州统计年鉴2007》. 北京: 中国统计出版社.

Guangzhou Bureau of Statistics. (2009). *Guangzhou statistics yearbook 2008*. Beijing: China Statistics Press. 广州市统计局, (2009).《广州统计年鉴2008》. 北京: 中国统计出版社.

Guangzhou Bureau of Statistics. (2010). *Guangzhou statistics yearbook 2009*. Beijing: China Statistics Press. 广州市统计局, (2010).《广州统计年鉴2009》. 北京: 中国统计出版社.

Guangzhou Bureau of Statistics. (2011). *Guangzhou statistics yearbook 2010*. Beijing: China Statistics Press. 广州市统计局, (2011).《广州统计年鉴2010》. 北京: 中国统计出版社.

Guangzhou Bureau of Statistics. (2012). *Guangzhou statistics yearbook 2011*. Beijing: China Statistics Press. 广州市统计局, (2012).《广州统计年鉴2011》. 北京: 中国统计出版社.

Guangzhou Bureau of Statistics. (2013). *Guangzhou statistics yearbook 2012*. Beijing: China Statistics Press. 广州市统计局, (2013).《广州统计年鉴2012》. 北京: 中国统计出版社.

Guangzhou Bureau of Statistics. (2014). *Guangzhou statistics yearbook 2013*. Beijing: China Statistics Press. 广州市统计局, (2014).《广州统计年鉴2013》. 北京: 中国统计出版社.

Huang, S. (2008). Characteristic analysis and countermeasure of floating population crime—a case study of Guangzhou. *Guangdong Social Science*, *4*, 178–182. 黄石鼎, (2008). 流动人员犯罪的特征分析与防控对策——以广州为例, 《广东社会科学》, 4:178-182.

Jian, X. (1996). Increasing pressure: Impacts of migration on cities. *China Population Today, 13*(5–6), 21.

Jiang, S., Land, K., & Wang, J. (2013). Social ties, collective efficacy and perceived neighborhood property crime in Guangzhou, China. *Asian Journal of Criminology, 8*(3), 207–223.

Liu, J. (2005). Crime patterns during the market transition in china. *The British Journal of Criminology, 45*(5), 613–633.

Liu, J. (2006). Modernization and crime patterns in China. *Journal of Criminal Justice, 34*(2), 119–130.

Liu, D., Song, W., & Xiu, C. (2014). Spatial patterns of violent crimes and neighborhood characteristics in Changchun, China. *Australian & New Zealand Journal of Criminology*, *0*(0), 1–20.

Mao, Y., & Dai, S. (2006). Spatial distribution and environmental characteristics of Crime—A Case Study of Shanghai. *Journal of Urban Planning*, *3*, 85–93. 毛媛媛, 戴慎志. (2006). 犯罪空间分布与环境特征——以上海市为例. 《城市规划学刊》. 3:85–93.

National Bureau of Statistics. (2014). *Chinese Statistics Yearbook 2014*. Beijing: China Statistics Press. 国家统计局,(2014).《中国统计年鉴2014》. 北京:中国统计出版社.

Sun, I., Hu, R., Wong, D., He, X., & Li, J. (2013). One country, three populations: Trust in police among migrants, villagers, and urbanites in China. *Social Science Research, 42*(6), 1737–1749.

Yao, H., Xu, X., & Xue, D. (2010). Change character and causal analysis of spatial distribution of floating population in Guangzhou. *Economic Geography, 30*(1), 40–45. 姚华松; 许学强; 薛德升, (2010). 广州流动人口空间分布变化特征及原因分析, 《经济地理》, 30(1), 40–45.

Ye, X., Xu, X., Lee, J., Zhu, X., & Wu, L. (2015). Space–time interaction of residential burglaries in Wuhan, China. *Applied Geography, 60*, 210–216.

Zhou, C., Liu, Y., & Zhu, H. (2006). Analysis of social district in transition period of Guangzhou. *Journal of Geography*, *61*(1). 周春山, 刘洋, 朱红. (2006), 转型时期广州市社会区分析. 《地理学报》, 61(1).

Chapter 5
Social Disorganization and Crime: A Case Study

5.1 General Description of Field-Work Sites

Generally speaking, living and practicing in a specific location is the foundation for investigating if a community is undergoing social disorganization. Fei says 'to make in-depth and meticulous research on the lives of people, researchers need to restrict their investigations within a small social unit, which is motivated by practical considerations. Investigators must be accessible to respondents for close observation in person.'

Since the reform and opening up, China has been facing a series of problems caused by rapid social change in high-speed development of economy—the spread of urban space, social disorganization, aggravated rich-poor polarization, poverty concentration, structural unemployment, frequent population flow, residential heterogeneity, etc. In such a process, China's tradition, morality, culture and even the whole social system has been greatly changed.

Through the aforementioned study on the spatial distribution of crimes in Guangzhou, we know that crimes in Guangzhou are generally in irregular structure and punctate distribution. Crime is a significant symbol, and possibly the most important symbol of social disorganization. We can deduce from punctate distribution of crimes that social disorganization distribution is not uniform and different regions and will show different social disorganization status. As far as the basic research unit—community—is concerned, there have been different types of communities. Some are elegant and orderly; some have complex social composition with residents from various stratums; some seem like severely disorganized communities described in classic textbooks—filled with broken shield housings, the noisy youths, waste and litters, graffiti, abandoned shop fronts, burned buildings, hugger-mugger vacant lots, strangers, drunkards, vagabonds, idle chairwarmers, prostitutes, noise, congestion, angry words, awful stink. Crime rates and crime

H. Xiong, *Urban Crime and Social Disorganization in China*,
DOI 10.1007/978-981-287-859-5_5

types of the three distinct areas are also different. Impact factors of social disorganization on crimes in different types of communities are also different.

The author selects three communities in Guangzhou—Village S, Community T and Community Q as investigating sites to describe the similarities and differences of impact factors of social disorganization on crimes in different types of communities—one socially disorganized, one just in social disorganization and the third without disorganization.

5.1.1 Social Disorganized Community: A Case of Village S

Village S is one of the largest and oldest urban villages in Guangzhou (Du et al. 2005), which is located in Western Tianhe District, and adjacent to two University. Village S is also one of the most famous urban villages in Guangzhou where 6 murders were committed with in the village in 1999 (Zheng 2007). In the 1990s, village S was still a typical suburban and rural area attracting a large number of the floating population because of the cheap rent and its adjacency to the urban center. Along with expansion of the city, Village S was gradually surrounded by the city, and became a "village in city". Even with the improved economic status, the security still maintains a problem. Therefore, Village S is selected as a model of a socially disorganized community to continue the field research.

1. Profile of Village S

(1) Geographic location and traffic

Street S, which Village S belongs to, has been set up in March 20, 1987. The whole area of the street is 4.3 km^2. The total population is nearly 300,000 people, including a registered permanent population of 100,219 people, a total of 26,571 registered permanent households, and an extraneous transient population of 118,042 people. There are additional 80,000 people staying temporarily without Temporary Residential Permit. The population density of Street S is about 70,000/km^2. With the city moving east, the geographical advantage of Village S is increasely highlighted. Villagers began to build low-cost rental houses in their homesteads on a larger scale, at the same time the community became the settlements of floating population.

(2) Landscape of village S

Village S is located in Tianhe District which is the new CBD of Guangzhou with lots of skyscrapers rising up into the clouds. However, it was once farmland out of the city. With the development of the city, farmlands were gradually devoured by commercial lands. Village S is now basically surrounded by business streets full of IT products. Buildings in Village S are essentially farm houses and the environment is more severe. Crowded and dilapidated kissing buildings give a strong sense of compression and restriction to residents. The plot ratio in village S amounts to 2.5, and the building density reaches about 40 % (Li et al. 2007).

Strangers might be easily lost numerous hand-in-hand buildings as the village acts like a maze. This also generates a series of social problems and a typical landscape: narrow and muddy streets, dreggy rivers, crowded and dilapidated buildings (Figs. 5.1 and 5.2), various advertisements, and even posters selling black market documents (Fig. 5.3). Some scholars think this is a kind of abnormal space during rural-urban transitions (Li et al. 2007).

(3) Population of Village S

We have talked about that the total population of Street S which Village S belongs to, is close to 300,000 people including a registered permanent population of 100,219 people and a total of 26,571 registered permanent households with an extraneous transient population of 118,042 people. There are an additional 80,000 people staying temporarily without Temporary Residential Permits. The population density of Street S is about 70,000 persons/km^2. As far as Village S is concerned–there are 4000 registered permanent households as well as 16,000 registered permanent residents in Village S, 70 % living on house rent. Furthermore, there is an extraneous transient population of 118,042 people in Village S. Because of this, it is clear that Village S is a highly crowded ghetto of extraneous floating population. The number of extraneous floating population has the absolute advantage over the local population.

Floating population in Village S hails from all part of the country. It gives the urban-village a sense of being pluralized. For example, you can find ubiquitous snacks in any urban village in Guangzhou: Chaoshan cuisine, Sichuan cuisine, Hunan cuisine, Shanxi cold noodle, Lanzhou hand-pulled noodles, Zhejiang small steamed bun, Xinjiang mutton shashlik, Shanghai snack. These items perfect showcases of cultural variety and ethnic diversity of this area.

2. Employment status

The main job of local residents in urban-villages is to rent their house.

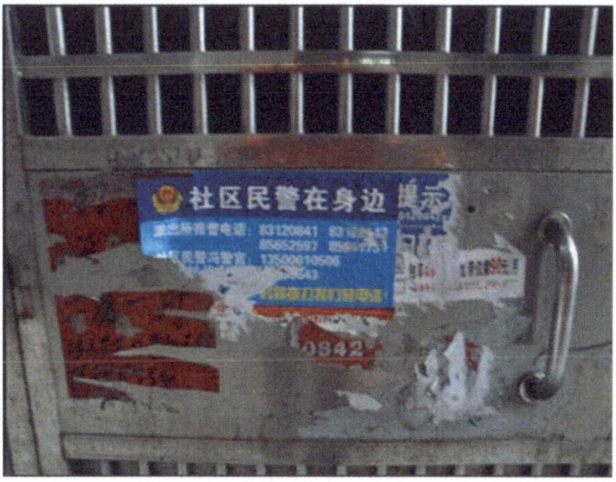

Fig. 5.1 Notice posted on iron gates of rental house in Village S (By Xiong 2014)

Fig. 5.2 Crowded and dilapidated hand-in-hand building in Village S (By Xiong 2014)

Case 25: LXL is a native of Guangzhou. In her own words, she is a "very authentic native of Guangzhou". LXL is a local of Village S as a child. Her husband is also a local villager. LXL still lived in her parents' home after marriage, although she has bought a set of commercial housing as the marriage house. But later, after having her daughter, LXL moved to live with her husband's father and mother. "Because of the needs of children care, we live together so it is easy to take care of my daughter. The house is very big. It is in homesteads, not commercial housing. So we can build a house standing four stories high with a lot of rooms. Child can walk a little more. There are several relatives in the street. We often drop around each other. You know, very happy. Sometimes if nobody in my house, I can let my relatives help to carry things. If I go out without keys I can call my neighbors to get the key back. Very happy, very satisfied. Many lessors are nearby. Many people have more than one building. One is occupied by the lessor himself, the other is rented out. Many outlanders, and many local people. I have a house rented to others. I treat them very well. I think they come here to work, and need a place to live."

Case 26: XH is just graduated out of College this year. "I'm Cantonese, from a small county in western Guangdong. My registered permanent residence is still in the hometown. I have been in Guangzhou for 4 years. Originally I went to the university to study in Guangzhou, and also chose to stay in Guangzhou. Because I have once been student in Guangzhou, so I am more familiar with the city and feel there are employment chances here. In the beginning I am very longing for living in Guangzhou, because Guangzhou is the capital of Guangdong Province, and belongs to the Pearl River Delta. It has developed economy, and gathers a lot of people. My current impression to Guangzhou is not so well

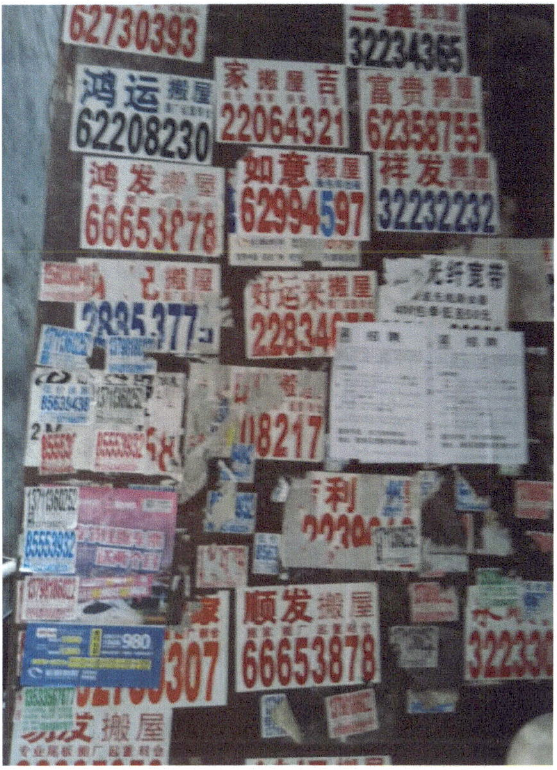

Fig. 5.3 Wall of a residential building in Village S are covered with small ads (By Xiong 2014)

as before, because there are too many people in Guangzhou, and the city is facing a lot of problems. One is traffic, the other is housing. I am not going to dwell in Guangzhou. I hope I can be in Guangzhou for one year or two years, and then I will choose another direction up to my working status." "I now live in Village S. The room is rented. Rental for me is quite expensive. Such a room probably about 10 m^2, its rental is 300 Yuan one month. I am satisfied with my room, especially from the security perspective, because the whole building is rented to students, graduated one year or two year ago. The rent requirement of the landlord is the tenant must be students or students graduated. So it is very safe. Tenants of the building I live in are basically students. The landlord is local villager. Houses on their own homesteads can be built up to 6 or 7 stories, all rental housing. Local villagers are can live very well just to rent houses, and are usually called '*Baozugong*, and *Baozupo*'".

After more and more extraneous population swarming into Village S, there is emerged restaurant, kindergarten, primary school, clinic, training institution, entertainment venue and so on aiming at them. Those are mostly managed by the extraneous population themselves. The occupations categories of extraneous population renting here are mainly as the following:

(1) Migrant workers (employees) in nearby factories, restaurants and shops etc.
(2) Clerks of Computer City.
(3) Small shopkeepers (including restaurants, grocery stores, and other private shops), night market venders.

(4) Practitioners in tertiary industry, including advertising, insurance, marketing personnel, also including some editors and reporters.
(5) Self-employed laborer, such as driver, actor, freelance and so on.
(6) White-collar in foreign-funded enterprises or private enterprise.
(7) University students or graduate students nearby.
(8) Hair salon practitioners. There are nearly a total of more than one hundred hair salons in Village S.
(9) Businessman in the central city.
(10) Construction workers, decoration workers, and some porters.
(11) Odd job workers whose job is most unstable, most coolies.
(12) Job hunters living with relatives and friends.
(13) Vagrants, who have no work, or even no residence.
(14) In addition, there are very few local native residents. Some of them temporarily live here because they have been marginalized for various reasons.

3. Inhabitation and food

Those floating population differ from each other greatly from the occupation, income, educational level, life style, and even taste of food. However, they still get mixed up. All sorts of people live together in spite of their social classes. Those whose jobs are relatively stable or their incomes are relatively high, generally live in more spacious rooms, equipped with some furniture, such as chairs, sofas, TV sets, and washing machines. Those without stable jobs or inadequate incomes always share rooms together, and their personal items are limited and simple.

> Case 8: HL is from Guangxi. His hometown is a small city in Guangxi province. His major was computer technology in the university. After graduating he ran a computer shop, and earned about 300,000 Yuan in a few years. Then HL "thought that it was much easier to make money in Guangzhou." But when he came to Guangzhou he found that the money was not so easy to earn. Store rental and salary are more expensive than those in Guangxi. "The shop has not been open until now. I am working in a computer company." "I rented a two-bedroom apartment in Village S shared with the others through internet. In the beginning we did not know each other. My flatmate lives with his girlfriend in a room, and I live in another room. The rental is too expensive for a person to rent the whole department, and it will be cheaper for two persons sharing a department."

5.1.2 Community in Social Disorganization: A Case of Community T

Community T is a large-scale anti-poverty community specially set up by the municipal government of Guangzhou to solve habitation difficulties of low-income groups. It covers an area of about 324,900 m^2. Community T is located in north of Village Tangxia of the Tianhe District.

1. Profile of Community T

(1) Geograpthic location and traffic

Community T belongs to the Street Tangxia. In a broad sense this area includes Village Tangxia, Village Shangshe, Village Tangdongt, and anti-poverty communities like Community T and Tai'an Garden. The location of Community T is still relatively in suburban Guangzhou. The north and west of the community are two expressways. South and east of the community are two famous urban villages. Relatively chaotic environment and poor public security in community T often make people live there complain that they are living in a "semi-slum".

(2) Landscape of Community T

As the largest anti-poverty community in Guangzhou or even in the whole country, internal environment of Community T is quite good except for the very old buildings. The foliage and greenery is adequate with a landscaping ratio up to 36 %. There are a kindergarten, a primary school, a middle school, a television university, two banks, a post office, a 24 h convenience store, and three vegetable markets with many small supermarkets nearby. A bus terminal is near the doorway of the community and more than ten bud lines commute people to urban central areas (Fig. 5.4).

Fig. 5.4 Diurnal landscape in Community T (By Xiong 2014)

Fig. 5.5 External environment of Community T (By Xiong 2014)

Adjacent to the two famous villages in city, Community T's external environment is very messy (Fig. 5.5). Illegal constructions stand everywhere as well as untidy parking is visible at any time (Fig. 5.6). In addition to the roadside stands, barbecues and night markets, Community T is like a large country fair and proves to be very noisy.

(3) Population of Community T

Community T is geographically divided into 2 areas by the transmeridional axis, wherein the south half of the community is the Tangdenan neighborhood committee, the north half of the community is the Tangdebei neighborhood committee. There are 11,875 people in 4750 households in the Tangdenan neighborhood committee, in which 1530 are floating population in 510 rental houses. In addition to this, there are 27 social relief households, 3 low-income households, 35 disabled persons, 4 mental patients, 21 elderly persons of no family. There are 12,500 people in 4843 households in Tangdenan neighborhood committee, and more than 500 households with low-income financial difficulties living in Cheap Renting houses. The prominent features of Community T are the large number of elderly residents, retired personnel, unemployed families and households in economic hardship. As for the composition of population, Community T is a mixed residential area of floating population, new Hakka and local population. The sources of residents in Community T are:

Fig. 5.6 Trucks parked in chaos outside Community T (By Xiong 2014)

The original anti-poverty housing residents: most of them are local natives; the other are registered permanent residents from other cities or other provinces.
The new commercial housing purchasers: most of them are new immigrants whose hometown in other cities or other provinces. Some have Guangzhou registered permanent residence, while some have not.
Tenants: most of them are floating population from other provinces. The majority are from Henan and Hunan, while a small amount of them are from other provinces.

Case 19: DXS is a home owner in Community T. He was once a laid-off worker of Guangzhou nitrogenous fertilizer factory and now he is one of the support crew in a company. In 1999, his Guangzhou nitrogenous fertilizer factory was facing bankruptcy, DXS did not want to go back to hometown and considered purchasing his own property to be a registered permanent resident. "I was unemployed, and couldn't afford commercial housing." With the certification given by the factory, DXS successfully applied the economically affordable housing in Community T. He bought a two-bedroom apartment of 63 km^2 at the price of 2470 Yuan per square meter. It cost a total of 160,000 Yuan. After 8 years, DXS "now lives in Guangzhou, and has a good life". In 2005 his economic conditions have changed a lot. The current apartment of 63 km^2 is not enough and he intends to buy a bigger apartment.

2. Employment status

Occupation constitution in Community T is relatively complicated. The job categories of the original anti-poverty housing residents mainly are the following:

(1) The unemployed personnel, including retirees, laid-off workers, and persons with disabilities. These kinds of the population are found more frequently in Community T;
(2) State-owned enterprise staff;
(3) Workers laid off from state-owned enterprises. Due to low education level and old age, they are engaged in office support, sanitation and other low income jobs;
(4) The staff of state units;

The occupations categories of new migrants who purchase commercial housing are mainly as the following:

(5) The staff of state units;
(6) Practitioners in the tertiary industry, including advertising, insurance, marketing personnel, also including some editors and reporters;
(7) Self-employed laborer such as artists, freelance and so on;
(8) Businessman in the central city;

The occupations categories of extraneous population renting here show as the following:

(9) Driver in name or taxi driver attached to Taxi Company;
(10) Employees in nearby factories, restaurants and shops etc;
(11) Small shopkeepers (including restaurants, grocery stores, and other private shops), night market venders;
(12) Businessman in the central city;
(13) Practitioners in tertiary industry, including advertising, insurance, marketing personnel, also including some editors and reporters;
(14) Self-employed laborer such as artists, freelance and so on;
(15) White-collar in foreign-funded enterprises or private enterprise;
(16) University students or graduate students nearby;
(17) Job hunters living with relatives and friends.

3. Inhabitation and food

Inhabitation conditions and other consumptions of residents in Community T differ from each other greatly depending on their occupation, income, and life style. Staff of state units and new migrants purchasing commercial housing whose jobs are relatively stable or incomes are relatively high generally decorate their departments in luxurious fashion. Oftentimes these apartments are equipped with furniture, such as chairs, sofas, TV sets, refrigerators, and washing machines. The original anti-poverty housing residents decorate their departments simply and economically, some even without decoration. As for the tenants, their living styles are distinct. Those in good economic status generally live in more spacious rooms with better decorations that are furnished and come with electrical household appliances. Those without stable jobs and enough incomes always share rooms together without decorations and equipped with simple furniture.

Case 24: LP, born in Xinyang Henan, with a degree of master and age of 38, residential registered in Guangzhou. He is in general family conditions and thinks himself belonging to the poor class. LP lives with his wife and daughter. He has worked in Guangzhou Procuratorate for 8 years. Considering of development opportunity he came to Guangzhou through civil service exam after graduation as a master 8 years ago. LP believes that he is living in "a rent flat in one of the largest slums in Guangzhou (laughing). The charge of the rent is very high and even doubled from original price. I think I am extorted by landlord for I am unwilling to move to another place. The flat is about 60 m^2 and looks just like a matchbox. I am greatly unsatisfied with this flat. Almost everything is bad here. My residential condition is too bad. The flat is almost not spruced up completely. It is in an old building with poor sunlight. The landlord provides nothing and nearly all furnitures are bought by myself. Some necessaries are in lack for we don't intend to stay here for a long time. That's just shortcoming of renting a flat."

There are no significant differences among residents in Community T on food. Their consumptions are daily, basic and thrifty. They would either buy some steamed stuffed buns and bags of soya-bean milk in the street side stalls or eat breakfast in their companies instead of consuming expensive meals. They often make dinner themselves after work, while young, single males often order fast food to satisfy their hunger needs.

5.1.3 Community without Social Disorganization: A Case of Community Q

1. Profile of Community Q

(1) Geographic location and traffic

Community Q is located in Town Nancun, District Panyu, composed of more than 200 sets of villas standing two or three stories high, surrounded by commercial buildings, clubs and management houses. From the view of traffic, Community Q is only suitable for car owners, because it is located in remote suburban Guangzhou. Neither bus station nor subway station is nearby.

(2) Landscape of Community Q

Community Q is a villa district. Its building is in Wannan dwelling style combined with modern modes (Figs. 5.7, 5.8, 5.9 and 5.10).

(3) Population of Community Q

Informed by local property service, Community Q covers an area of 10,000 m^2 with only 200 sets of housings that contains only 700 people.

2. Employment status

People dwellings in Community Q are generally economically elevated persons with higher income and higher education. The main categories of occupations are as the following:

Fig. 5.7 Safeguard standing beside the entrance of Community Q (By Xiong 2014)

Fig. 5.8 Villa exterior in Community Q (By Xiong 2014)

(1) Businessmen, private owners;
(2) Officials, state-owned enterprise leaders;
(3) Senior executives in IT, trade, financial and securities vocations;
(4) Denizen and people from Hong Kong, Macao and Taiwan;
(5) College teachers, lawyers, accountants, and freelancers.

3. Inhabitation and food

Residential environment and housing conditions are quite superior in Community Q. Case 17 uncovers the clean and elegant living environment and luxury housing conditions.

> Case 17: CFL, 42 years old, was born in Guangzhou with a registered permanent residence. He returned to Guangzhou after he graduated from Beijing University in the1980s,

Fig. 5.9 Chinese courtyard in Community Q (By Xiong 2014)

Fig. 5.10 Living room of an example in Community Q (By Xiong 2014)

and worked in the Propaganda Department of Provincial Party Committee. Then he resigned and went into business. Now he owns more than 10 houses in Guangzhou and a plant in Dongguan. He lives in a three-floor villa of 400 m^2 with his wife and daughter and his servant. CFL's living conditions are superior. He is quite satisfied with the inhabitation. The reason lies in that "living space is enough, decoration style is my selection and the redwood furniture is my favorite."

Ordinary people cannot afford expensive daily consumption in Villa district. The author also interviewed an owner of unoccupied villa. The owner has the economic ability to buy a villa, but could not withstand living expenses in villa, so he moved out to live in an apartment in city center.

5.2 Empirical Analysis

5.2.1 Village S

1. Employment and unemployment

Most interviewees in Village S have experienced unemployment. However, local villagers of village S are rich. If they are unemployed they also have houses to rent and dividends distributed by collective economic organizations. So unemployment to them is not a big problem. Some local villagers do not work and in long-term unemployment, but their livings are not in trouble.

> Case 25: LXL is a resident in village S. She grew up in village S and was married with another villager in village S. LXL 'works in a law firm with quite a snug income. I had some short-term unemployed experiences all lasting no more than three months. I will basically do a job for a long time. Unemployment affects me little for I was relatively young when I was out of work before, and there was not a very long time unemployed, so it can also be tolerable. I think it is due to the person himself if he was unemployed in Guangzhou. In fact, many people unemployed are just looking for a more suitable or more professional job for themselves. I will never commit crimes when I lost my job. Absolutely some people would do. Lots of people around me have this thought and some even committed crimes. Some people's lives are so senseless that they would rather stay in home than go out for a job. People in Guangzhou formerly have this social mentality. I mean, they just sit at home every day, drink Chinese Tea every day, as well as play mahjong immediately after eating up breakfast, and then return home for sleep. They spend time in vain day after day and have not a penny in their pockets. This type of people actually exists, especially in the inner city.

For the main inhabitants of village S—migrant workers, their poor economic conditions and disadvantaged status in employment will cause them great difficulties in life. They widely express that there is no way to live if unemployed in Guangzhou. "Unemployment will be very painful." It is visible that reactions to unemployment are relative to an individual specific economic situation. If the economic condition is very poor, short-term unemployment will cause pressure on their life; and conversely, if the economic condition is good, long-term unemployment will cause no pressure on their life.

> Case 5: JYQ is from Hubei with a Hubei rural *hukou*. "A relative bought a flat in Guangzhou and asked me do decoration for him. Then I stay here to see if there is any chance to make money in this city." "I am not in a rich family, just middle in rural areas. I have a wife and a son in my family." JYQ can be said as a skilled worker with a special craft," "I studied decorating houses following a master worker after graduating from junior high school, and now I do decoration myself". Therefore JYQ's income is decent in migrant workers. "I just come to Guangzhou to do room decoration and I must seek job opportunity myself. I could earn 3000 or 4000 yuan per month. The earning is actually almost equal to that in hometown.' The purpose JYQ stays in Guangzhou is to see 'if there is any chance.' Turning to the unemployment problem, JYQ said, 'I am not unemployed in Guangzhou so far. If there is no job chance, I'll go back home. My wife and child are both at home and it is also easy to pop back home. I have farms in hometown, and farming will make me avoid the danger of starvation."

Case 7: WLH is from Hunan, who was a rural woman before coming to Guangzhou and usually did farming and housework at home. She came to Guangzhou with her kid following her husband. 'My husband was a teacher in the village school in hometown, and later he got a master degree from a university. After graduation he got a job in Guangzhou, and then I followed my husband coming here. At the beginning I had no job, and later I got jobs as parking lot porter and then supermarket clerk. Salary for parking lot porter is 800 yuan per month, and for supermarket clerk comes up to about 1000 yuan per month.' When asked about the views of unemployment, WLH admits unemployed experience in Guangzhou before, 'I will have no income if losing job, but fortunately my husband has good salary so I do not have to worry about bread and cheese.'

Persons in good economic situation generally show unwilling to use illegal means making profits when unemployed, and think the others will basically never use illegal means to make profits too. "I never think I will use illegal means to make profits when unemployed, and the ratio of other people who think so is relatively very small". While individuals in poor economic situation generally show that they will use illegal means to make profits when unemployed, and think that the others will basically use illegal means to make profits, too. "I think I will try to find some money to buy something to eat, at least to get enough money to go back to home town. The others would certainly think so. Or they will starve to death." (see Interview Record 4).

2. Marriage and family

In the interview process, I found that marriage and the family of local villagers in village S appear not big questions. While marriage and family of extraneous tenants are in some trouble, and has caused the wide attention of the society. Extraneous tenants living in Village S are mostly unmarried single, young people. There are still some older migrant workers but the majority are young. Although these migrant are already married, their poor economic status as well as restrictions on household registrations prevent the whole family from moving to Guangzhou. They are forced to leave their wives and children in hometown farming and looking after the elderly. Therefore, despite being married, they are still in a long-term separation conditions. JYQ in Case 5 has been in Guangzhou for almost a year, but his wife and son remain in hometown. Case 14 is an example that long-term separation leading to divorce.

Case 14: CF is from Hubei, "My family is fairly wealthy in the countryside. I live with my parents in hometown and I am the only child of them. I am 27 years old now. I joined army in Fuzhou after graduating from junior high school. Then I learned driving and got driving license during this period. Later I was promoted to volunteer soldier and got monthly wage of 800 yuan. So a few years later I also saved some money. After returning from troops by a fellow villager's introduction I got a job of driving truck in a factory in Guangzhou managed by another fellow of villager with a salary of 2000 yuan a month, which is even higher than that of civil servants in hometown. Later I met a girl immigrant worker in Guangzhou, whose hometown is adjacent to mine. We got married in my hometown soon. Now I come here, leaving my wife home. We love each other deeply, but my parents want us to divorce. I feel great pressure. And we divorced finally. I feel very sorry for her. I actually do not want to leave her."

Although the selection of community is mainly decided by the economic status of residents, the marriage status and marriage itself are strong enough to affect people's living area. Whether married or not, the respondents generally think their marriages and families are happy. It is obvious that various individuals have their own understanding on "happiness". During the interview process, the author finds an interesting phenomenon. Even if having earned enough money, single youth prefer to renting rooms to live, and to saving up money until marriage. Case 8 mentioned above is just a perfect example. HL's economic condition is not too bad, but he prefers to share an apartment in urban village with strangers to save money.

Case 8: HL mentioned that he once had the opportunity to buy a flat in Guangzhou. "Housing price in Guangzhou had never been so far off the mark in 2004. I have a friend whose company had flats to sell with 3000 yuan/m^2. So an apartment of 100 m^2 only sold 300,000 yuan. In fact, I can afford it at that time. The community was perfectly equipped with swimming pool, tennis courts, etc. And there were very few people living in it. Sometimes I went there to swim I felt it a private swimming pool for there are only we guys in it. You know that's so cool! The reason I didn't purchase a flat is mainly that I hadn't a girlfriend that time. I didn't know if my future wife would be satisfied with the flat. So what I could do was just waiting. And the matter is lasted to nowadays. I have still not found a girlfriend while the housing price rose up rapidly. A second-hand flat is almost charged 30,000 yuan/m^2. It is beyond my pocket now."

Most single female interviewees tend willing to be tenants. Most of them hope to change living condition either through marrying with rich man, or through collaboration with spouses after marriage. In the interview, the author actually found that there are women leaving original living areas and moving to relatively more expensive community through marriage, such as Case 23.

Case 7: WLH is from Hunan, who was a rural woman before coming to Guangzhou and usually did farming and housework at home. She came to Guangzhou with her kid following her husband. 'My husband was a teacher in the village school in hometown, and later he got a master degree from a university. After graduation he got a job in Guangzhou, and then I followed my husband coming here. Because WLH and her son's have still rural *hukou*, if her son want to go to public primary school in Guangzhou, she need to pay a large amount of money as grant in aid. However, her family is in poor economic condition, so WLH has to send her son to a civilian-run school nearby. This school is located in the edge of a urban-village and the most enrolled are children of immigrant workers. WLH herself also greatly takes unkindly to this situation, 'Students enrolled in this school are mostly children of immigrate workers renting in urban-villages nearby. They are useless to my son. Teachers there are in low levels too. Most of them work there just because they cannot find a job in other place. An accident happened not long ago.A teacher was arrested for child molestation in his class. Soon WLH and her son got Guangzhou *hukou*. She transferred her son to a public primary school as soon as possible. As to the victimized boy, according to WLH, 'he is suffered greatly from the criminal behavior. However, his parents have no ability to send him to public primary school while they are afraid to send him still to a civilian-run school, so he is sent back to hometown and cared by his old grandfather.'

Case 13: YL is from Hubei. He was born and grew up in Hubei rural. Like many other rural children, his parents left hometown as immigrant workers when YL was a little boy. Although the family was not particularly poor, YL stopped schooling without finishing junior school course for disgusting study and poor grades in exams. He came to Guangzhou to stay with parents, doing odd jobs. 'I was too young and too naïve at that time, only 16 years old. Oh, I was hanging out with some peer friends in Tianhe Park and saw a pair of lovers sitting in a dark corner. We went up to ask the man to give us his mobile with a knife pointing him. Actually we did that just for fun at that time. However we were arrested for robbery and I was sentenced an imprisonment of 3 years as a juvenile. I feel it utterly mortifying to return hometown so I still stay in Guangzhou. Actually I am unwilling to go back home. I am the only son of my parents. Their hair turned to white with broken hearts after I was imprisoned. I think they would lose face if I go back home.

3. Resident stability and heterogeneity

As a village in city, residents in Village S of are frequently floating. "Residents are very instable. They are basically renting here, and often move here and there." (see Interview Record 23). Residents in Village S think residents they are extremely mobile. At the same time, in the interview we also find that many residents of the village themselves are often eager to move. It can be said, one reason of great mobility of residents in Village S is the bad living conditions. Lots of people just treat Village S as a temporary stance, and will leave if their conditions were slightly better. On the other hand, Village S brings together a large number of mobile residents.

About the ethnic heterogeneity problems, due to Chinese historical traditions and cultures it basically shows pattern of "small colonies in large sympolyandria" among various ethnic groups. Same patterns exist in Guangzhou. Basically each minority lives together with same nationalities, while some minorities live mixed in the Han areas. There are few ethnic minorities in Village S. At the same time because most minorities are sinicized deeply on costume, diet and living habits, it is difficult to recognize between the Han people and the minorities. Ethnic heterogeneity based on nationality is not significant. "I have no impression about the minority. I even don't know who the minority is." As for the minorities they can obviously be distinguished from clothing and appearance, some problems can be found from the talks of most interviewees. "There are some people from Xinjiang (in the community). The other minority is not easy to distinguish. The Xinjiang people are very brutal, we (the Hans) dare not to provoke them."

Along with the frequent intercourse between Guangzhou and international cities, problems of ethnic heterogeneity on race also emerge. In Guangzhou, most communities will mix some foreigners living in groups in spatial distribution. There are also few foreigners living in Village S. Residents in Village S treat foreigners more objectively. "I feel that there are good guys or bad guys in every country. And the foreigners will not definitively commit crimes." "I think crime is a problem of criminals themselves, not a problem of their nations."

LXL in Case 25 does not consider house-renters as residents in the community, so although she sees that "there are many people in the area, many leasers, local people, and many outlanders", but she still thinks that, "households are ultra stable, because the house is owned by villagers themselves". Even extraneous tenants themselves also feel that many crimes in Guangzhou are committed by outlanders.

"Outlanders especially who can not find a job are easier to commit crimes". The author finds that differences between the local and the outlanders in Village S are quite large. "There may be more outlanders with low qualities in our village. Many migrant workers, construction workers and many factories are nearby. Thus, those kinds of people are generally higher in number." Some local people even don't consider renting people as residents in the community in abstract. They hold the opinion that only local villagers with registered permanent residences are 'formal' residents in the community.

4. Social justice

(1) Satisfaction

Village S is in tremendous contrast with surrounding communities in appearance and resident income level. However, when asked about question of social justice, most of the interviewees, whether local or extraneous, think that the society is fair. "The social gap between the rich and the poor is large, but it is fairly impartial. One's success mainly relies on its own struggle." Although some believe that society is unfair, they recognize social injustice as a normal social phenomenon. "There must be unfairness. I feel that God is fair to everyone. They live a luxurious life, because they worked very hard before." At the same time the interviewees mostly agree the old saying "in the land of the blind, the one-eyed man is king", so that social discontent will reduce, while self-satisfaction will increase.

(2) Social discrimination

In regards to discrimination, residents in Village S generally feel social discrimination. This is decided by their economic status, occupation type and social status. As before-mentioned, personnel occupations of tenants in Village S include migrant workers (employees) in nearby factories, restaurants and shops, clerks of Computer City, small shopkeepers (including restaurants, grocery stores, and other private shops), night market venders, practitioners in tertiary industry, self-employed laborer, university students, job hunters and vagrants. Except for a few people such as white-collar workers and college students, housing-renters in Village S are almost always engaged in dirty, tired, and hard work with low pay and poor benefits. Extraneous tenants in village S basically belong to the bottom of social class in low social status, and endure discrimination by others. People renting houses in village S normally think they are "poor, uneducated, extraneous, and migrant workers".

Dealing with discrimination, most interviewees in Village S think they are discriminated. "Sometimes I feel discrimination. Some people are very snobbish." JYQ in Case 08 also tells the author the discrimination once he experienced. "Once my relatives took me to buy clothes in a Jeanwest store, everyone could try any clothes except me. When I tried it, the salesman came to prevent me. I know a lot of people look down on us migrant workers."

Discrimination of villagers is a little bit more complex. On one hand they express clear discrimination on the outlanders. "I can answer with a definite Yes! I actually look down on the outlanders. If a local native of Guangzhou is not good, then the outlander is much worse. They often spit on the streets." On the other hand, they feel discrimination when facing higher social class even though the latter are outlanders too. "When I just entered the law firm my colleagues including my boss were all basically new migrants. They are Mandarin speakers, and they are more confident. Personnel in this field always have more confidence. You have to adapt to the life style and the environment. If you cannot speak Mandarin they will think you are in low quality and speak poor Chinese."

The author also finds that the feeling of discrimination is correlated with individual occupation, personality, experience and social interaction. CF in Case 14 was a driver and had been a soldier in Fuzhou before coming to Guangzhou. He had life experiences in big city. In his own words, "I have seen the elephant". CF recognized that "I was sometimes treated as outlander in Guangzhou but mainly because I couldn't speak Cantonese. Basically there is no discrimination. Outlanders are treated well in Guangzhou." HL in Case 8 is a white-collar in company. Before came to Guangzhou he was once a company boss in his hometown with some savings, and had a comfortable income. In addition that HL himself is Cantonese, "nobody knows I am an outlander", HL think people do not discriminate against him. FD in Case 12 is a master from a prestigious university. Even though his income is lower, he still has an advantage in psychology because of high education, and he also feels no discrimination. It is visible that although in the general sense people will discriminate those living in disorganized areas, but discrimination is decided by individual socio-demographic factors such as economic status, social class, occupation, educational degree and other factors. Although both renting in Village S, the dominant groups in same economic class with similar occupation and education degree do not feel discrimination, and do not feel they should be discriminated against. While disadvantaged groups such as migrant workers, decoration workers, waiters and others would not only feel, but also experience discrimination, and they are psychologically self-contemptuous.

(3) Institutional injustice

Institutional injustice felt by residents in Village S includes the household registration system and the primary education system. Due to the poor economy, and despite the existence of institutional injustice, there are no strong opposition to the institutional injustice from residents in Village S. They cannot buy even a single room in Guangzhou, so they do not care about preferential policies for the citizens of Guangzhou about house purchase; they cannot afford children's education fee in Guangzhou and have to leave their kids in hometown, so they are also indifferent about injustice of education system. "It's actually not fair, and is discrimination to outlander. But it doesn't matter to me. I will not buy a house in Guangzhou." It is obvious that institutional injustice is in relationship with the distance of individual interest. If the interest is not directly affected by institutional injustice is too far, the individual will not have strong dissatisfaction with it.

While beneficiaries of institutional injustice though believe that the present education system is unfair and it is discrimination on outlanders that primary schools enroll students with registered permanent residence, they still feel that this system is in the nature of things, and is "good". "It is unfair that primary schools charge sponsorship fee, and most of us feel it is discriminatory. But it is also actually good for us beneficiaries. My son is enrolled according to registered permanent residence." What is more, some institutional injustice beneficiaries consider inequality brought by institutional injustice as mark of identity promotion. "It is actually not fair, but we also got the registered permanent residence by hard work. This is my only difference with the migrant laborer."

5. Social capital

Generally speaking, tenants in Village S generally consider themselves have little "*guangxi*" in Guangzhou. They have few friends and relatives in residential community except local villagers. They almost do not participate in any formal or informal programs. Their friends circle basically includes individuals with same occupation and social status. The circle of friends for university graduates is composed of "former classmates or alumni". Local villagers living in Village S are quite well in economy, and have better "*guanxi*[1]" than extraneous tenants. While put in the whole social networks in the city, local villagers as the residents in urban-villages are still politically and socially in a weak position. LXL in Case 25 feels that "I cannot reach the senior within the social hierarchy you mentioned, such as the official, the rich and famous. I'm not contact with this class". In short, regardless of how the economic status is, residents in such a disorganized community as Village S are in disadvantageous positions of social capital.

When in trouble, residents in Village S would first seek help from former classmates, friends and home fellows. Among migrant worker interviewees, only one person would seek help from relatives, because "he has no social relations", his friends are all countrymen. While his relatives "works in public security department." The other participants have no such a relatives working in government, mainly social related with migrant workers in similar economic and social status. When confronted with difficulties they appear extremely helpless. Residents in Village S with richer social capital are more active to earn a living. They even dare to do some illegal business to increase incomes.

Residents in Village S hardly participate in some social activities. Migrant workers basically play mah-jongg or play cards in dormitory after work with colleagues. University graduates will be slightly involved in more versatile activities. They "often participate in several gatherings of friends, go swimming or play badminton." However, their overall social activities are still relatively simple.

6. Social order and social control

Through the author's field observation, Village S is generally a rough part of urbern relatively weak social control, and social control is relatively weak. The winding alleys, shabby houses and bevy of scantily clad young women make the whole urban village filled with an ambiguous air. With leaflets about security and adlets

---

[1]Guanxi (Chinese: 关系; *Pingyin*: guānxì) means personal relationship and connections in a society.

selling fake certificates dramatically posted together, social control of the community looks more unreliable. However, different views on social order and social control in village S exist between local villagers and extrangeous tenants.

Extraneous tenants generally think Village S is relatively in great disorder. Case 07 and Case 08 are obviously not satisfied with the community per se. "The environment of urban-village is terrible! There are too many people along with a lot of miscellaneous items. It is easy to trigger potential delinquent juveniles." While the local villagers in Village S believe both social order and social control are in good conditions. Case 25 thinks their village is perfectly "adequate". "I believe my family when they tell me that there is no prostitution and crimes like robbery in our living street. The community is under effective social control." In fact, case 25 admits that there are frauds happening in Village S, but she does not think that "fraud could embody the social disorder in a community for fraud is mainly caused by victim's greed. It is personal motives driving these behaviors". As to such a seriously disorganized community as Village S, why there exists so much diversity between local villages and extraneous tenants on its social order and social control remains unknown. The author analyses that it is because of different effects on residents' experiences by an acquaintance or stranger to the society.

7. Social isolation and social exclusion

Such a disorganized community as Village S is impossibe a closed circulation, while the other communities around Village S are basically gated. It can be said Village S is segregated and exclusive from the surrounding neighborhoods. However, residents in Village S, whether local or extraneous, almost unanimously support changing Village S into a gated community. The perspective of Case 25 is representative: "(If gated,) it would be inconvenient, but crime would be decreased." For extraneous tenants, "security and peace of mind were part of the reason (to prefer a gated community.)" Obviously, although outsiders regard village-in-city such as Village S as crime hot spot, residents in Village S still think "outsiders" bring crime into their community. With fear of crime, residents in Village S expect the community to be gated, although it will cause access inconvenience.

Social exclusion is simply examined through consumption frequency and the feeling to expensive amusement places in this book. The author finds that the residents of village S are socially excluded not only spatially but also psychologically. When asked about consumption frequency in expensive amusement places, answers of most of the interviewees as residents of village S are "not many", "no", "few", "basically rarely". One of the interviewees specially flaunts his only experience once to an expensive amusement place. It can be said that residents in Village S, especially extraneous tenants, are in long distance from the general public consumption places, let alone expensive amusement places.

8. Community cohesion, trust and fear

Local villagers and extraneous renters are different when asked about community cohesion. Although the entire community gives a feel of no cohesion, Local villagers in Village S insist they are cohesive to each other. LXL in Case 25 considers herself a member of the community, because she "would meet many relatives on the way home." When asked for the trust between neighbors, LXL answers without hesitation that they are "extremely trustworthy, for we are all relatives." LXL also expresses her trust to the neighborhood committee and peddlers in community because they "have been familiar with each other for more than sixty years." While asked the trust of strangers, LXL seems uncertain about them. It can be deduced that, Village S is partly an acquaintance society, even as a general stranger society. The acquaintance society and the semi—acquaintance society is the important field of the Chinese interpersonal trust. Local villagers belong to one family with the same surname, same ancestry, as well as same customs and traditions. Some traditional folk activities would be held in the village and it is just these activities, customs and traditions tie them together. They are cohesive, and trust each other with little fear of crime. As for extraneous tenants, they generally admit lack of cohesion in Village S, as well as mutual distrust among neighbors. They also show distrust on strangers and traders in general. It is obvious that for extraneous renters, Village S is not only unattractive, but even strongly centrifugal. They hope to leave the area as soon as possible, rather than "become a member there".

9. Tradition, moral and belief

Residents in Village S insist that traditions are well preserved in it. The village will hold some traditional ceremonies on festivals such as Chinese New Year, the Dragon Boat Festival, the Lantern Festival, etc. While for those extraneous renter interviewees, these traditions are just the villagers' traditions. These traditions and ceremonies as ancestral temple, spirit tablets, Tomb-sweeping in Pure Brightness Festival, encircling meal in Dragon Boat Festival, ancestor worship in the Winter Solstice, are going on around them, but simply tell them such traditions are saved and carried out in Village S. The traditions are visible, but do not belong to them, and they have no way to participate. While their own traditions have been abandoned as their distant hometowns are too far away, and despite those traditions belonging to them, they cannot participate in those activities anymore.

Most extraneous people think that there are "no traditions in this community", or just tell the author expressionlessly "the ancestral temple is well preserved". When asked about money and moral views, extraneous renters in Village S generally worship money, or believe that both money and morality should be taken into account. "Gentlemen's love Choi, to the way".[2] Some participants attribute their living in such a poor area to the lack of money. Some interviewees express that moral issues are not in the calendar in the current economic condition, and money is the basic survival need. Local villagers are economically richer, so they emphasize more on the importance of ethics.

[2]A Chinese idiom means a decent person would love money, but gets it in legal and moral methods.

In view of belief, Chinese especially the Hanrians are widespread lack of faith, and residents in Village S are no exception. All of the participants say they have no faith. "Faith for us Chinese is not very important." The interviewees hold the belief that this has positive significance on China's existing security, morality and a series of social problems.

10. Language

In general, languages used in Village S are not uniform. Cantonese, Mandarin and various dialects coexist in the urban village. Extraneous renters generally speak Mandarin when going out, while dialects among fellow-townsmen. Most local villagers also can speak Mandarin with Mandarin speakers, but there are still a few cannot speak Mandarin. Because Guangzhou is a Cantonese society, most interviewees who cannot speak Cantonese present that language will produce negative affect on their work and life. GJ in a trademark firm says "now I am unable to speak Cantonese. I feel it is difficult to communicate with customers." But outlanders who can speak Cantonese distinctly express much less trouble in life. XH also works in the trademark firm, who can speak Cantonese, so that "language itself has no effect on my life." In the interview, the author find that discrimination and social communication disorder induced by language barriers affect not only extraneous tenants, but also local residents who speak dominant language. This is beyond the author's expectations. The author thought that local original residents have more advantages in their ingrained native language environment than the outlanders. But the fact is that some local residents even once in a while suffer discrimination, even dismissal, due to incapability of speaking Mandarin. "Language greatly influences my life. I am native of Guangzhou; my studying is not going very well. My Mandarin is very poor. I still remember that I lost my first job in the office because of Mandarin."

It is obvious that language also appears heterogeneous tendency due to individual speaking different dialects mixing together with social transition, resident migration and frequent social intercourse. Language heterogeneity affects not only extraneous residents but also original local inhabitants. It would generate social discrimination or even affect their jobs and incomes directly.

5.2.2 Community T

1. Employment and unemployment

As a community just experiencing social disorganization, residents in Community T come from various social classes. For example, some are either middle class in society such as government officials, state-owned enterprise workers, white-collar workers in foreign invested enterprises, or economically emerging classes such as private owners, lawyers and accountants. There are still a large number of unemployed, laid-off workers and migrant workers in the lower social stratum.

These personnel with different incomes, different occupations, and different social classes have different views on unemployment. As for interviewees in better economic conditions, experience of unemployment is just a conceptual framework. These persons generally think unemployment does not impact their lives greatly when losing job. While the others, even have jobs, still fear for unemployment. Generally, panic of unemployment becoming more prevalent in community T.

Case 1: WDW is from Hubei and his *hukou* is still in Wuhan. WDW has an enviable job in bank after graduating from a famous faculty of law. However unsatisfied with the salary of inland bank, WDW resigned quite a stable job and went to Guangzhou as a lawyer. He has a wife and a kid at home. He has a monthly family income about 20,000 or so, but unstable. So WDW thinks his family is not rich, "I am doing legal work with a not so high income. At the beginning I was a member of 'moonlight clan', then my economic status became gradually better and better and there are some savings now." "Although I had not experienced unemployment, I have to admit that unemployment is quite miserable in Guangzhou. Because daily life costs are so high, and commodity price in Guangzhou is so expensive." WDW accepted that "Actually there is hidden unemployment for me", "sometimes there are several continuous months without income, but you still need to spend money on necessities. At this time I always suffer both economic and spiritual stress, and want to do something to cover up my insecurities."

Case 2: HY is from Hubei with a *hukou* in Guangzhou. "Family condition is OK. Parents are both civil servants, and do not need us to afford anything. Our annual family income is about 300,000 yuan. We have a little baby to feed. I could also go to university in Shanghai after graduating as a master of law. I think Guangzhou has higher wage than Shanghai so I chose Guangzhou as job site. In fact, as far as the city itself I prefer Shanghai to Guangzhou. I became civil servant with an ordinary income. I got only less than 3000 yuan in the first year of internship after deducting common reserve fund. What fortunate was that I was provided good welfare. I enjoyed public rented room with a very low rate of 150 yuan per month and free public medical service. And I only need to pay 2 yuan for a meal in our dining room. My payment became higher and higher gradually, and reached 8000 yuan per month now. Unemployment for me does not exist. We have an 'iron rice bowl' unless we resign by ourselves. I think it would affect me greatly if unemployed. After all, Guangzhou is a city with high-level consumption. The unemployed would be greatly miserable."

Case 26: LLS was born in Guilin with *hukou* in Shenzhen. "My family is in very general conditions. I worked in Shenzhen after graduation doing law-relative job. I came to Guangzhou less than 2 years ago. I have a very bad impression of Guangzhou before, because they say that public security is very bad in Guangzhou. I feel it become better than before when I come here. I do intend to continue to live in Guangzhou. I am a lawyer now and have not experienced unemployment. I think unemployment should make life difficult. In fact, Guangzhou is still a city holding tolerant attitude towards persons with highly developed business. As far as illegal means to say, I am sure that somebody would adopt it to make living."

Case 3: ZL was born in Hubei with a Jinan *hukou*. "My father is managing a clinic, and my mother is a farmer. My family condition is medium. I am 29 years old with a bachelor degree. I was born in the countryside, went to high school in a small city, and then entered college in a big city. I like big city so after graduation I tried to get a job in big city. I think my current life is ok. My company has a project in Guangzhou and one of my previous leaders is a project manager here, so I just come here with my husband together.

Guangzhou has highly economic development and plenty of employment opportunities. It is proved that my decision is right. I am an engineer in this project with monthly after-tax income of 5500 yuan. I have been once unemployed for two months, but I was seldom affected by unemployment. I feel as long as you are diligent in Guangzhou you will get high income. Even a pancake vendor in the street would almost earn as much as me per month. I never think to use illegal means to get profit. There are no people around me do engage in illegal jobs and there should be no such thoughts."

Case 20: CC was born in Jiangxi and her *hukou* is in Guangzhou. "I was born in a civil servant family in common level. I have parents and an elder brother at home." CC is 31 years old, still single and has a bachelor degree. "I have been in Guangzhou for almost 10 years. I feel there are more job opportunities here. And more important is that I feel not exclusive here. At the beginning, I worked as a lawyer assistant, while the starting salary was somewhat low. Then it increased slowly but gradually. Later I became a civil servant and the salary increased to 8000 yuan per month. I have been unemployed for a short time. My former boss heard that I was going to leave the law firm then he fired me. I actually felt no pressure at that time for almost no psychological panic. But I was suffered economic difficulty indeed. However, I had still some savings and the out-of-work period was very short, so it would not influence my normal life."

However, it is known that some with great ability consider unemployment as a good thing meaning new opportunity.

Case 4: GEZ is from Fujian province and have a *hukou* in Guangzhou now. "It should be said that my family condition is good and life quality is also well. Currently I am single in Guangzhou with monthly income of about 8000 yuan. I have a master degree of law. After graduation I became a judge in Guangzhou. Now I passed the admission exam as a doctoral degree candidate in Southwest University. The course is part-time and I still have my current job. My income is stable and the salary is increasing continuously.' GEZ has not experienced employment, but she thinks 'employment sometimes even means new chance. My current income is not low while is not high too. If I resign my current job I could certainly earn big money. Almost all civil servants are unwilling to lose current jobs for they are too stable and comfortable. If unemployed, we would all come out to earn money ourselves. I hear some colleagues left to be a lawyer, and earned more than one million yuan a year."

There are interviewees expressing their concern about the life state of low income groups, especially migrant workers in unemployment. HY in Case 2 says, "No kidding, I really want to use illegal means to get profit without unemployment, such as bribery." CC in Case 20 also says that he will not commit a crime when unemployment, but he hears that "there was a migrant worker that killed a man for 2000 Yuan." Interviewees in community T, if the economic situation is not positive, regardless of occupation, education and social status, have expressed fear of unemployment, and indicated willing to adopt illegal means to make their survival in Guangzhou when unemployment.

Case 24: LP, mentioned above, "I have never been unemployed. I think unemployment is simple for immigrant workers. They certainly cannot make living in Guangzhou and have to leave. Nowadays the city of Guangzhou suffers severe unemployment. Some large state-owned enterprises as well as private companies have to shed labour. A large number of factories close down which results in reduced employment opportunities. I am sure that there should be some people using illegal methods to seek a livelihood. There is such a big difference between urban and rural areas. Nobody wants to return to undeveloped

Midwest. If I was unemployed I would never come back to till the land again. I would have some evil thought in case that I cannot survive in this bustling metropolis. How do you think about it?"

Case 9: XP is from Henan Province. He was born in Henan and still has Henan *hukou*. "My home is in countryside in bad condition. My parents and three brothers are living there now. I am 22-year-old. I went out for work after graduating from junior school, and now I am a security guard in a public organization. They pay me 1200 yuan per month inclusive food and accommodation. But I had found a new job in Dongguan. You know, here is a dormitory area of a public organization and girls living here are all graduated from university, so how can I find a girlfriend here? I'm looking for a position as security guard in a garment factory in Dongguan inside which the woman workers are easy to chase. I have not worked for two months. Unemployment means no money earning, and it is a big problem to make a living. Fortunately, I got job in the third month, or else I do not know what I would do then. I think I would break the law in long-term unemployment."

2. Marriage and family

Residents in Community T are generally in good marriage and family status which relates to the individual condition of Community T. From the description of field work site in the last chapter, we already know that there are three types of residents in Community T. The original anti-poverty housing residents mainly include aged retirees, laid-off workers and persons with disabilities, state-owned enterprise staff, workers laid off from state-owned enterprises and state personnel. The new migrants who purchase commercial housing mainly include state personnel, practitioners in tertiary industry, self-employed laborer and businessman in the central city. The extraneous population however, that are renting here include taxi drivers, employees in nearby factories, restaurants and shops, small shopkeepers, and night market venders. Among the three types of residents, marriage and family of original anti-poverty housing residents are relatively stable. Because aged retirees, laid-off workers, persons with disabilities, workers and workers that have been laid off from state-owned enterprises have less ability to change their marriages. State-owned enterprise staff and state unit staff are restricted by moral, discipline and evaluation factors of their companies and colleagues, while marriage and family are relatively stable. The new migrants are mainly youth. These youth are unmarried or recently married and are in honeymoon period, full of hope and image to the future. Therefore this part of residents' marriage and family are also very stable. The most part of the extraneous population renting here are taxi drivers, and some small shopkeepers, night market venders. Because their personal incomes are adequate to support a whole family, these three kinds of people often live together with their whole families in relative happiness. Compared with tenants in Village S, there are relatively few separations, and marriage and family are relatively more stable.

3. Resident stability and heterogeneity

Due to a large number of renting-house outsiders, residents in Community T are not particularly stable. "It is in great mobility. Because there are mostly rented houses and transitional houses, it is an anti-poverty community." However, because of the great quantity residents that have bought their houses in Community T, residential mobility is more stable in comparison to village S. Residents in Community T who are have extensive mobility prior to purchase of a house. As far as the issue of ethnic heterogeneity, there are few ethnic minorities in Community T. This is because most minorities are sinicized deeply on costume, diet and living habits, it is difficult to recognize who are Han people while who are the minorities remain without further contact. Ethnic heterogeneity based on nationality is not a significant problem. "I have no opinion of the minority; I even don't know who the minority is." As for the minorities which can obviously be distinguished from clothing and appearance we can find some problems from the talks of most interviewees especially the Hui nationality and the Uyghur.

There are few foreigners living in Community T, especially the Africa. So a lot of the interviewees talk about impression to foreigners in Guangzhou, especially blacks. "I never met a particularly bad foreigner, because of no special contact. Primarily their color is not same as ours. The overall impression is not good for blacks. Foreigner crimes are almost always by blacks. This is only hearsay."

On relationship between ethnic group and crime, more interviewees hold the opinion that "outlanders are related more to crime". While some think the blacks related more to crime. There are still interviewees believe that crime and ethnic relationship are not in necessary connection.

4. Social justice

(1) Social satisfaction

Objectively speaking, relative poverty in Community T is much more significant. It has been said before that Community T is a mixed residential area of extraneous floating population, new Hakka and local population. The local population mainly is the original anti-poverty housing residents in low education level, coupled with the lack of skill, which makes them incapable to change their housing. They can only passively stay in Community T. Commercial housing residents are generally in households in above average incomes, attracted by the indemnificatory-housing price. Besides, a great many owners purchase other commercial housing in suburbs or other place with relatively better condition and rent their housing in Community T. The tenants here are mainly taxi drivers and their families as well as businessmen in the Tangxia area, and pedlars from Henan. Generally speaking, sense of social injustice in mixed areas will be stronger. However, when asked about social justice, most of the interviewees, whether local residents or extraneous renters, regardless of being the upstart in middle class or laid-off workers, basically think society is fair. Although some believe that society is unfair, they recognize the social injustice is a normal social phenomenon, and think that changing the unfair reality relies on their own efforts. The author analyses that it is because villages-in-city surrounding Community T is much worse. In addition, inside and outside contrast displays residentials' relative satisfaction. The interviewees mostly agree with the old Chinese saying "In the land of blind the one-eyed man is king". Thus social discontent will reduce, and self-satisfaction will increase.

Case 10: NYP was born in Jiangxi. "I grow up in a common family in a small county. My parents are both workers. Besides parents there is still a younger sister in hometown. I am 32 years old, and was graduated from a medical school. After graduating I worked in county hospital in hometown. Then I went to Guangzhou as a nurse by introduction of my friends for higher wages. Actually I find that income in Guangzhou is higher than inland, but consumption here is also higher. And there are too many people to find a good job. So it is not easy for us inlanders moving in Guangzhou to survive here. Generally salary for nurse here is above 3000 yuan a month, but you still cannot afford buying a flat here. I have moved in Guangzhou four or five times. I was living in rent rooms before being married. I feel stabilized just after marriage." NYP shows great satisfied of marriage and family. "My husband and I got married very late. I was 30 years old when married. It is difficult to find a suitable person to be married with. My husband is a civil servant who has his own flat in Guangzhou. I am quite satisfied with our flat and residential environment."

(2) Social discrimination

Regards to discrimination, although Community T is a mixed residential area with big gap between the rich and the poor, participants in Community T generally feel no discrimination. This is because of living habits of residents in Community T. Although Community T in general is mixed of groups from each social class, the residents basically live orderly lives according to their personal income, occupation and social class. They generally only affiliate with people of their own groups, so that individual pride will increase. At the same time people in their own groups are rarely encountered discrimination or discriminate the others, and rarely feel discrimination. Of course, as widespread feelings in society, residents in Community T will "despise the poor and hold favor with the rich". Some residents still show discrimination on underprivileged population, especially migrant workers, and believe that their qualities are not high.

(3) Institutional injustice

Due to obvious distinction among individual characteristics, the attitudes of residents in Community T on institutional injustice are not exactly same. As residents living in Community T are in good economic situations, they can afford one family in the cost of living in Guangzhou. So that even outlanders are generally living together with his wife and children. It involves a lot of problems regarding social welfare and social policy. Preferential policies for school children and the elderly are directed to local residents with registered permanent residence of Guangzhou. Without a registered permanent residence, you are unable to use these benefits.

In front of the realistic interests, the stakeholders in Community T respond more strongly about social injustice. While for the individuals who are basically not in need of these privileges, or do not use these privileges regardless of the income, cannot enjoy preferential policies, they are able to tolerate those institutional injustices. The beneficiaries of institutional injustice consider it as a matter of course. "It is normal that preferential policies aimed primarily at citizens of

Guangzhou. Guangzhou cannot take in the increasing outsiders. This is normal. If all enjoy it, then Guangzhou cannot afford it. If so, many outlanders will come to Guangzhou, as well as public security in Guangzhou will naturally worsen."

5. Social capital

Social capital of residents in Community T is relative to individual economic condition, personal character, occupation and social status. For middle class, although they have few relatives in Guangzhou, they have many friends, former classmates, and colleagues. Thus, they have moderate social capital. Individuals in lower social classes in Guangzhou have relatively less social capital. XP in Case 9 as a security guard of Community T says he "has no *guanxi* in Guangzhou". Residents in Community T will firstly seek help from family members when facing difficulty. The friend circles are formed with those in equivalent social status.

Regardless of economic status and occupation, residents in Community T basically do not participate in any societies. While people in good economic situation would often take part in some activities, mainly dinner, classmate's party, school reunions and so on. The retired elderly's amateur life is relatively monotonous, as they almost do not participate in any association, or participate in any activities. People in relatively poor economic conditions "do not often parttake activities, because they have no money." While individuals have no much spare time "do not often take part in such activities, because they have no time."

6. Social order and social control

From the author's understanding and field observation, the order of the Community T is in its diversity. More adequate buildings than Village S are approached by broad roads. Grassy lawns are located in center community. Although it is an old community, it is clean and clear. However, due to the surrounding urban villages, the outside of the community is very chaotic and noisy with dawdling pedestrians and bargaining vendors here and there. It is clearly lack of order. Even in the interior of the community, social order shows obvious diversity. Old local residents, new immigrants and extraneous tenants all have occupied a considerable proportion. As living habits, economic status and occupational characteristic are not identical of these three types of residents, Community T shows distinctly different landscapes in day and night. During the daylight, when most of the residents are going out to work, few people can be seen in the empty neighborhood. Occasionally a group of local elders who play cards or mahjong in the overhead layer of the buildings make people yearn for this happy life. However, once after the dinner, the whole community is just like a big trade market. Almost all people go out in the opening for activities, even residents in outside urban-village flood into Community T. Walking dogs, kicking shuttlecocks, playing badminton, jogging, playing cards, playing mahjong, and drinking, are all activities that take pace in the community which and gives people a feeling of strange mixture.

Renters in Community T have different views on social order. Renting-housing individuals in middle class occupations, income and education think social order in Community T is very poor. While renters in low social class such as security guards, waiters and families of sole proprietorship are satisfied with social order as well as social control in the community. Householders think that social order and social control in Community T is good. The author analyses it may be by reason of that householders pay more attention to the satisfaction of the house, and pay less attention the community, so that relatively their requirements will be lower. Of course there are still some householders expressing discontentment on social order in Community T.

> Case 24 LP is unsatisfied with his neighborhood. "Poor environment. Almost all residents are temporary tenant. Most part of them is from Henan. There are almost no leisure centers in this community. All people are out playing badminton or shuttlecock on the road. It is full of people. Neighbors often play Mahjong, especially the porter of the bike shed on the first floor. He always invites people to play mahjong every night just upright below my bedroom. The noise prevents me from sleep all the night. I once could not tolerate any more so I threw a beer bottle downstairs then they just stopped for one night. The next day they restarted Mahjong again. To speak fairly it is clean and neat, especially during the daytime when most part of the residents go out to work. You can see some garbage here, but not too much. I have not seen the police, but the security can be seen in this community. But securities here are all arrogant, because residents here are mostly tenants from other cities. Securities are often seen chatting up *Dagongmei.*[3]"

> Case 1 is not satisfied with the community, but in fact the main reason is the flat he living in, "Actually I pay more attention to the size of the room. Our flat is too small. However, the community is also decent and there is not much noise and no bad boys. But some garbage and waste can be seen. And there are no public facilities in the community. No police station. But there are police office, neighborhood committee, and property management companies. Police can often be seen in the community, let alone securities. There are plenty of securities. Leaflets of security knowledge or other public safety messages could be distributed in the community. But it is not so often."

7. Social segregation and social exclusion

Community is a semi-gated community surrounded by a wall and has an entrance that is guarded. But the security guards never prevent strangers into the community. Its residential environment is much better than regions nearby. It causes residents in near urban village infuxing into the community. They share the environment and resources with residents in Community T, and bring series of public security problems. Ordinarily, residents in Community T should be quite agreeable with closed neighborhood. However, in the interview, the author finds out that most of the interviewees do no say yes or no on this question, it seems like it does not matter to them. There are only two female participants who support full-gated community.

Social exclusion is examined through consumption frequency and the feeling to expensive amusement places of interviewees. The author finds that different residents feel different of social exclusion. When asked about frequency

[3]Dagonmei (Chinese: 打工妹; pinyin: dǎgōngmèi) refers women factory workers especially from rural area to the urban.

of consumption in high end places, Middle class interviewees in Community T respond basically as "not much", "medium", "rarely", "moderate", "sometimes", "once in a while". When asked about feelings of high-level entertainment place, they basically do not feel anything special. Low class interviewees respond similar as most of interviewees in Village S, "I have not been there, and feel it is a very mysterious place. But I don't dare to enter. I am afraid I cannot afford it." Obviously, for middle class interviewees living in Community T, on one hand because their economic power is not enough, there is still a certain distance in real life from high-class estalishment. On the other hand, psychologically, they do not think they are far away from such places, and are little affected by social exclusion. While lower class residents feel like villagers in Village S and most of the residents are in poor economic situation and psychological inferiority, they would feel strong social exclusion.

8. Community cohesion, trust and fear

About community cohesion, feels of residents in Community T are various. Some feel a strong sense of community cohesion, while others think that there is little cohesion. However, one who actively takes part in the community would obviously feel more cohesive. About trust, no consensus of opinion is formed in participants in Community T. Despite housing status, income level and occupation type, one who lives alone in the community and do not know the neighbors would then do not trust neighbors and strangers in the neighborhood. If it is gregarious in the community, such as the original house distributed in housing system reform, the neighbors are the original official colleagues, or a group of people renting together such as security guards, waiters, and taxi drivers. As everyone is familiar with each other, the trust will behave more intense. XP in Case 9 as a security guard expresses trust on his neighbors and the neighborhood committee. All of the participants express distrust with strangers. However, there is still an exception. For traders, almost all of the participants express trust. The author analyses the reason may be that traders in this community are relatively stable compared with residents in it. Traders have dealings with almost all of the residents here, and are familiar with everybody. Thus it is easier to form a relationship of trust.

9. Tradition, morality and belief

Participants in Community T mostly think Chinese traditions are not well preserved, and this is not a phenomenon merely in Community T. While because Community T is an old neighborhood, and living in a part of local people, it still preserves parts of the traditional. The loss of Chinese traditions is now a widespread phenomenon all over China. In the process of rapid social transition, the fall of tradition inevitably emerges when the old traditions are abandoned while new ethical values have not formed. Participants in Community T believe it is normal. When asked about money and morality, the interviewees in Community T respond diversely. Some worship money, some advocate morality, while the others balance money and morality. Only the older members prefer morals over money, "firstly morality, secondly money."

When asked about money and morality, the interviewees in Community T respond diversely. Some worship money, some advocate morality, some balance money and morality. Only the older prefer more moral than money, "morality is above money."

In view of belief, Chinese are widespread lack of faith; the same Village S. T community participants have no faith. All the young participants bluntly say they have no belief. Older people experienced more severe social changes are more contradictory in the belief. "Now I am more confused".

10. Language

Generally, languages used in Community T are not uniform, including in Mandarin, Cantonese and various local dialects. New immigrants generally speak Mandarin, while speaking dialects among fellow-townsmen. Local natives mainly speak Cantonese. Because Guangzhou is a Cantonese society, most interviewees who cannot speak Cantonese represent that language will produce effect for their work and life.

However the language effect on residents in Community T is not so obvious. Residents in Community T depend less on language because of their education degree, economic capacity and occupation type. "At the beginning it had a little influence on me. Now there are basically no effects. I am seldom engaged in the local people's case, so Mandarin can be enough." (By Case 1). And from some of the interviewee's words, the author feels some residents in Community T have more initiative in front of different languages. Some of the new immigrants even despise those can only speak Cantonese and cannot speak Mandarin. "If I meet those speaking Cantonese to me, I will tell him directly I don't understand. Please speak mandarin!"

5.2.3 Community Q

1. Employment and unemployment

Residents in Community Q belong to social upper class economically. Their average annual income is over one million Yuan. They commonly are business people, leaders of state-owned enterprises or governmental offices, university teachers, and freelancers. Unemployment has no impact on them. Some of them may spend three years on a single business without payment, who also can be said to be in the long-term unemployed; some unemployed person herself is a full-time housewife, and is enough to lead a decent life by her husband's income. To residents in Community Q, unemployment affects them inconspicuously, unless economic bankruptcy. Otherwise their existing wealth is enough for the whole family maintaining a comfortable life for a long time.

Case 17: CFL was born in Guangzhou with a Guangzhou *hukou*. "42-year-old. Bachelor. After graduation from Beijing University I returned to Guangzhou to work

> in the provincial propaganda department, and later resigned to go into business. As to my income, how to say, now I have a dozen of houses in Guangzhou and a factory in Dongguan. Look at this set of mahogany furniture. It cost more than three million yuan. My family condition is good. I have been very satisfied with current status. My wife and two daughters live with me." CFL believes that "unemployment means broken source of income to the poor, but it is not a matter to the rich. The rich can do not go out for work in several years." In fact, according to my understanding, CFL also did not go out to work these years, but he is not worried about the problem of unemployment.

Participants in Community Q hold more objective attitudes to unemployment. WCZ in Case 21 thinks "unemployment and reemployment are normal flow of laber force." Some respondents even concern about living conditions of the poor in unemployment. CFL in Case 7 believes that, "people who have no money would commit crime". LHP in Case 22 believes that unemployment effects seriously on the poor, "if his basic life is in trouble, you can't expect he would not commit crime. He must solve the basic living problem."

2. Marriage and family

Young interviewees in Community Q are generally in good marriage and happy family status. For middle-aged participants, some are divorced, but basically can find good remarried objects. CFL in Case 17 divorced his wife for various reasons prior to his success; after he became rich he met a university girl and soon married after the girl graduated. Now they have a good life with their daughters. Although with relatively high divorce and remarry rates, there are few problem children in family within Community Q. Case 17 CFL's two half-blood daughters are very clever and docile.

3. Resident stability and ethnic heterogeneity

Residents in Community Q are very stable. "Basically almost all are private housing. Few renting houses are rented long-term." Residents living in Community Q differ not quite on social status. They are basically in the upper status of society.

On ethnic heterogeneity, there are few minorities in the community. "Even almost none". So that ethnic heterogeneity based on domestic nationality is not significant. About the racial ethnic heterogeneity, foreigner residents in Community Q are not a large percentage of the population. "If any, they are quite successful." Thus ethnic heterogeneity on race is also not significant. When asked the relationship between crime and ethnic groups, most of the interviewees believe that crime is not necessarily linked to ethnic groups, but to the economy and education degree.

4. Social justice

(1) Satisfaction

Participants in Community Q are satisfied with their lives. The self-made successful persons think the society is fair. The most frequent sentence said by CFL in Case 17 in conversations with the author is: "I have been very satisfied with the present situation." He believes that "society is fair, and life is a deadly struggle in which only the fittest survive." He repeatedly stresses that he is "very satisfied".

(2) Social discrimination

Due to high income, excellent education, and decent jobs, belonging to the upper class of society, participants in Community Q do not feel discrimination, and basically represent "a sense of superiority" compared with others. WCZ in Case 21 came from Hubei to Guangzhou just a few years ago, but he has not suffered from discrimination as an outlander.

(3) Institutional injustice

Interviewees in Community Q encounter little institutional injustice. Even if it is present, it is not a problem for them. Institutional injustice they encounter can easily be solved with money or *guanxi*.

5. Social capital

In three types of communities surveyed, residents in Community Q have the most abundant social capital. CFL in Case 17 thinks he has "a wide range of social relations in Guangzhou." When faced with difficulty they would resolve it by themselves first. Residents in Community Q regardless of economic status and occupations basically do not participate in any associations, while they would often take part in some activities, mainly dinner or various entertainments. As for Interviewees as living in Community Q, "social relations are relatively simple, mainly in one circle." Although with simple *guanxi*, they also think that the social relation networks are relatively on high levels, "people I am in contact with are of very high quality."

6. Social order and social control

Community Q is found in good order through field observation. The interviewees also agree with me. As for social control, both formal social control and informal social control are weak in Community Q. Policemen do generally not emerge in the community; let alone official social control mechanism like police stations or public security bureaus. "Security guards basically stay in the gated area; they do not go about inside the community." However, crime rates in Community Q are the lowest in the three selected communities. It is almost zero. Thus the good order of the community can only be attributed to the strict closed management and social isolation.

7. Social isolation and social exclusion

Community Q is under strict closed management. The author feels it profoundly when entering Community Q. The security guards at the gate ensure there is an appointment via contacting the owners by telephone. Then they let the author in. Interviewees in Community Q strongly support the closed management. They also do not feel the social exclusion.

8. Cohesion, trust and fear

Residents in Community Q feel the strongest neighborhood cohesion among the three selected communities. Interviewees in Community Q think they are the members of the community with no exception. The cohesion is also higher than that in Village S and Community T. Fear of crime in Community Q is in minimum. The interviewees generally say they would not fear and do not worry about encountering crime in the community. But as for trust, they generally still express distrust to their neighbors and strangers.

9. Tradition, morality and belief

As mentioned above, architectural style of Community Q is of the traditional Wannan style. However, not many interviewees think Community Q preserves a bit of Chinese traditions. Of course, this view is resasonable considering the universal loss of tradition in China. China maintains the relative cultural self-contempt brought out by long-term economic weakness, which makes the new generation reluctant to inherit the tradition from the old, whether good or bad. As for the relations between money and morality, participants in Community Q tend to present that both them are co-existing. When the both are incompatible they would select moral.

"A mature society should probably be that: either the public or officials should reverence spiritual belief (neither religion, nor so-called '-ism', but the most basic moral bottom line as a man), as well as have the scruple about institutional constraint. Scruple, who can without fear. However, in current Chinese society, these two aspects are lost" (Zhang 2007). Thanks to the absence of belief of religion its validity is getting declined continually. Except for an interviewee admitting himself as a believer, interviewees in Community Q are generally atheist. Slightly different with interviewees in Village S and Community T, interviewees in Community Q are able to recognize the problem, and associate it with the social problems in China.

10. Language

As a whole, residents in Community Q use both Mandarin and Cantonese as daily language. Language has no effect on them, and they also show no discrimination against groups using different languages.

References

Du, Q., Chen, L., & Chang, C. (2005). Shipai village in Guangzhou City: Urban village reform exploration—village committee replaced by village enterprise. *China Economic Weekly* (27). 杜青耘, 陈丽科, 常菁, (2005). 广州市石牌村: "城中村"改制探索——村企业取代村委会,《中国经济周刊》, 2005, 27.

Li, Y., Chen, Y., & Li, H. (2007). Closed or open: Spatial analysis of urban village—A case study of village Chebei in Guangzhou. *City Issues*, *7*(144), 63–70. 黎云, 陈洋, 李郇. (2007). 封闭与开放: 城中村空间解析——以广州市车陂村为例, 《城市问题》, (7): 33.

Zheng, H. (2007). *Social discrimination and people-oriented a sociological analysis: Costs reduction and improvement promotion, sociology and its deep philosophy* (p. 193). Beijing: Beijing Normal University Press. 郑杭生. (2007). 社会歧视和以人为本——一个社会学的分析, 减缩代价与增促进步, 《社会学及其深层理念》, 北京: 北京师范大学出版社, 193.

Chapter 6
Conclusions and Future

6.1 Conclusions

6.1.1 Economy and Crime

We can draw a conclusion from aforementioned analysis that social stratification has emerged on economic basis in Chinese society. People in the same social status dwell in same neighborhoods for similar personal income. Thus residential areas for different social status emerge geographically in urban space, such as rich districts, civilian areas and slums. The relationship between economy and crime is still puzzling. Actually I cannot induce the concrete micro-relationship between crime and economy through criminal spatial distribution and the interviews I have done previously. I cannot conclude whether economy determines crime, or if crime affects economy. What I have found, is that the total number of various crimes in rich districts is much lower than it in the slums. It is not that the rich commits less crime than the poor; it is that better safety precautions as well as strict community closure excluding the outlanders in rich districts. However, economic conditions of the rich are much better than the poor; they have no issues with one another. Thus, the rich would not break the law for basic survival whereas it can be conceived that the poor would.

6.1.2 Cultural Conflict and Symbiosis

In periods of social transition with rapid economic growth, a community is neither as stable as a Chinese traditional rural village, nor composed of a single homogeneous group. There exists acculturation in the three types of communities

H. Xiong, *Urban Crime and Social Disorganization in China*,
DOI 10.1007/978-981-287-859-5_6

examined. Individuals or groups with different cultural background enter a community and produce direct or indirect contact and influence. Large-scale changes occur on cultural traits of one or more varied groups. Some increase, some decrease, and some disappear by substitution. Cultural conflict and symbiosis are inevitable during colonial acculturation. This kind of cultural conflict and symbiosis is mostly between local culture and immigrant culture.

People in Village S and Community T both can be divided into two groups, one local group, and the other immigrant group. As for the local group, residential individuals are much closer to high population homogeneity, especially local residents in Village S. As they are belonging to a natural village society originally, and are descendants of the four original families; they are relatives of each other and do more social intercourse. They have common living areas and life styles, same traditions and culture, as well as use same language. Thus they jointly constitute a wholly stable unity. With the acceleration of social transition, population mobility is more frequent as well as immigrant population more and more enter the community. The total of immigrant population catches up and even preponderates over local population. Then cultural conflict appears when two or more kinds of culture meet together. As each type of culture cannot conquer the others, the outcome must be culture symbiosis and coexisting. Either Village S as an urban-village, Community T as an anti-poverty community, or Community Q with residents of similar cultural source, local culture is in a dominant situation. Although the total of the immigrant population would outnumber local population, they are from different provinces and diversified by different types of culture, such as Northeast culture, Northwest culture, Lianghu culture, etc. Thus each immigrant culture is weaker than local culture in intensity and influence. Basically, the current culture in each community is a new formed culture with multiplicity, complexity and otherness.

In general, Chinese culture is basically homogeneous inheriting Confucianism. As for religion, most Chinese are antitheists. Believers mainly believe in religions with comparably more inclusiveness such as Buddhism, Taoism and Christianism. However, cultural conflict based on religion and race difference still exists, and gradually become a problem that should be treated seriously along with the reform and internationalization of Guangzhou.

6.1.3 Label, Discrimination and Belongingness

Conflict usually comes into being when people in different economic status, social status and cultural background gather together. This conflict is embodied by stress, discrimination, fear and repugnance. On a worldwide scale, racially discriminatory laws have been abolished along with the erection of the black regime in South Africa. Special ethnic discrimination symbols in some countries are only the extension of traditional customs and are not legally accepted. But in actual social life discrimination based on nationality and racism still exists. For example, in the interview, many Chinese think that blacks are relatively more related with crime, while whites are not. Many Hanrians think Xinjiang people, Uyghur and Hui are closely linked with crime. This is an evident label.

This so-called "label" is in actuality a social stereotype, which is a fixed belief about specific social groups or types of individual in the cognitive process, and used as a foundation to judge and evaluate their personality. Stereotypes can have both negative and positive impact on individuals. Labels are not necessarily correct, and may not necessarily have factual basis. "Labeling" is just a cognitive process. An incorrect label will produce discrimination among different groups, and strengthen this kind of discrimination. From the interview the author finds that the labels by the native to outlanders may be: easier to commit crime, more prostitution, of relatively low quality, poor, and illiterate. Outlanders would label the native as; snobbish and indifferent. Hanrians may label minorities especially Uyghur and Hui as: easier to commit crime, arbitrary, involved in AI-Qaida, troublesome, discord, selling lamb shashlik and hand-pulled noodles, and many say they think the government should halt affirmative-action programs for minorities. Chinese may label the black as: prone to commit crime, from poor countries and regions, smelly body odour with unattractive skin colors. While other labels to the white are completely different: much richer, fewer crimes, good education, and decent occupation.

On the whole, discrimination based solely on race, nationality does not really exist. Though foreigners, Uyghur, Tibetan, Hui and so on can be distinguished from appearance and clothing, difference of appearance and dress are not the root of the label. Its truth lies in the difference of social status including economic condition, occupation and education. As the president of an African country says, "gold has no skin color". Among the groups in the same economic class with similar occupation and educational degree, even if there are labels to each other, mutual discrimination will be much less. As a group, why the local people discriminate against outlanders, Chinese discriminate against the black and respect the white, and Hanrians discriminate against minorities? It is nothing more than that the latters are considered "poor" with lower personal income, inferior occupation, lower education degree. This kind of discrimination is particularly evident in the lower income areas such as Village S and Community T that people are living in. Outlanders in Village S are basically floating workers, and feel strong social discrimination themselves. While outlanders in high-end residential Community Q are basically social elite, so there are no problems of discrimination.

Besides the discrimination on aspects of economic and social class, another type of discrimination is hard to overcome for the individual. It is institutional discrimination. In present Chinese society, the most obvious institutional discrimination is the registered permanent residence system. A strict separation system between urban and rural had been implemented in China for long. Thus to change an agricultural registered permanent residence to urban is almost impossible. This kind of situation basically behaves the primary level in reforming and opening.

It is also very difficult to change registered permanent residence from one city to another. Although with frequent population migration and the relaxation of registered permanent residence system, difference between the urban and rural is gradually disappearing. Registered permanent residence no longer has the original symbolic meaning of identity, but it still to some extent means different social classes, marking higher income, better living conditions, more preferential conditions of admission to school for children and more convenient public services, and more public welfare.

In addition to the institutional discrimination such as household registration system, separation effects of language cannot be ignored. China has a vast territory and an extremely long history. The dialects differ large between each other, unlike American English which only differs with accents. For all people, other local dialects are sometimes impossible to understand, let alone to speak. The author once spoke with a local taxi driver. He was resisting popularization of Mandarin, because learning Mandarin to him is just like "learning a foreign language". From the language it is easy to distinguish individual's social identity. "One speaking Cantonese is a native Canton, or stays in Guangzhou for a long time; one speaking Mandarin is an outlander. Good Mandarin generally goes with good education. One speaking dialect is fairly new in Guangzhou, perhaps did not go to the University, as University men now all speak just mandarin." Thus the language imperceptibly becomes a prominent label.

The population categorised by labels have some classificatory characteristics, and would not form a close-knit group even within a neighborhood. Moreover, the label's meaning is significant. These labeled categories, especially the discriminatorily labeled category, will feel the difference with other demographic categories in many aspects of social life. Ethnic heterogeneity and racial heterogeneity, of course, are mainly cultural heterogeneity caused by differences in economy and social class, resulting in discrimination, stress and conflict, and is one of the factors influencing crime.

Cultural conflict is probably one of reasons the floating population have no strong sense of belonging in the community. But we must see that in my survey of the three communities, besides local villagers in Village S, interviewees regardless of economic conditions and whether settling in Guangzhou all express no sense of belonging. As for this problem, economic condition no longer appears to be a fundamental factor. The interaction between people and informal social control of community organizations will have more important influence on sense of belonging. This sense of belonging within the community is closely related to the community environment, living condition, interpersonal interaction, resident satisfaction, frequency and effect of community activities, and the length of time settling in the area.

In previous criminal spatial geographic analysis the author has concluded that the crime rate is relatively higher in transient floating population dwelling areas. The author here tries to analyze the reasons as the end of the discussion. First of all, outlanders leave their original community and come to Guangzhou. Due to the economic and institutional reasons, they are unable to settle in Guangzhou and also cannot get registered permanent residence. Thus the outlanders without registered permanent residence are called "floating population". The floating population has gotten out from original control, while they cannot really integrate into the social life of new community. They have no housing, no *hukou*, and cannot regard themselves as real members of the community. Coupled with the harsh residential environment, they are eager to move out. Hence, these members have no real sense of belonging to the community.

Relaxed regulation and control render criminals and offenders totally unrestricted. While the lack of a sense of belonging makes nobody preventing crime in the neighborhood. No one pays attention to public interest, as well as fear of crime would spread throughout the whole community. Estrangement and discrimination are generated by cultural conflict as well as the psychological sense of inferiority. A large part of persons in unhealthy emotion are hostile to other groups or even the whole society. It can also generate crime and deviance. The extraneous population lives in a small circle, which are mostly based on fellow-townsman or colleague relationships. Furthermore, their fellow-townsmen or colleagues themselves are often left at the bottom of heap, and can give them little social support. Due to institutional discrimination and policy tendency, extraneous population, especially floating population faces problems in governmental and social assistance. Strain and stress are easily generated due to poor economic condition, relatively limited social resource and restricted human capital. Extraneous population would encounter huge pressure in process of cultural adaptation and localization. Once the basic living runs into trouble, crime and deviance would possibly take place.

6.2 Future

At this point, my research has come to an end. However, study is just beginning on spatial distribution characteristics of urban crime and relationship between crime and social disorganization on community level.

The main research defect of this book is about data. Officially public criminal data is only the total number of criminal cases and police offences every year. Only Haizhu, Yuexiu, Tianhe and Liwan publicly publish their criminal case-filing number on level of district. As far as District Baiyun with "the largest criminal case-filling number", its actual criminal case-filling number cannot be obtained. So that case density map cannot be made according to official criminal data at the level of district. Criminal data on level of street are more difficult to get through official channels. Therefore, research can be continued only through news gathering method in such cases.

Research shortcomings are in data, and the author tries to adopt various methods to make the conclusion reflect the realistic regulations to a certain extent. News reports were in long duration, and covered most of published ordinary criminal cases and police offences, so that information bias generated by news filter can be avoided to a certain degree in spite of defective case representation. On one hand, due to the sensitivity of news work, cases not considered as crimes or even police offences by police would be reported by newspapers, so that the cases not included in official data are detailed included in news-gathered data. On the other hand, this paper focuses on the question of e relationship between crime and social disorganization. While social disorganization is not only reflected in crimes defined by criminal law, but also reflected in deviant behaviors and is not considered as crimes by criminal law, cases calculated in this book should accurately be "criminal and deviant cases". Although the collected samples are limited in number, and can only reflect real regulations to a certain extent, whose comprehensiveness and accuracy need to be improved, especially that the reliability is questionable, this kind of method can ensure the research to be carried on although accurate criminal materials are basically not available, as well as to afford a kind of research method to develop spatial criminology in China. Especially in China where criminal data is treated as national secret, researchers can try to use news gathering method to carry on relative study of criminology.

From the spatial distribution of cases reported in SMD, crime paradigm is different between Guangzhou and Chicago. Urban spatial distribution of crime in Chicago shows a clear pattern of concentric circles. Business district are the core. Close to the business district is the transition zone, which is affected by the outward expansion of the central business district. Outside the transition zone is the workers living area, mainly compiled of collective buildings. These households mainly migrate from the transition zone, so they can be more easily accessible and continue out-migrating employment places. The next is a medium-end residential area which is mainly inhabited by the middle class. They are usually small businessmen, professionals, managers and government officials, dwelling in separate houses, service flats and hotels. The outer ring is a rich area with a high-quality residential area. The upper class and Belgravia's suburb residence is located here. There are a number of small satellite cities. People living here are mostly working in the central business district, commuting within the two places. The transition zone was once a wealthy upper-class residential district, and later as a result of the invasion the central business district, the living environment has deteriorated. Upper-class families gradually moved out, as well as lower-class people migrated inwards. Once elegant residential areas became slums inhabited by the poor immigrants. This area also became the area in city of most severe poverty, corruption, and crime.

As for Guangzhou, spatial distribution of crime shows irregular layered-circle pattern. Urban center commercial district has the highest crime rate, which is decreased gradually from the center to the outward. And the layered circle is not uniform gradient, with hot spots existing. Hot spots in urban center are mostly commercial areas, old residential districts and urban villages.

The afore-mentioned Chicago school is one of the earliest explorers of urban sociology. They do commendable work; however, it is difficult to avoid the theoretical deficiencies. When introducing the ecological method to analyze urban structure, although Park also has realized that human society is different from the plant and animal world, in the actual research he imperceptibly copies the competition rules dominating the ecological world. Park thinks economic competition is the only factor deciding the distribution of urban population and institutions. In fact, in the human society, cultural factors such as the residents' analysis of the residential area and traditions can all affect the utilization form of urban land. Especially in such a country extremely respecting collectivism as China, the law make excludes individuals from land ownership. The ownership of state-owned land belongs to the state, while collective land ownership belongs to the villagers collectively in unit of village. Therefore, the urban expansion process is not only an economically decided "natural" phenomenon. It is where the institutional policy factors play the largest roles. As for the urban village, land in it owned by all villagers collectively, is not in free flow and free trade. While there are almost no developers that could integrally move it with sufficient economic power. So urban village remains in its place, regardless of whether developing into rich areas or reducing to slums. Consequently "transition zone" formed by natural invasion and succession of residents does not appear in Chinese cities. On the contrary there are several criminal black spots existing in urban China.

Differences between Guangzhou and Chicago reveal that no theory can cover every field and contain everything. There is also no urban feature can be fully applied to another city. It must be "concrete analysis of concrete problem" in our study and policy formulation. Specific detailed investigation should be done under the guidance of macroscopic theory, which is especially deficient in social science in current China.

As for the problem of the relationship between crime and social disorganization, the fundamental concepts are confused and indistinct. "Social disorganization" in this book is divided into two levels: spatial structural disorganization and social structural disorganization, which makes a new interpretation of the social disorganization theory, and promotes the most complex concept of "social disorganization" a step forward to more clearly defined.

This book tries to cover various impact factors related to social disorganization, including economic status, marriage and family, resident mobility and ethnic heterogeneity, justice and discrimination, social capital, social order and social control, social isolation and social exclusion, community cohesion, trust and fear, tradition, morality and religion, as well as language. Although it is inevitable that discussion on all factors is not deep enough, this preliminary analysis could lay the foundation for later research and make the future research to be conducted on a more in-depth analysis. In addition, when studying problems of Chinese social disorganization, it needs to be considered in future criminological research how to closely link criminology with sociology, demography, spatial geography, urban ecology and other related disciplines.

The study may be improved if two types of data and analyses in the book can be linked more tightly. Recently, a new research direction is to integrate the spatial analysis with the community research on crime. A spatial pattern of crime has emerged through the spatial analysis in the study. A critical question is why such a pattern is observed. For instance, why do the northern districts had more criminal cases reported than those in the southern districts of the city? In other words, why does the spatial distribution point to a certain direction in the city? To answer the question, research may be needed to examine the community structural characteristics and processes in different districts. People could speculate the answers in terms of their daily experience or common sense, however, a rigorous study is needed to collect valid and reliable data to address the issue. The study has two types of data and analyses. One is the data gathered from the reports of criminal cases by the newspaper Southern Metropolis Daily during January 1 to December 31, 2014 and the spatial analysis of 1483 criminal cases reported. The other is the information collected from the author's field work in three communities of the city and the qualitative analysis of the information. Linking these two types of analyses may indeed represent significant contribution to the literature. However, due to limitation of time, fund support and material obtaining, it would be focus work of the further research.

Appendix A
Table of Case Classification[1]

Place	Place type	Case	Behaviorer
Jingtai Street, Baiyun	A	Leaped to his own death	A 40-year-old taxi driver
Songzhou Street, Baiyun	A	Sudden death due to drug abuse	A middle-aged man
Songzhou Street, Baiyun	A	Leaped to her own death	A 18-year-old girl
Tangjing Street, Baiyun	A	Accidentally fall dead	A 25-year-old woman from Jilin
Tonghe Street, Baiyun	A	Electrocuted accidentally	A 54-year-old dweller
Xinshi Street, Baiyun	A	Murder and throwing body	35-year-old man without any identity
Xinshi Street, Baiyun	A	Accidentally fall dead	34-year-old shopkeeper from Fujian
Zhongluotan Street, Baiyun	A	Dead accidentally	22-year-old male dweller
Dashi Street, Panyu	A	Suicide	Middle-aged female dweller
Panyu	A	Burglary	20-year-old man
Panyu	A	Intentional injury	Debtor
Panyu	C	Traffic accident	Security guard
Dashi Street, Panyu	A	Gun robbery	Three men
Dashi Street, Panyu	A	Leaped to his own death	A drunk man
Dashi Street, Panyu	A	Suicide	Female dweller
Panyu	A	Leaped to her death	50-year-old woman
Nancun Street, Panyu	A	Home invasion robbery	A criminal group
Shiqi Street, Panyu	A	Vandalizing and intentional injury	Four men with west Guangxi accent

A means residential land, B means commercial land, C means land for road and square, etc.

[1]Two pages are cited from the whole table.

H. Xiong, *Urban Crime and Social Disorganization in China*,
DOI 10.1007/978-981-287-859-5

Appendix B
Table of Case Number on Level of Street

H. Xiong, *Urban Crime and Social Disorganization in China*,
DOI 10.1007/978-981-287-859-5

Yuexiu: 125	Huangpu: 30	Liwan: 71	Haiyzhu: 161	Tianhe: 197	Baiyun: 250	Panyu: 111	Huadu 60	Luogang: 25	Nansha: 10
Hongqiao 8	Yuzhu 4	Shamian 1	Chigang 18	Shahe 8	Sanyuanli 7	Shiqiao 28	Xinhua 29	Xiagang 1	Nansha 2
Guangwei 4	Huangpu 1	Hualin 6	Xingang 12	Wushan 10	Songzhou 11	Qiaonan 0	Timian 0	Lianhe 8	Wanqingsha 1
Beijing 10	Nangang 3	Duobao 2	Binjiang 33	Chebei 19	Jingtai 9	Donghuan 0	Huashan 1	Dongqu 2	Hengli 1
Liurong 2	Dasha 10	Changhua 4	Sushe 2	Yuancun 24	Tongde 1	Shatou 1	Tanbu 1	Luogang 5	Huangge 6
Liuhua 22	Wenchong 4	Fengyuan 2	Haizhuang 4	Shipai 11	Huangshi 20	Luopu 0	Chini 2	Jiulong 4	
Dongfeng 4	Hongshan 2	Longjin 3	Fengyang 9	Tianhenan 7	Tangjing 7	Dashi 24	Shiling 22	Yonghe 2	
Guangta 3	Shuidong 2	Jinhua 1	Longfeng 4	Linhe 9	Xinshi 28	Xiaoguwei 12	Huadong 2		
Shishu 2	Changzhou 0	Caihong 3	Shayuan 3	Shadong 1	Tonghe 10	Nancun 1	Yayao 0		
Daxin 2	Lilian 0	Nanyuan 2	Ruibao 11	Xinghua 15	Jingxi 14	Zhongcun 6			
Renmin 9		Xicun 3	Jianghai 5	Tangxia 14	Yongping 14	Shawan 3			
Donghu 7		Zhanqian 3	Nanhuaxi 1	Liede 2	Jinsha 3	Shiqi 9			
Nonglin 4		Lingnan 4	Nanshitou 1	Xiancun 16	Shijing 29	Shilou 4			
Dadong 1		Qiaozhong 7	Jiangnanzhong 3	Tianyuan 8	Jiahe 16	Xinzao 1			
Datang 3		Weikou 1	Changgang 8	Huangcun 2	Junhe 9	Hualong 0			
Zhuguang 2		Huadi 1	Nanzhou 21	Yuangang 2	Jianggao 9	Lanhe 2			
Baiyun 5		Chajiao 0	Pazhou 5	Zhuji 5	Renhe 8	Dongcong 3			
Jianshe 0		Baihedong 2	Guanzhou 6	Xintang 1	Zhongluotan 13	Dagang 3			
Huale 1		Shiweitang 10	Huazhou 7	Longdong 19	Taihe 30				
Meihuacun 7		Dongjiao 1		Fenghuang 1					
Huanghuagang 7		Dongsha 2		Qianjin 4					
Kuangquan 4		Hailong 2		Changan 0					
Dengfeng 4		Zhongnan 1							

Appendix C
Table of Population, Area and Density of Case

Baiyun	Number of cases	Areas (km^2)	Population (10,000 persons)	Case/area	Case/ population
Sanyuanli	6	6.8	8.5	0.88	0.71
Songzhou	12	9.5	2.2	1.26	5.45
Jingtai	9	11.4	7.17	0.79	1.26
Tongde	1	3.59	11.2	0.28	0.09
Huangshi	20	5.71	2.4	3.50	8.33
Tangjing	7	4.18	10	1.67	0.70
Xinshi	27	10	8	2.70	3.38
Tonghe	11	24.25	5.2	0.45	2.12
Jingxi	14	5.51	4	2.54	3.50
Yongping	14	16.3	2	0.86	7.00
Jinsha	3	10.2	1.07	0.29	2.80
Shijing	29	39.28	6.5	0.74	4.46
Jiahe	16	9.8	2.66	1.63	6.02
Junhe	2	19.8	2.8	0.10	0.71
Jianggao	9	95.71	11.1	0.09	0.81
Renhe	8	74.39	12	0.11	0.67
Taihe	30	155.37	7.13	0.19	4.21
Zhongluotan	13	169.4	3.4	0.08	3.82

H. Xiong, *Urban Crime and Social Disorganization in China*,
DOI 10.1007/978-981-287-859-5

Appendix D
Interview Outline 1

1. Q: Excuse me, where are you from? Where are you born? Where is your household residence?
2. Q: How about your family condition? Please introduce your family members?
3. Q: Please briefly introduce your personal status: age, education, growth experience.
4. Q: How many years have you been in Guangzhou?
5. Q: Why did you come to Guangzhou formerly?
6. Q: How did you come to Guangzhou? For example, did you come here by yourself, or with relatives, friends, fellow-townsmen? Or introduced by classmates?
7. Q: What's your impression to Guangzhou formerly?
8. Q: What's your impression to Guangzhou now?
9. Q: Are you going to live in Guangzhou permanently?
10. Q: Which job do you have after coming to Guangzhou? And how about the income?
11. Q: Have you been unemployed? How do you think about unemployment in Guangzhou?
12. Q: Have you thought about making profit through illegal means? And how about the others?
13. Q: Which community do you live in?
14. Q: Is the house you living in purchased or rented?
15. Q: Introduce the area and structure of your house. How many people live in your house? What is the relationship with your roommates?
16. Q: Are you satisfied with your house? What is the reason?
17. Q: Your marital status? Have you a happy family?
18. Q: How long are you living in this community? How many times did you move house in Guangzhou?
19. Q: Whether are residents in the community stable? Do you feel the neighbors often change?

H. Xiong, *Urban Crime and Social Disorganization in China*,
DOI 10.1007/978-981-287-859-5

20. Q: Are there many outlanders in this community? Talk about your perception to them.
21. Q: Are there many foreigners in this community? Talk about your perception to them.
22. Q: Are there many minorities in this community? Talk about your perception to them.
23. Q: What relationship do you think between foreigners, outlanders, minorities and crime?
24. Q: What types of communities are there near your neighborhood? (Are there high-end residential neighborhoods or slums?) Do you feel fair comparing with communities nearby?
25. Q: How about your social networks in Guangzhou?
26. Q: How many your relatives and friends in your community?
27. Q: Have you participated in any societies? Do you often take part in any activities?
28. Q: What kind of persons are there in your friend circle?
29. Q: Whom would you turn to first when you encounter difficulties?
30. Q: Are you satisfied with your community? And the reasons?
31. Q: Is your community noisy? Will Neighbors often have a noisy party or play mahjong?
32. Q: Are there many deviant juvenile in your community?
33. Q: Are there drunk or bum wandering in your community?
34. Q: Is there clean and tidy in your community? Are there any garbage and waste?
35. Q: Are public facilities well preserved in your community? Are there any graffiti and small posters?
36. Q: Is there any police station in your community?
37. Q: Are there any other judicial organs or administrative organs in or around your community?
38. Q: Can you often see the police in your community?
39. Q: Can you often see security guards or public security patrol in your community?
40. Q: Have safety knowledge leaflets or other public safety messages been distributed in your community?
41. Q: Is your community under closed management? Are there any restrictions to outsiders?
42. Q: Are communities nearby under closed management? Are there any restrictions to outsiders?
43. Q: How frequent do you consume in high-end places?
44. Q: Have you any experiences refused to enter somewhere? Talk about your feelings.
45. Q: Have you considered yourself as citizen of Guangzhou?
46. Q: Have you been treated as outlander when going out, such as shopping, repast, etc. Do you feel discriminated or misunderstood?

47. Q: There are some preferential policies for persons with household residence in Guangzhou. Please talk about your perception.
48. Q: What is the social care you mostly need as a outlander?
49. Q: How do you think about public security of Guangzhou?
50. Q: How do you think about public security in your community? How about crime rate in it?
51. Q: Have you heard of surrounding neighbor committing crime?
52. Q: Do you worry about encountering crimes in your community?
53. Q: Do you fear about walking alone at night in your community?
54. Q: Will you come to prevent if you see somebody encountering crime (be stolen, robbed, killed or other)?
55. Q: Do you think you are member of your community?
56. Q: Do you trust your neighbor? For example, will you let him/her to care children for you?
57. Q: Do you trust strangers in the community? Do you think they will not pose a threat to you?
58. Q: Do you trust the neighborhood committee? Do you think the members actually serve for the community? Do you think they won't corrupt or commit irregularities?
59. Q: Do you trust traders in the community? Do you think they don't cheat?
60. Q: Talk about your views on tradition. Is Chinese tradition well preserved in your community?
61. Q: Talk about your views on moral. Which do you prefer between money and moral?
62. Q: Talk about your views on religion. Have your beliefs changed or disappeared? How about your ideal?
63. Q: What is the language you usually use?
64. Q: What is the popular language in your community? Cantonese or Mandarin?
65. Q: How do you think about people speaking Cantonese, Mandarin or foreign dialects?
66. Q: Talk about how language affects you.

Appendix E
Interview Outline 2

1. Talk about your basic status.
2. Talk about your employment.
3. Talk about your housing conditions.
4. Talk about your family.
5. Are residents in your community stable?
6. Talk about your views on outlanders, foreigners and minorities in your community. What is the relationship do you think between crime and them?
7. What types of communities are there near your neighborhood? (Are there high-end residential neighborhoods or slums?) Do you feel fair comparing with communities nearby?
8. How about your social networks in Guangzhou?
9. How about social order in your community? Are you satisfied with your community?
10. Is the neighborhood committee efficient? Why? How do you think to promote the management?
11. How do you think about police in community? And the security guards?
12. Talk about your views on enclosed management of community.
13. How frequent do you consume in high-end places? Talk about your feels.
14. Have you been treated as outlander when going out, such as shopping, repast, etc.? Do you feel discriminated or misunderstood?
15. Will you discriminate outlander?
16. There are some preferential policies for persons with household residence in Guangzhou. Please talk about your perception.
17. How do you think about public security of Guangzhou?
18. How do you think about public security in your community? Do you fear?
19. Have you heard of surrounding neighbors or friends encountering crime?
20. Will you come to prevent if you see somebody encountering crime?
21. Do you feel cohesion of your community? Do you think you are member of your community? Please talk in details.

H. Xiong, *Urban Crime and Social Disorganization in China*,
DOI 10.1007/978-981-287-859-5

22. Do you trust your neighbor? For example, will you let him/her to care children for you?
23. Do you trust strangers in the community? Do you think they will not pose a threat to you?
24. Do you trust the neighborhood committee? Do you think the members actually serve for the community? Do you think they won't corrupt or commit irregularities?
25. Do you trust traders in the community? Do you think they don't cheat?
26. Talk about your views on tradition. Is Chinese tradition well preserved in your community?
27. Talk about your views on moral. Which do you prefer between money and moral?
28. Talk about your views on religion. Have your beliefs changed or disappeared? How about your ideal?
29. Talk about how language affects you.
30. Talk about how life style affects you.
31. How do you treat social disorganization in China? Do you think it would be better or worse?
32. How would you suggest about social disorganization in China? What do you think should be done by government, society and personnel to slow down social disorganization process?

Appendix F
Example of Interview Record

访谈记录24

1. 谈谈您的基本情况。
   出生在河南信阳，户口在广州，家庭条件一般，属于贫困阶层。家里有父母老婆孩子。现在在xx工作有八年,但是从参加工作算起已经有十五年了。学历硕士,年龄三十八。在广州已经八年了。当初到广州来是想着广州有发展机会,毕业后公务员考试过来的。之前对广州的印象还行,对广州不了解,传说很发达。现在对广州的印象从经济发展来讲还可以,但是整体城市规划太差,从个人发展来讲从全国来比已经没有什么优势。应该会在广州常住。
2. 谈谈您的工作情况。
   过来之后在xx工作,收入一般。没有失业过。如果外来人失业很简单,可以走人了嘛,肯定呆不下去。广州现在失业现象比较严重,一些大国企还有民营企业纷纷裁员,特别一些私营老板素质比较低,在经营模式上是二十年不变的,是很落后那种模式,导致就业机会减少,大批工厂倒闭。失业后通过非法手段来牟利的肯定有,城乡差别这么大,在广州呆着的话一个月肯定有几千块钱,很多中西部一年也拿不到两三千块钱,如果走出来之后谁还愿意回去,人的心理上的对比落差非常大的,如果是我的话,我出来之后让我回去种田那肯定是不行的嘛。如果在没法生存的情况下,在没有什么特长的话肯定会动一些邪念的,你说是不是?
3. 您的住房状况。
   住在广州最大的贫困区(笑),房子是租的,租金比较贵,涨了一倍了,因为我不想搬,被房东要挟了。房子六十来平方,结构也就是那种火柴盒,三个人住,同屋是家属。我对房子不满意,太差了,哪里都差。我居住的条件太差了,房子没怎么装修,光线不好,房子太老旧,所有东西都是自己买的,因为不打算长住,所以很多东西都没有配齐,租房子就是这点不好。
4. 谈谈您的家庭情况。
   已婚,一般。
5. 您居住的小区里居民稳定么?
   在这里住了六年。在广州搬了三次家。流动性比较大,因为这里大部分是租房子的,还有就是过渡房,是解困小区。

H. Xiong, *Urban Crime and Social Disorganization in China*,
DOI 10.1007/978-981-287-859-5

6. 谈谈您对小区里的外地人、外国人和少数民族的看法。您认为他们跟犯罪有多大关系?
   外地人多,总体上来讲,在这儿住的素质都不是很高的,有一部分是打工的,还有一部分
   外国人不多,没有见到。少数民族不知道多不多,因为分辨不出来。
   我觉得犯罪跟这些族群没有必然的联系,而是跟经济有关,人穷了就会犯罪,要生存嘛。
7. 你所居住的小区附近有些什么样的小区呢?(有没有很高档的小区/贫民窟之类的)您对那些小区的看法?您对那些小区居民的看法?您觉得这个社会公平么,有没有"劫富济贫"之类的想法?
   附近比较高档的就是天朗民居了。社会本来就是不公平的,关键是给每个人的机会是公平的,我现在就要抓住这些机会。
8. 你在广州的社会关系网怎样?
   还行,比不上广州本地人,但是跟同时来的差不多的相比我认识的人要多多了。没有参加什么社团,平时饭局比较多。
9. 您居住的小区社会秩序怎样?您满意么?
   比较乱,不是很满意。
10. 小区里的居委会管不管事儿?为什么?您觉得应该怎样促进管理?
    不太了解,我觉得居委会应该多听听业主的意见。
11. 您对小区里的警察有什么看法?保安呢?
    警察还可以,小区里就有一个警务室。保安也还不错,虽然比较拽,但是有什么事情打电话给他们他们还是很快会过来的。
12. 谈谈您对小区封闭管理的看法。
    这个小区太大了,没有办法封闭管理,要是封闭管理的话出行会很不方便。我觉得有条件的话还是要封闭管理,比较安全。
13. 去高档场所消费的频率?看见高档场所气派的门厅会不会有望而生畏的感觉?谈谈感受。
    偶尔。这种地方有钱就去呗,没有觉得什么特别的,我还是比较喜欢在家里吃饭舒服些。
14. 出去的时候会不会被当作外地人对待?有没有觉得被歧视或误解?
    会,因为不会说粤语啊。没有觉得被歧视,不过有些广州人看不起说普通话的。
15. 您会不会看不起外地人?
    不会,有些外地人也很厉害的。
16. 广州市有些针对广州户口居民的优惠政策,谈谈感想。
    这个是正常的,如果都享受的话,广州市也负担不起,而且这样一来很多外地人都会跑到广州来,广州的治安啊资源啊会更加恶化。

1. 您觉得广州的治安怎么样?

   可以。
17. 您觉得所在小区的治安怎么样?您怕么?
    一般。很少发生犯罪,偶尔出现盗窃。晚上走夜路不怕,以前怕。
18. 有否听说周围的邻居或朋友遭遇犯罪(被抢、被偷、被杀或其他)?
19. 如果您看见小区内有人正在遭遇犯罪(被抢、被偷、被杀或其他),您会上前制止么?

会。看什么情况下,如果有人拿刀,我一个人没办法制止的情况下会报警,喊叫,或者叫保安,不会漠视不管,在我的能力范围内会的。

20. 您觉得所在的小区有没有凝聚力?您觉得自己是小区的一分子么?具体讲讲。
好像没有什么凝聚力,因为这个小区流动性比较大,不是像单位那一种,它是很大的解困小区,而且是周转性的,租的人太多了。没有把自己看做小区的一分子,因为我在这里是租的房子。
21. 您信任您的邻居么?比如您会让他/她帮您接送小孩么?
很信任不会,不是朋友不会信任,对他们的放心就是大家不会相互干扰,他们不会来偷你的东西。
22. 您信任小区里的陌生人么?您觉得陌生人不会对您构成威胁?
没有信任感。
23. 您信任小区里的居委会么?您觉得他们的确是在为小区服务的?他们不会贪污或者徇私舞弊?
不信任。我对小区居委会向来个人的偏向就是不信任。因为我觉得他们根本不是为业主的利益考虑。
24. 您信任小区里的商贩么?您觉得他们不会欺诈?
信任。小区外面的不信任,经常缺斤短两。小区里面的商贩是固定的有门面的,大家都很熟了,有一个基本的诚信,这是中国经商的一个基本道理,就是相互熟的之间他是不会骗你的。
25. 讲讲您关于传统的看法。您所在的小区里很好地保存了中国的传统么?
总的来讲中国的传统文化像尊老爱幼啊,还有相互之间的、邻里之间的相互帮忙啊,这种热情助人是比较值得提倡的,但是很多中国的传统文化已经消失了。小区里没有保存什么传统,都是外地人,广州本地的文化传统保存的还是不错的。中国的传统继承要分几个方面,对于那种比较封闭、比较落后的地方保存的还是比较好的;对于一些开放的地方、文化素质比较高的地方放而保存的不好。
那传统的沦丧对社会来讲是好还是不好呢?
有利有弊。如果从中国的民族凝聚力、从中国的民族文化民族发展来讲,传统的沦丧就是一种破坏;如果从世界经济的发展来讲就是比较进步的。
26. 讲讲您关于道德的看法。金钱和道德您更崇尚哪个?
道德是有幅度的,道德自身也在不断地改变,比如说八十年代在信息和交往不发达的情况下,大家是比较淳朴的,那个时候谈恋爱都是很严肃的,拉拉手都是不道德的,现在呢,同居根本不算什么。现在人的思想开放了,接触的西方的东西比较多,或者说世界性的东西比较多,行为也受到影响,所以道德水平下降了。不同时代的道德是没有可比性的,大家都接受的就是道德。金钱和道德没有什么更崇尚的问题,金钱是在道德的范围内去谋取。
27. 讲讲您关于信仰的看法。您的信仰有否改变,或者消失了?
没有信仰。如果说主义、宗教是没有的,如果从崇尚讲我觉得中国应该有个民族精神在。
谈谈理想?

理想是小孩子的东西,我们现在已经没有理想了,我们只有对生活和工作的规划问题,谈不上理想。小时候的理想是当一名将军,没当上是因为自身的条件,一个是要上学,一个是眼睛近视,不符合体检要求。

28. 谈谈语言对您的影响。
语言的话,对我是有一定影响的,在广州这个地方工作生活中白话的影响很大。很多人是讲白话的,听不懂普通话。在生活上会造成一些本地人对外地人的歧视。

29. 谈谈生活方式对您的影响。
生活方式对自己有一定的影响,基本上融合了当地的那种生活方式。

30. 您怎样看待中国的社会解组,您觉得会好转还是会恶化?
从政治制度来讲呢发生了很大的变革,抛开主义来讲,从真正的人和人的制度来讲中国的社会制度要发生很大的变化,以前的那种专制化或者人治化的东西在慢慢地减少,社会生活对制度的影响是越来越大,就是从民主的进程上来讲。我觉得这不是规范沦丧的问题,这是社会制度的衔接问题,不是沦丧,我个人认为。像堕胎啊、吸毒啊,这种任何年代都存在的,在任何社会都有的。跟刚解放比呢,没办法比,人的思想状况是不一样的,就像我刚才讲的,道德也是不停地在变的。这和经济条件、生活方式、社会的稳定程度有关的,也可以说跟人的物质满足是有关系的,像吸毒的,很多方面就是跟物质生活方式有关系的。相比以前来讲经济条件好多了,有的人精神空虚嘛。
应该会好转,这是现实嘛,看得到的。以前那种人治化的东西越来越少了。人的法制意识和民主意识不断增强,而且人和人的交往也不像原来那样了,什么崇管啦、什么崇富心理,这些都没有了。

31. 您对于中国的社会解组有什么样的建议呢?您觉得政府、社会和个人应该做些什么来减缓社会解组?
这个问题太大了,要全民努力,政府要在体制上改善,更多是关心民心,制度的建立不在于多少的问题,而是适不适合这个社会发展的问题。中国的制度在很多方面已经流于形式了。整个社会是每个人的兴趣是不一样的,他必须是有组织的,在组织的群体内,对社会解组产生影响。个人在自己的职责范围内,按照自己应尽的权利义务来做,得到整个社会认可,个人的行为都在影响社会,如果大家都崇尚一个和谐的美满的社会,大家都这样做,那社会肯定会进步。

Appendix G
Assumption of Interview Analysis Process[2]

Topic	Interview summary	
1. Resident stability	Village S	1. 在这里住了1年。刚来的时候在本科的一个同学那里落脚,后来找到房子就搬到这里来了。这个小区里的住民不稳定,邻居经常换人
	Community T	1. 不算特别稳定。因为是买的是以前国企的老房子,大部分是出租了。剩下的都是老弱病穷买不起新房子的。出租的房子一般1年租期。 2. 基本稳定,因为是房改房,很多老居民变动很小。除少数卖掉其它基本没变动。
	Community Q	1. 基本上都是自有房屋者,有少量租住的,也都是长期租住。
2. Heterogeneity	Village S	1. 外地人多,大部分是打工仔、打工妹,也有少数像我这样刚毕业的大学生。没有看到什么外国人,至于少数民族我不是很分得清,跟汉族都差不多吧。 2. 从表面看我觉得外国人不会犯罪,因为他们都是从其它国家过来的,都是为了生存,我就知道广州的黑人很多,他们都是以前国家的生存条件很恶劣过到广州来,他们觉得广州很好,他们可能会为了生活而留在这里,我想不会犯罪。外地人会是会有犯罪。外省的少数民族可能会因为宗教的冲突而犯罪。
	Community T	1. 我分辨不出来。只知道卖羊肉串的是维族,卖拉面的是回族。这两个民族比较喜欢闹事。不过我们小区里很少啦,石牌计算机城那里比较多维族, 经常因为占道经营跟城管发生冲突呢。 2. 有时候看得到,能见到,主要是黑人。我看他们也是忙忙碌碌的,玩的也不多,走路也很快。 3. 感觉外地人跟犯罪有很大关系。经济发达的地区通常很吸引犯罪分子,包括街头的职业乞丐,扒手,抢劫。

[2]Only 6 variables of social disorganization are cited from the interview record as examples, for the interview records are too many that they are listed in about 600 pages. It is too long to attach them all.

H. Xiong, *Urban Crime and Social Disorganization in China*,
DOI 10.1007/978-981-287-859-5

Topic	Interview summary	
	Community Q	1. 少数民族几乎没有。 2. 外国人我见过一两个,不算多。外国人入住这小区的话,我觉得会更好地改善外国人与这个小区之间的交流。 3. 觉得本地人、外地人、外国人、少数民族这些身份跟犯罪之间没有必然的联系,关键是看生活的环境条件以及接受教育的程度。
3. Social justice	Village S	1. 就是贫富差距大一点啰, 应该还算公平吧,主要靠自己奋斗啰。 2. 从学校出来之后因为走过的地方也挺多的,会有不公平。我觉得上天对每个人都是公平的,他们过着高档的生活,那是因为他们之前也很努力。 3. 一看就知道我是外地人。本地人不大看得起我们,就是外来的也看不起我们这样的打工仔。 4. 他跟你接触你不会说普通话他就会觉得你素质差,说你学历水平差,说你普通话不标准。 5. 没有户口小孩上学要交赞助费,是不公平。不过全国都一样啊,广州的小孩到我老家上小学一样要交赞助费的。本地人买房子有优惠啊?不去想它,反正我不会在广州买房子,那么贵。
	Community T	1. 我觉得是公平的,政策就是让一部分人先富起来,你富不起来是你的问题。心理是平衡的。 2. 基本不会受歧视。就算会当作外地人也没关系,反正很多店的老板、老板娘都是外地人。 3. 这个小区是解困房小区,很多房东都有其它房子,所以这里的房子大部分都出租了。小区里很多外地人,都是租在这里的,都是打工或者在附近开小餐馆的,素质都不高,乱糟糟的。 4. 政策只针对本地人确实是对外地人的歧视和打击,很多外地人在广州生活了很多年,对广州的贡献很大,广州社会财富的获得有外地人的贡献,但外地人享受不到这些优惠,是不公平的,不对的。 5. 我自己都有享受这些优惠政策的,现在住的房子就是买的单位福利房。怎么说呢,得了便宜就不要再卖乖了吧。是不公平,但是中国人那么多,不交赞助费的话大家都往大城市挤了。
	Community Q	1. 我记得我有一次去我家附近的窗帘店去买一块布,就跟老板娘闲聊,老板娘说有一些居民真的很贫困,他们贫困到家徒四壁。我自己没有见到。我觉得社会还是比较公平的,多劳多得嘛。 2. 哈哈。没啥歧视或误解吧,应该仰视咱们吧。去菜场买菜,我还没开口,摊主都主动跟我讲普通话了。似乎一眼看出我不懂粤语。 3. 广州已经给了我挣钱的机会,这些优惠要不要无所谓。是不公平,但是我交得起。
4. Social capital	Village S	1. 刚来的时候除了老公的同事外我都不认识什么人,后来去超市上班后也认识了一些人,我的同事。 2. 自己还没有到一个层次吧,就是徘徊在自己的亲戚、朋友、同学、同事啊这些方面,但是你说去到一个层次,就是一些官啊、一些有钱人啊,我又没到这个层次啊

Topic	Interview summary	
	Community T	1. 社会关系还可以吧,方方面面的人都认识。是不是本地人这真的不影响。只要勤奋,本地外地关系不大。 2. 在广州没有什么关系。
	Community Q	1. 在广州社会关系广泛。我本来就是广州军区部队大院长大的,叔叔伯伯同学的一大堆。又是从省委出来的,关系比较广。经常有饭局,谈事情的多。什么人都有,政府官员、商界精英,刚毕业的大学生,都有。遇到困难自己解决。
5. Social order and social control	Village S	1. 城中村的环境太差,住的人也太杂。小区很吵闹,隔壁经常打麻将,要么就是一群人在那里鬼叫鬼叫的。不良少年多,有醉汉或流浪汉游荡,小区不干净,到处有垃圾。小区没有什么公共设施,到处都是乱涂乱画和小广告。小区里没有派出所,也没有其它司法机关或行政机关?居委会、业委会之类的也没有。 2. 我觉得我们那边还好吧,我听家里的人说我们那边是没有嫖的,街头犯罪,像抢东西这些是没有的,那边管制还可以,因为我们自己村里面的那个管的还可以。小区里的居委会管事儿。他们安排的很好的,我们村里面是有钱的,他们每年都拿那个钱的利息来做一些事情。就是小区里没有见到什么警察,见到很多协管员,还有那些保安。现在我们附近的村前后都会有一些铁栏,每个地方都有一个保安亭。保安很好,经常看到他们在巡逻,所以抢东西的比较少,但是骗人的多。骗人跟抢东西是两回事,骗人是你自己的事情。他会找一些东西掉在地上说'哎,是你的东西么?','一起分赃'之类的啰。
	Community T	1. 满意,就是离市区远了点。不过好在单位有班车接送上下班。小区不吵,而且干净整洁,绿化很好。有派出所、居委会、业委会,很少看到警察但经常看到保安,小区治安不错。 2. 不满意。环境太差,都是出租的,河南人很多。小区没有什么活动场所,一到晚上,所有的人都出来在马路上踢毽子打羽毛球,密密麻麻,到处都是人。邻居经常打麻将,特别是一楼看自行车棚的,天天晚上喊人在下面打麻将,吵得人一晚上都睡不着。我有次实在忍不住,扔了个啤酒瓶下去他们才停了一晚上,第二天又打起来了。还算干净整洁,特别是白天大家都上班去了,小区空荡荡的,看上去还不错。垃圾也有,不多。没有看到过警察,能看到保安。不过这里的保安都盛气凌人的,因为这里租住的外来人多。经常看到保安跟租在这里的打工妹搭讪。
	Community Q	1. 环境好,别墅区,住的都是比较成功的,氛围也好。很安静、也很干净。 2. 有一次我家做的橱柜没用几天就坏了,我打电话让装橱柜的到我家来看,结果保安不让他进来,说是要物业公司批准。我就说那我以朋友的身份请他上门,这总是我的权利吧,结果保安还是不让他进,这侵犯了我的权益。

Name Index

H. Xiong, *Urban Crime and Social Disorganization in China*,
DOI 10.1007/978-981-287-859-5

Subject Index

H. Xiong, *Urban Crime and Social Disorganization in China*,
DOI 10.1007/978-981-287-859-5

The manufacturer's authorised representative in the EU is Springer Nature Customer Service Centre GmbH, Europaplatz 3, 69115 Heidelberg, Germany. If you have any concerns regarding our products, please contact ProductSafety@springernature.com

Printed and bound by CPI Group (UK) Ltd, Croydon, CR0 4YY
30/09/2026
02225448-0003